Monopoly and Competition in British Telecommunications

Monopoly and Competition in British Telecommunications

The Past, the Present and the Future

John Harper

PINTER

London and Washington

PINTER
A Cassell Imprint
Wellington House, 125 Strand, London WC2R 0BB
PO Box 605, Herndon, VA 20172

First published in 1997

© J. M. Harper 1997

British Library Cataloguing in Publication Data
A catalogue record for this book is available from the British Library.
ISBN 1 85567 455 6

Library of Congress Cataloging-in-Publication Data
Harper, J. M. (John M.)
    Monopoly and competition in British telecommunications : the past,
the present, and the future / John Harper.
        p. cm.
    Includes bibliographical references and index.
    ISBN 1-85567-455-6 (hardcover)
    1. Telecommunication policy—Great Britain—History.
2. Telecommunication systems—Great Britain—History.   3. British Telecom—
History.   4. Privatization—Great Britain—History.
5. Competition—Great Britain—History.   I. Title
HE8095.H37 1997
384.1'3—dc20
                                                                    96–34968
                                                                         CIP

Typeset by Ben Cracknell Studios
Printed and bound in Great Britain by Biddles Ltd, Guildford and King's Lynn

Contents

List of Figures

Foreword

Privatization and deregulation are rightly seen as two of the major policy achievements of the Thatcher government in the 1980s. Even the most committed opponents of Thatcherism have to acknowledge the remarkable gains in productivity which took place in many of the previously state-owned corporations. But this process is too often presented in black-and-white terms, as a sudden transformation from incompetent, Civil-Service-dominated management on one day to thrusting commercialism on the next. What is forgotten is the extent to which, in some cases, the period before and after privatization showed a high degree of continuity. This is particularly true of telecommunications, where the groundwork for the modernization of the British telephone network and for improvements in service to the customer was laid in the 1960s and 1970s, long before privatization had ever been seriously contemplated. Much of the credit for the system as it now exists goes to those who joined the old Post Office when it was still a government department, oversaw its transition into a free-standing public corporation and brought it into the modern age.

An understanding of this earlier history is essential if privatization is to be seen in a balanced perspective. Few people are as well placed to contribute to this understanding as John Harper, who as a senior manager in the Post Office and then British Telecom was closely involved in many of the pre-Thatcher reforms of the British telecommunications industry; with his subsequent experience as an adviser to telecommunications manufacturing companies, he is ideally qualified to present an informed but objective account of events which can easily be obscured by prejudice and ideology.

Harper shows in this book that, as a state-owned monopoly, the Post Office was far more efficient and commercially minded than it is given credit for, especially after the structural reforms of 1969, and that the record of productivity growth in the 1970s was not much different from what was achieved after privatization in 1984. This is not to deny that privatization brought with it many advantages, not least an end to the unpredictable interference from Ministers which made running the old regime so difficult, or that the emphasis which the Thatcher government placed on competition and consumer choice was highly beneficial. A more liberal framework, coinciding with a period of rapid technological change, helped to stimulate innovation among the growing number of independent service and equipment providers. But many of these advances built on what was already in train before Mrs Thatcher entered office.

The importance of this book lies not only in its description of the performance of the Post Office and British Telecom over the past thirty years; it also looks to the future. In telecommunications, as in Britain's other privatized industries, the regulatory system is still evolving, and it would be surprising if precisely the right balance between competition and supervision had already been arrived at. A particularly difficult issue in telecommunications is the role which competition should play in the basic infrastructure of the system. While Harper does not question the value of competition in the provision of private network services, he makes a powerful case for a single organization, subject to national regulation, to control and manage the public network. This is a radical proposal, but it is one which deserves to be taken seriously at a time when relations between British Telecom and its regulator are going through a period of turbulence and uncertainty, and when government decisions on telecommunications policy are awaited.

These are issues which, thanks to the changes which took place in the 1980s, can be analysed on the basis of what makes commercial and technical sense, with the interests of the customer always being paramount. No one, least of all Harper, is suggesting that the clock should be turned back; but privatization was not the end of the story. The next steps in the development of the regulatory arrangements will be no less important to the future of Britain's telecommunications industry.

Sir Geoffrey Owen

Preface

It is characteristic of the public utilities and services in Britain that the most important forces for change are political. Publicly owned enterprises have to accept the right of publicly elected governments to determine their fate; and insiders in any industry have to recognize that people outside are often able to see the reality of what is going on more clearly than they can. But it is common sense to take account of the point of view of the insiders, who by definition know most about the industry.

Many books have been written about the Post Office and many no doubt will be written about BT. But very few except official documents have been written by people from inside. Circumstances gave me thirty years' experience inside the PO and BT and then positions on various other vantage points within the telecommunications industry for a further twelve. I decided it was time one of us put a personal point of view across. If one boards a London tube train in the rush-hour the odds are that there is at least one Post Office or BT employee in each carriage. Posts and telecommunications have always been like that. They are run by ordinary people for ordinary people. In this book I have tried to tell something of our story.

The prospect facing the observer of UK telecommunications changed abruptly in the early 1980s. Up to then the real action had been confined to the PO, the government, the three main suppliers and the principal PO unions. Most power had lain along a single axis, between government and the monopoly operator. I had had a place on this axis myself in various senior positions; and I can write about it as an insider. But suddenly things changed. A whole new set of actors came on the scene – competing operators, competing suppliers, the regulator, consumer bodies and so on – all of whom were contributing to the advance of events and all of whom had to be watched. In trying to understand what was happening I found advantage in the fact that I had left BT and was moving around the industry. I got a better perspective than if I had stayed in one place.

The sequence of change in British telecommunications which is still working itself through today really started in 1964. The first initiatives in it were due to two people who came at the question from very different angles – the Rt Hon. Anthony Wedgwood Benn and Sir William Ryland, the latter now sadly dead. In 1964 Tony Benn was Postmaster General and Bill Ryland was a senior Civil Servant in the old GPO. The latter later became the second Chairman of the Post Office Corporation. The objective they shared and which runs through the story was to transform posts and telecommunications into business operations standing on their own feet free of government manipulation. It is no coincidence that Sir Iain Vallance, who has presided successfully over BT plc since 1987, was trained by Ryland, as indeed I was myself. I believe both of us would want a tribute to him to stand on the record.

There was nothing else in Britain quite like the Post Office of 1980; and there never will be again. It was an arthritic, musclebound dinosaur, uncomfortably yoking two major businesses – posts and telecommunications – and one medium-sized one – Giro – which were in urgent need to go their separate ways. It inspired in many of us who worked in it a rueful affection; but that did not mean we were blind to its faults – indeed rather the reverse. On the other hand its achievements were real and they should not just be buried in oblivion.

That BT is better now than Post Office telecommunications were in the 1970s there is no question. But researching and writing this book led me to a conclusion which I had not expected. I now believe that the most significant changes which came from government in the 1980s were not privatization, regulation, or competition in the form they have taken so far, but the separation of posts from telecommunications and the national industrial relations reforms. This is confirmed by the success of the mail and counter services in the last decade, even though they remained organized on a monopoly basis in the public sector. We shall never know what a similar state management free to concentrate on telecommunications might have done in the equivalent industrial relations environment. Both these reforms stand to the credit of the early Thatcher governments, even though they are usually overlooked by present-day commentators where BT is concerned.

Set against the facts, the attempt to load the main credit for the improvements in telecommunications since 1984 on to privatization and competition looks contrived. What really happened was that with the help of the separation of the businesses and the industrial relations reforms the private sector management picked up and ran successfully with a ball which was already well in play. As Part II demonstrates, the ground gained in UK telecommunications between 1969 and 1980 was at least as great as that gained between 1984 and 1995.

It is common practice to assess bodies like the PO and BT by reference to the performance of their peers in other countries. I first became involved with the problems of inter-country comparison of telecommunications operators in 1956; and on and off I have been wrestling with them ever since. Carefully researched comparisons in fields where circumstances match with sufficient accuracy can tell one a lot. Work done by the consultants McKinsey in the late 1970s showed that on a like-for-like basis NYNEX (as it now is) used 20 per cent fewer staff than we did on exchange maintenance. This told us things we needed to know – and did not like – specific to our maintenance practices for exchange equipment. Detailed comparisons of this kind in specific areas of activity can be of great value. But after forty years of trying to make them stick my conclusion is that broad-brush comparisons of the overall performance of telecommunications operators at global level are a waste of time. Circumstances and the scope of operator functions are always too different between the different countries and can never properly be factored out.

Global manpower comparisons are a telling case in point. In 1980 29 per cent of total BT engineering field staff were staff employed on capital account or on servicing growth in lines. Graphs in the book show how markedly the BT capital and customer growth workloads have fluctuated over the subsequent fifteen years. The workloads of other operators will obviously have varied to similar extents, according to the particular patterns of growth and modernization in the networks concerned. If, as Appendix 3 suggests in the BT case, such work is outsourced to outside contractors, the criteria on which this is done may vary markedly between different operators.

There are other traditional differences arising from variations in the boundary of the operator's functions. The predecessor of France Telecom, for example, was never involved in provision of customer apparatus, where the PO exercised a *de facto* monopoly in that respect; and the respective staffing levels varied accordingly.

Financially based comparisons can be the most unsafe of all. Who is to say what is the 'true' exchange rate between the dollar, the franc and the pound? And exchange rate fluctuations can make nonsense of findings within a matter of weeks.

In such circumstances it is amateurish to attempt global inter-operator comparisons. I make no apology for avoiding them here. What matters is to get simple first-order measures of the performance of a particular operator and then to look critically at trends in its behaviour over time. If BT's expenditure per line improves over five years, all the odds are the company has genuinely become more efficient and vice versa. This is the approach I have used in this book.

Since I left BT I have spent twelve years in the fiercely competitive environment of world telecommunications manufacturing. I have run my own consultancy business now for several years. These experiences have underlined my belief in the principles of the open market for end-customers and in their application in our industry. The character of telecommunications in the twenty-first century is going to be quite different from that in the 1980s when the present UK regime was devised. Parts V and VI take a critical look at the working of this regime and test it against what we can foresee of the requirements of this future. They conclude that it does not measure up and that it has not solved the problem of making the market work in telecommunications.

The trouble lies partly in the basic structure of the operating industry, which is obsolete; and partly in the policy of competing network infrastructures. I was Managing Director of BT's inland operations at the time when competition of this kind was first introduced in the UK, and I organized our responses to it. I welcomed it because I believed what I was told about its potential as a stimulus to our efficiency. After fifteen years' experience of its working I now think I was wrong to do so. In the last Part of the book I suggest an alternative approach.

Two things struck me with particular force as I pieced together the account in this book.

The first was the hurried, chancy and contradictory character of the policy processes which formed the present British telecommunications regime, especially considering what has been built since on their foundations. As Joe Rogaly has pointed out in the *Financial Times* (see Chapter 15), the privatization of BT itself arose as much from events as from premeditation. Margaret Thatcher wanted to break BT up in 1982 and was restrained mainly on grounds of time. The Beesley Report, revered as the bible of carrier competition, actually said that economic evidence for replication of infrastructure was poor. The White Paper on Cable Systems and Services (see Chapter 15), which set out the basis for competing local infrastructure based on combining cable TV and telecommunications, expressly looked forward to BT being 'free to compete' in the very market in which today it labours under hobbling constraints.

The second was the sheer vigour and fertility of the world telecommunications engineering community in the last fifteen years or so of monopoly. Between the mid-1960s and the early 1980s the scientists and engineers of the USA and Europe devised reed and digital electronic switching, digital transmission, cellular radio, the

Prestel family of services, a whole new generation of customer apparatus and many ancilliaries. Taken as a whole this period in telecommunications must surely have been one of the most creative in the whole history of technology.

I want to pay a particular personal tribute to the designers and creators of System X, the British digital exchange system. I am not a professional engineer. But on and off in various capacities as a GPO administrator and as a PO operating manager I worked with Roy Harris, David Leakey, Martin Ward, Jock Marsh, John Martin and many others too numerous to mention and watched what they were doing through most of our joint careers. What they produced was one of the best switching systems ever. Events in Britain in the early 1980s deprived them of the recognition they deserve. If this book can do something to retrieve this it will have achieved an important aim.

Finally I want to make a point about the Bell companies of the USA and their generosity towards people like me. I owe them a considerable debt. I started learning from them in 1958. I am still learning from them today and I have many friends among their senior people. Their arrival as competitors may well turn out to be the best thing that ever happened to European telecommunications. I want to see nothing but success for them on fair and sensible terms. But the present set-up into which they have been drawn in Britain is as wrong for them as it is for us.

The book is about telecommunications domestic to Britain. I did not set out to deal with the part which our national operator has played over the years in the development of the world's international network and services, with the ventures overseas of the PO and BT or with the wave of re-grouping which is developing in the international business carrier market as I write. These deserve separate treatment, which I hope one day they will get.

John Harper
Seaford, May 1996

Acknowledgements

This book and the policy proposals in it are my responsibility. but a large number of people helped me write the historical Parts I to IV. In a real sense they have been a collective effort by representatives of a generation in UK telecommunications. Some of these people are quoted verbatim in their own name and right in the text; I am particularly grateful to them for allowing me to use their words. I hope I may be forgiven for not trying to list all the others who have helped me here and for expressing my warm thanks to them in a general way. But I do want to single out certain individuals for special recognition. Jenny Barton helped me with the basic historical research without which I could not even have got to first base. By challenging me on the proposals in Chapter 19, Cor Berben of DG XIII in the European Commission helped me to make a major improvement in them. Professor Nicholas Garnham of the University of Westminster helped me greatly to improve the effectiveness of the argument. Sir Geoffrey Owen took time to guide me in trying to write to the exacting standards of the world of affairs and contributed an important Foreword. Jeff Wheatley not only provided key statistics but kept me on track with the critique of a professional economist. Above all Gordon Pocock kept me going over seven years of observation, research, drafting and discussion. Thanks for the Index go to my wife, Berry Harper.

The principal sources for the book were my own diaries, recollections and observations, plus fifteen interviews recorded on tape with senior people who had been concerned in the PO, BT, the manufacturing industry and the unions. The people concerned were Sir William Barlow, Sir Edward Fennessy, Peter Benton, Kenneth Cadbury, John Flint, Clive Foxell, Kenneth Glynn, David Leakey, Ron Martin, Gordon Pocock, Mel Price, Peter Shaw, Bryan Stanley, Henry Tilling and Don Wratten. I am most grateful to all of them for the time and trouble they took. The tapes, which contain a wealth of historical material beyond that actually used in the book, are being deposited with the Archivist of the Institution of Electrical Engineers in London who should be approached by those who wish to consult them.

I am indebted to the *Financial Times* for permission to quote material within its copyright; to Macmillan General Books for permission to quote the passage on pages 147–9 from *Conflict of Loyalty* by Geoffrey Howe; and to Faber & Faber for permission to quote the passages from *The Turbulent Years* by Kenneth Baker on pages 137 and 149–50. I am grateful also to Her Majesty's Stationery Office for permission to reproduce the extensive extracts from Crown Copyright material.

With one or two exceptions which are indicated all the statistics and financial results used in the book are taken from successive PO and BT Reports and Accounts, from the publication *BT Statistics 1983* or from the *Blue Book* of the UK Central Statistical Office.

List of Abbreviations

ADSL	Adaptive Digital Subscriber Loop technology
AEI	Associated Electrical Industries
AGD	Accountant General's Department
AGSD	Advisory Group on Systems Definition
ASTMS	Association of Scientific, Technical and Management Staffs
AT&E	Automatic Telephone and Engineering Company
ATM	(former) Automatic Telephone Manufacturing Company
ATM	(modern) Asynchronous Transfer Mode (packet switching)
AT&T	American Telephone and Telegraph Company (USA)
BBC	British Broadcasting Corporation
BPO	British Post Office
BSA	Bulk Supplies Agreement
BT	British Telecommunications
BT plc	British Telecommunications public limited company
CAD/CAM	Computer Aided Design/Computer Aided Manufacturing
CCITT	International Consultative Committee for Telegraph and Telephone (ITU)
CHQ	Central Headquarters (of the PO)
DCF	Discounted Cash Flow
DoI	Department of Industry
DTI	Department of Trade and Industry
ED	Engineering Department (of the GPO)
E-in-C	Engineer-in-Chief
EO	Executive Officer
EU	European Union
GDP	Gross Domestic Product
GEC	General Electric Company (of the UK)
GPO	General Post Office

GSC	Group Switching Centre
IRC	Industrial Reorganization Corporation
ISDN	Integrated Services Digital Network
ITD	Inland Telecommunications Department (of the GPO)
ITT	International Telephone and Telegraph
JERA	Joint Electronic Research Agreement
MACs	Measurement and Analysis Centres
MDCT	Managing Director's Committee Telecommunications
ME	Marketing Executive (of the PO)
MPT	Ministry of Post and Telecommunications
MSA	Management Services Association
NCU	National Communications Union
NDPS	National Data Processing Service (of the PO)
NE	Network Executive (of the PO)
NN	National Networks (in the PO)
NPD	Network Planning Department (of the PO)
NPV	Net Present Value
OED	*Oxford English Dictionary*
OFTEL	Office of Telecommunications
OPD	Operational Programming Department (of the PO)
PABX	Private Automatic Branch Exchange
PAM	Pulse Amplitude Modulation
PCM	Pulse Code Modulation
PDI	Personal Disposable Income
PM	Prime Minister
PMG	Postmaster General
PO	Post Office
POEU	Post Office Engineering Union
POUNC	Post Office Users National Council
PRU	Pay Research Unit
PSBR	Public Sector Borrowing Requirement
P&SD	Purchasing and Supply Department (of the PO)
PTL	Plessey Telecommunications Ltd
PTT	Posts, Telegraphs and Telephones (typical monopoly operator title round the world)
RHQs	Regional Headquarters (of the GPO and the PO)
RoD	Reorganization Department (of the GPO)
SDH	Synchronous Digital (transmission) Hierarchy

SPC	Stored Programme Control
SPOE	Society of PO Engineers
STC	Standard Telephones and Cables Ltd
STD	Subscriber Trunk Dialling
STE	Society of Telecommunications Executives
TCL	Telephone Cables Ltd (GEC)
TDM	Time Division Multiplex
THQ	Telecommunications Headquarters (of the PO)
TIPs	Telecommunications Improvement Programmes
TMKD	Telecommunications Marketing Department (of the PO)
TMRs	Telecommunications Monthly Reports
TO	Technical Officer
T2A	Technician Class 2A
TUC	Trade Union Congress
TXD	BT standard digital exchange system (System X)
TXE2	PO small reed local exchange system
TXE4	PO large reed local exchange system
TXK1	PO standard local crossbar exchange system (GEC and Plessey)
TXK2	PO standard trunk crossbar exchange system (GEC and Plessey)
TXK3	PO standard local crossbar exchange system (STC)
TXK4	PO standard trunk crossbar (transit) system (STC)
TXS	PO strowger exchange system
UKAEA	United Kingdom Atomic Energy Authority
UPW	Union of Post Office Workers
VANS	Value Added Network Services

1 Introduction

Most difficult and most lasting [of Mrs Thatcher's earlier triumphs] was the dismantling of the malign, if unspoken compact between state ownership and monopoly trade unionism in Britain's bloated public sector.

Lord Howe, *Financial Times*, October 1993

With his superb English Lord Howe paints a picture of the process of privatization in Britain which is accepted across the world. For some industries no doubt it was accurate. But the picture is too much a broad-brush one. Many of the state industries were much more efficient than Lord Howe implies and much more deserving of balanced understanding. By the same token the time has come for balanced scrutiny of the corresponding privatized regimes created by Lord Howe and his colleagues.

In 1996 the world telecommunications industry stands on the threshold of a completely new era, whose problems and opportunities are only just beginning to be charted. In the thirty years since 1965 Britain has had as wide an experience of constitutional arrangements for telecommunications as any country in the world. The UK operation has acted as a test bed for the replacement of direct government control by ownership by a state corporation and of that in turn by privatization; and of monopoly by competition. The present British regime has served as a model for change in many other countries. It has particularly influenced the thinking of the European Commission on telecommunications matters. National governments across the European Union are now giving effect to the resulting policies. We in Britain have a responsibility to put as accurate a view of our experience on record as we can, not coloured by prejudice or political considerations.

Telecommunications is a business with a long lead time, whose rhythms can be properly assessed only over decades. This book is about the British telecommunications operating and manufacturing industries in the 1960s and 1970s, about privatization and the introduction of competition in the early 1980s, about the successes and limitations of both public and private regimes and about the lessons to be drawn for the future from the whole story.

The Parliamentary milestones on the road of change were the Post Office (PO) Act 1969, which created the nationalized PO Corporation with responsibility both for posts and for telecommunications; the British Telecommunications (BT) Act 1981, which introduced competition, separated telecommunications from posts and created BT as a short-lived nationalized Board in its own right; and the Telecommunications Act 1984, which converted BT into a Companies Act company all of whose shares were owned by Government and paved the way for the initial sale of just over fifty per cent of the equity on the market.

Part I of the book briefly describes the General Post Office (GPO), as it then was, as it stood at the end of the 1960s.

Part II is about the twelve years between 1969 and 1981. With a very small number of distinguished exceptions from the outside world, the management who ran PO telecommunications throughout this period had all started life as established Civil Servants. Many of us had originally chosen and been chosen specifically for policy work, with no aspirations as managers. The majority of us had been brought up in the headquarters environment of an orthodox Ministerial department. The particular permutation of a group of former senior Civil Servants running a major public service in the nationalized sector is most unlikely ever to be repeated. We accomplished a remarkable task. In 1968 GPO telecommunications had formed a quarter of the government machine, steeped in Civil Service ways of doing things. In the years which followed we built it up into an operation which in 1984 qualified for world attention as the object of one of the largest and most successful private company launches in history. This experience is highly topical in the Britain of today, as more and more of the remaining executive functions of Whitehall are hived off.

Part III tells the story of the British telecommunications equipment-supplying industry and its relations with the PO, culminating in the mixed success and failure of System X, the British digital exchange system.

The PO organism resisted all attempts to change it until Sir George Jefferson finally implanted the quite different philosophies of private business, in a collision of cultures which was the final climax of the history of telecommunications in the state sector. The state-owned organization he took on in 1980 was a sitting target for the onslaught of Conservative political doctrine. But there were other much less theoretical forces at work also. Telecommunications operations were (and are) highly profitable. Business people saw a long-awaited chance at last to make money out of them as operating competitors. The stock market wanted a big piece of the action, which it was denied while telecommunications was a public sector organization and for which it was eager to pay. And the funds which privatization offered to the public purse were there for the Government to take.

The collision of cultures overseen by Jefferson is described in Part IV, which also deals with the creation of BT, with the introduction of competition and with privatization. It forms a centrepiece to the book.

Part V examines the working in practice of the regime which was then created in Britain. It includes analyses of the performance of BT plc over the years 1984 to 1995, supported by two detailed financial and statistical Appendices; and of the working of the regime as a whole. It concludes that the British experiment with competing telecommunications infrastructures is developing in a basically unsatisfactory way.

Part VI deals with the future. Following the Bangemann Report, the European Commission and the Council of Ministers have embarked upon policies directed to the promotion of telecommunications competition through competing infrastructures. Part VI proposes a new and different approach to the organization of competition and to the future structure of the industry.

Part I
The Last Days of the GPO

2 The GPO

it was decided to opt for complete government take-over in 1912 on the expiry of the National Telephone Company's licence. The Tory Chamberlain and the economically orthodox Murray saw this as the best – i.e. the least expensive – escape route from a generation of misconceived policy towards the telephone, not as an opportunity to expand the corporate state.

C.R. Perry, *The Victorian Post Office*[1]

In 1960 the General Post Office (GPO) was a Government department like any other within the British system of government. It was headed by the Postmaster General (PMG), a Minister directly answerable to Parliament, supported by career Civil Servants. A Post Office Board had been set up in the 1930s, but it was no more than a formalized organ for discussion between the PMG and his senior officials. All responsibility rested with him.

The office of Postmaster General dated from the seventeenth century. The GPO had been married into the uniform Civil Service system in the second half of the nineteenth century. The reforms of Northcote and Trevelyan had set their mark on it just like the rest of the service. But a distinct 'Post Office' self-esteem survived. Senior GPO officials were used to being lumped along with Customs and Excise and the (then) Ministry of Works at the bottom of the Whitehall scale of values. But they retained an enduring pride in their own tradition.

Telecommunications was already more than a hundred years old. The telegraph service had grown up as a private sector activity in the first half of the nineteenth century. The government took a state monopoly of the conveyance of telegrams in 1868. The reason was fear that they would damage the revenues of the postal service, coupled with serious dissatisfaction among the business community about the service being given by competing private interests. When the telephone was introduced in the 1870s the GPO took operating responsibility only for the trunk service between cities. Local telephone service was provided by private companies. The government finally took over local services as well (with the exception of those in Kingston-upon-Hull) in 1912. The state operating monopoly thus created was to last sixty-nine years, to 1981.

During the 1920s serious public dissatisfaction built up with the GPO. The Bridgeman Committee was appointed in 1932 to enquire into the management. The government accepted the findings, and the work of implementation began in 1933. It was interrupted by the Second World War. The changes due to Bridgeman were not finally completed until some fifteen years after their inception.

The war brought out the true potential of telecommunications. By 1945 far-sighted people in the industry were beginning to perceive something of the future. Nevertheless the situation of the telephone service in the 1950s was a national disgrace. There was a waiting list of half a million for service on a system of some three million.

In 1955 the government published the White Paper Report on Post Office Development and Finance. Paragraph 22 said:

> The nub of the reforms ensuing from the Bridgeman Committee of 1932 was self-contained finance, involving a limit on the use of Post Office finances as a revenue producing instrument for the Exchequer. It meant the fixing of a definite contribution to the Exchequer beyond which any net earnings were at the disposal of the Post Office. The objects were to give the Post Office an opportunity to show that it could run its services with enterprise and economy, to promote better understanding by the public of the commercial basis of its activities, and to facilitate a less meticulous Treasury control of the Post Office.[2]

The last sentence provides no bad curtain-raiser for the next few chapters of this book. This was what the officials of the PO saw themselves as trying to accomplish from then on. But they had to wrestle with a wholly unsuitable system. The logic and imprint of the main Civil Service pervaded everything. The GPO was at this time responsible for broadcasting policy, which was prestigious in the administrative scale of values and took up a good bit of Ministers' time. This added to the Whitehall atmosphere of GPO headquarters. In telecommunications the result was a daunting degree of under-management and misplaced effort.

Senior GPO officials had been restless about the situation for a long time. They wanted to do a good job and they could not do it. They had yardsticks for their dissatisfaction. It was generally recognized that the Bell system in the USA was one of the best telecommunications operations in the world, if not the best. Bell was also reckoned to be one of the best-managed companies in the United States. It was of course a private company and completely independent of government. The Swedish administration was generally reckoned to be the best in Europe. Swedish telecommunications were organized under the Royal Swedish Board of Telecommunications, under a formula particular to Sweden which placed telecommunications and other utilities separate from the government machine, even though they were state-owned.

All the indications were that separation from government and Civil Service was an absolute prerequisite for real efficiency of operation. But the GPO headquarters within which the officials worked and thought these thoughts was structured and run on the orthodox Whitehall model. To do anything about the situation they had to change the system of which they were themselves part.

Great importance attached to industrial relations and to staff consultation. In 1946 the then Director General, Sir Alexander Little, had defined a philosophy which in essentials was to operate for three decades to come. The starting proposition was that GPO operations were so labour-intensive that a good industrial relations climate was essential. Industrial relations were good right up to the end of the 1960s. Inflation was still relatively low and serious pay disputes were rare.

The GPO followed Civil Service industrial relations practice, based on the 'Whitley' system. The GPO had two separate and equal national Whitley Councils, one for engineering staff and one for the rest. The councils themselves rarely if ever met. Most of the work was done in committees and other subordinate organs of these councils.

As Bryan Stanley, who was to be General Secretary of the Post Office Engineering Union (POEU) throughout the 1970s says:

> The [Civil Service] Whitley Council procedure was a really great procedure in the sense that it allowed both sides to sit round the table discussing the general issues, not necessarily always in a deadlock situation or seeking to resolve a crisis but to talk about every part of the work we were doing. So by covering the range of occupational issues and also every condition of service by a sub-committee of the Whitley Council we were able by simply doing our homework on both sides to have meaningful informed discussions on every aspect of the work that was being done and of the conditions of the staff. The one thing of course that was not covered by that was the pay and hours negotiation which was often quite sharp, even in those days.

The GPO still bore a strong stamp of the days before the First World War. Peter Shaw, who was to be a POEU-nominated member of the Industrial Democracy Board of the PO in the late 1970s, paints a vivid picture of how it looked to him as a union official at the time:

> What struck me most about the levels I dealt with in the GPO at that time was its almost caricatures of Civil Servants, very straight laced, very proper, very set ideas about master/servant relationships, that kind of thing. I really was surprised at how close to the truth the caricature was. Very formal minutes of meetings, very little relaxation. It wasn't for some time, until the later sixties or the early seventies, that I thought people were beginning to relax a bit.

Nevertheless, in line with the Little doctrine the GPO hierarchy went to a lot of trouble to keep industrial relations on an even keel. Stanley again:

> The Director General and the Engineer-in-Chief were the significant people in the last event. The Director General used to hold meetings from time to time and explain to us exactly what he saw as the future; and in the event of total disagreement the Director General was available, if he thought it was a genuine disagreement, to actually discuss with us our problems. We could look to him for a final decision.

Pay negotiations in those days were a complicated business. Stanley again:

> [Pay] was not entirely in the control of the Post Office negotiators and therefore there were constant interferences, as we both termed it, by government. Intervention by government, government pay policies, pay freezes, pay restraints and various bodies set up to review every claim. There was a whole succession of these events, under both governments. It was not only the Conservative government, although in the fifties it was; but later there was a similar arrangement when Labour was in office.
>
> So as far as negotiations were concerned apart from pay those negotiations were in my view constructive and solved many problems before they became difficulties. There were two effects from that – one, the staff had confidence that they could get representation for their problems. They put their problems up to the head office of the union if they could not solve them locally or regionally and there was a channel through which they could be dealt with. Not always successful from the union point of view of course, but things were dealt with and usually a solution was agreed.

On the pay issues things were very much sharper, for the reasons that I have given. Indeed we felt, I think with some justice, that in the fifties the engineering staff, the technicians, the Technical Officers that we represented were underpaid; and that they were not receiving the kind of remuneration that they deserved as a result of their training and technical knowledge. For that reason we tried to use the Civil Service pay research channel which emerged in the fifties as a possibility. And so we began to establish under Charles Smith's leadership [later Lord Delacourt-Smith] the finest Research Department that could be put together.

We were very fortunate in getting the services of Ted Webb, who had previously been involved in the TUC and who was a quite exceptional, excellent person. He understood exactly what we needed and therefore his research was if anything better than the research which was going on through the [official] Pay Research unit. He was meticulous in his approach and his contacts were tremendously effective. So we found that channel of comparison could be used very effectively; and therefore, when that became true, some of the conflict was taken out of the pay negotiations as well. The Pay Research procedure was one that, if we put the facts together and produced the evidence, could lead to a better settlement than plain straightforward horse bargaining.

At that time we also had the rather good Civil Service arbitration procedure. They were truly neutral and stood against interference from the government or being identified with the employer and were very fair we felt in their adjudication.

The same hierarchical criteria governed thinking at engineering management level. Kenneth Glynn, later General Secretary of the STE,[3] says:

The central problem in the union in pay terms and on status issues as well was that when Leonard Leese [his predecessor] had become General Secretary of the then Society of Telecommunications Engineers, the first-line supervisor engineering had had a status and pay comparable with the Clerical Officer; and the top POEU grade compared with the Clerical Assistant [the most junior clerical grade in the Civil Service], if you make allowances for the sex discrimination at the time. They were exactly lined up. By the time I came in 1960 the main STE grade, which had emerged from the earlier reorganization and provided three-quarters of the staff of the first-line supervision grade, was better paid than the Executive Officer grade. This of course caused a lot of tension and friction and trouble, not only between the union and the GPO but also with the other unions.

My period in office simply continued that. Obviously we were in very good market conditions. PO-type engineers were in short supply. I was able to exploit pay research in the sixties. Throughout my term of office I could show that the PO was unable to meet its own recruitment standards. As a government department I would cite the liberality of the UKAEA.

Treasury for their part were concerned about the relativities of specialized GPO grades with general Civil Service grades. The danger from their point of view was that pay concessions to PO grades, which might be justified by outside comparisons or by arguments specific to the GPO and which the GPO might feel it could afford, would lead to pressure for comparable grades across the Civil Service which could not be resisted and would cost a great deal of money. Such public sector considerations continued to constrain GPO and later PO Corporation and BT negotiators right up to the time of privatization in 1984.

The momentum which the union strategies created in respect of the pay of the engineering staff and their first-line managers was to have an important influence on future events. It created a set of expectations and a basic confidence in their own strength among the union memberships which were to last long beyond the point where the original objective was accomplished of equity of treatment compared with the rest of the staff. As we shall see in later chapters, the resulting attitudes were to be formative on a much broader canvas than just pay in the late 1970s; and were only finally to spend their force when they hit the industrial relations reforms of the early Thatcher governments in the 1980s.

Token 'Commercial Accounts' for the GPO had been published since 1912. The idea of 'self-contained financing' had been central to the Bridgeman proposals. The 1955 White Paper introduced new financial arrangements on a trial basis for the five years up to 1961.

Two important appointments were made at the end of 1955. Gordon (later Sir Gordon) Radley was appointed Director General. He was the first engineer to become permanent secretary of a government department. At the same time Kenneth (later Sir Kenneth) Anderson was appointed Comptroller and Accountant General. Anderson was Treasury-trained. The 1955 White Paper represented real progress, but Radley and Anderson were very far from satisfied. The priority was to build on the five-year trial to secure proper legal separation of GPO finances from the Exchequer. The Post Office Act 1961 formally separated them out and provided the first proper foundation for commercial operation of the services.

What none of the authors of these early reforms appears to have realised was just how unsatisfactory were the accounting foundations on which they rested. The experience of nineteenth-century GPO officials had been that there were few things more damaging to their careers than suggestions of irregularities in bookkeeping. A criticism by the Public Accounts Committee could be the kiss of death. The priorities of the old GPO accounting system were the safeguarding of public money and indeed literally of cash; and the requirements of Parliamentary estimates and appropriation accounting. Managerial requirements were accorded hardly any attention at all.

A number of changes were made to financial and accounting systems following the 1961 Act, with the assistance of the City firm of Peat Marwick. Quarterly forecasts were introduced of expected revenue and expenditure out-turns for the current year; and of expectations for the following year. But events were to prove the system quite inadequate to the requirements for running telecommunications in a modern economy.

Also in 1961 the Government published a White Paper, The Financial and Economic Obligations of the Nationalised Industries.[4] Paragraph 23 of this White Paper says:

> the State, as owner and guarantor of the capital of the nationalized industries, (which are investing over £800m a year, more than half of which comes from the Exchequer) would expect capital employed in this kind of business to earn a higher rate of return than the cost of the money to the Exchequer. The objective for each undertaking will be determined in the light of its own circumstances, needs and capabilities in relation to the criteria in paragraph 19. For some the objectives may be expressed in terms of progress towards an appropriate level of self-financing of their capital

expenditure. For others, the objective may be in terms of a specified rate of return on capital employed.

The targets prescribed in this way were not intended to be statutory. The target for telecommunications was set in terms of return on capital employed. The policy set out in this paragraph in this White Paper was to drive PO telecommunications finances, and through them the operations of the business, throughout the twenty-three years up to privatization.

In the world of engineering the standing of the GPO, of its Engineers-in-Chief and of its Engineering Department had always been high. Working closely together, the GPO Research Department and laboratories in the supplying firms had made Britain a world-class centre of innovation in technology. They had made basic contributions to carrier telephony and microwave transmission. In development of submarine cable and satellite systems they were an equal partner of Bell Telephone Laboratories in the USA. Trail-blazing work on the underlying concepts of electronic exchanges had begun on the benches at the GPO Research Station at Dollis Hill as soon as the war ended.

As the demands of public service telecommunications had become apparent, engineering standards had risen to meet them. The telecommunications manufacturing sector grew up almost as a client state of the GPO Engineering Department. The cachet 'GPO Approved' came to be greatly valued by the carefully selected engineering suppliers who were authorized to use it. Nevertheless the Engineering Department was held in a subordinate position inside the GPO. In Headquarters the engineers were supposed to be under the policy control of the administrators, although in reality they were not. Call charging policy in Britain was influenced right through to the 1990s by a series of detailed design compromises decided on by middle-ranking engineers in the late 1950s. In the field the subordination of the engineers was hardly even nominal. Chief Regional Engineers with great practical power and responsibility for engineering operations over hundreds and often thousands of square miles answered to ten Regional Directors who were not much more than administrators, responsible for posts as well as telecommunications over the same territory. A minority of the Regional Directors had been engineers; but most had postal or other backgrounds.

At local level Telephone Managers led some fifty Telephone Areas. Formal responsibility for all that happened in the Area rested with the Telephone Managers. But the core of their operations and of their staff was engineering. The Engineer-in-Chiefs and under them the Chief Regional Engineers had a recognized 'dotted line' relationship on technical matters with the engineers in the Areas. So much of the work was technical in content that the Engineering Department exerted much *de facto* managerial authority as well. It had its own Organization Branch, concerned with many details of management in the field. A weak Telephone Manager could become little more than a staff and money administrator. A stronger one would spend much of the time in profitless conflict with the engineering line of command. The situation was not necessarily improved if, as often, the Telephone Manager was personally a professional engineer.

One energetic attempt had already been made to jolt the GPO out of its traditional mould. Ernest Marples, a Conservative businessman with a distinguished record in the construction industry, was appointed PMG in the late 1950s. He took to the

GPO like a duck to water. In 1958 he caused the department to publish the study called *The Friendly Telephone*, based on examination of the practices of the Bell system. It included proposals, both of which were adopted, for the first luxury telephone in Britain, the Trimphone, and for telephone credit cards. It also said for the first time in GPO history that users should be called 'customers' rather than 'subscribers'. The approach did good out of proportion to its content. But Marples was a Minister, not a Chief Executive, and there were strict limits to the effect he could have.

Despite the 1961 Act the GPO of 1964 was quite profoundly unsuited to the tasks it had to face. Its atmosphere still bore the imprint of the Edwardian Civil Service and of the discipline called forth by two world wars. It was staffed by hierarchies fated to conflict and led by officials wrestling with their own system. On the telecommunications side it was sitting on a bomb of technology and growth. The situation could not be allowed to go on. The next chapter describes the first serious attempt at change.

Notes

1. C.R. Perry, *The Victorian Post Office* (Royal Historical Society, The Boydell Press, Woodbridge, 1992), p. 185.
2. Report on Post Office Development and Finance, Cmd 9576 (HMSO, London, 1955).
3. The structure of the unions representing engineering management and similar grades had a complicated history vividly reflecting the complexity of the Civil Service hierarchical system. Originally professional engineers in the GPO were represented by the Institution of Professional Civil Servants (IPCS). The Society of Post Office Engineers (SPOE) broke away from the IPCS in 1961. The Society of Telecommunications Engineers, which originally represented engineering supervisors below professional level, merged with the Telecommunications Traffic Association representing the bulk of the Traffic departmental grade in 1968 and with SPOE in 1972 to form the Society of PO Executives. This combined union changed its name to the Society of Telecommunications Executives (STE) in 1983. For the sake of simplicity the union group concerned is referred to as STE throughout this book.
4. The Financial and Economic Obligations of the Nationalised Industries, Cmnd 1337 (HMSO, London, 1961).

3 Farewell to Whitehall

If you are efficient you do not need a monopoly. If you are inefficient you do not deserve a monopoly.

> John Harper to Maurice Tinniswood,
> Director of Reorganization in the GPO, 1968

Ministers will never consider doing away with the PO telecoms monopoly.

> Tinniswood to Harper

Labour came to power in the autumn of 1964. Tony Benn had had an interest in the GPO for some time. Just before the election the *Manchester Guardian* had carried a short article by him in which he set out what he thought ought to happen to it. Benn was now appointed PMG.

It soon became apparent that he was not going to see eye to eye at all with the GPO old guard. In *Out of the Wilderness* he recalls a dinner he attended when he first arrived:

> The whole general directorate were there . . . The first speaker, Mr De Grouchy, made a characteristic PO speech in which he poured scorn on the automatic telephones as if they were new fangled devices. He said the PO had always been run by broad-minded ignoramuses at the top.
>
> Replying, I drew attention to two occasions when the PO had been wrong in opposing innovation. One was the introduction of mail coaches in 1784 and the other was the statement in 1879 by Sir William Preece, the Engineer-in-Chief to the PO, when he said he saw no future for the telephone. I said we had a lot to learn from those who opposed change.[1]

One afternoon not long after, I was with Ronald German, the Director General of the time, in his office. The DG suddenly burst out: 'That b——y young fool' (he meant Benn) 'sits down there dictating twenty-six-page Cabinet papers off the top of his head. He hasn't the faintest idea what he is talking about.' I could not help wondering what Benn was thinking, sitting as it happened in the PMG's chair physically just fifteen feet below.

Benn's encounters with the manufacturing industry (see Part III) had a similar flavour of conflict about them. He recounts in *Out of the Wilderness* that at the 1965 annual dinner of the Telecommunications Engineering and Manufacturing Association, the manufacturers' trade association, he 'sat next to a tough guy called John Clark of Plessey who was wildly right wing and greatly resented having to meet me'.[2] Benn now impelled the government to begin serious study of the possibility of transferring the GPO to nationalized industry status.

There was no precedent for the mind-boggling idea of changing the status of something like half the Civil Service in one go. The potential repercussions not only for the GPO itself but for Whitehall and for the Parliamentary process were totally uncharted. With Labour in power the question of the attitude of the unions and of the staff bulked large in thinking. And what would be the implications of loss of Crown status and legal privilege for an undertaking which had never operated without them in four hundred years? Post Office counters provided an essential channel for enormous sums of money paid out by the social security system. What was to be done about these?

On 26 May 1966 the House of Commons decided that the recently formed Select Committee on Nationalised Industries should examine the GPO. The government took the decision in principle to proceed with reorganization. On 3 August 1966 the PMG (by now Edward Short) made the following statement to the House of Commons:

During recent years the Post Office has developed into a complex of vast business enterprises. It now faces considerable problems of expansion, modernization and re-organization if it is to meet the growing demands of the economy.

In considering whether or not the Civil Service context in which the Post Office functions is appropriate in present circumstances the Government have carried out a fundamental survey of its management, structure and functions. After the most careful consideration it has been decided that the time has come to make a change, and that, instead of being a Department of State, with a Minister at its head, the Post Office should become a public Corporation, the members of which would be appointed by and responsible to a Minister.

Within this Corporation the management of the various services would have an opportunity to develop on more independent lines but always with a primary responsibility for the maintenance of comprehensive national services available to all citizens in all parts of the country.

A final decision on the exact form of the re-organization and of the internal management structure must await publication of the Report of the Select Committee on Nationalised Industries which is now examining the Post Office and the fullest consultations with the representatives of the staff. These consultations will now be put in hand, and a White Paper will be presented to the House in due course setting out the government's final proposals.

The Government believes that this decision to modernise the status and management of the Post Office will make a considerable contribution to its efficiency, and the efficiency of Britain, in the years ahead.[3]

Paul Bryan, the Conservative shadow PMG, replied to the statement as follows:

Is the right hon. Gentleman aware that we on this side of the house welcome this statement, which seems to us a development of the policies which we started and in particular the ideas of my right hon. Friend the Member for Wallasey [Ernest Marples]?[4]

In his reply Edward Short said: 'I agree that this is a logical third step from the two steps which the Conservative administration took in 1956 and 1961'.[5] The headquarters of the various unions wanted to believe that their members would do better in terms of pay and conditions if they could get out from under the direct control of Ministers. They therefore raised no serious opposition in principle to the idea of transfer to nationalized industry status.

The attitudes of the staff themselves differed. The engineering unions and their members had few reservations. They had a good idea of the going rates of pay for their skills and of the perks available outside. Years of subordination and of frustration within the system had left them in little doubt about getting out of the Civil Service. Many of them had joined the Service primarily for security in the aftermath of the Depression. In the affluent society now forming round them their priorities had changed. The general service executive and clerical staff on the other hand had serious misgivings. As they saw things, ever since the war they had been fighting to hold their position in terms of pay and status against a steadily rising tide of advance by engineers and other specialists. Within the Service they had had the protection of the hierarchical structure, which operated across all Departments and was not easily set aside. In the new Corporation their position had to be less secure.

The Civil Service as a whole had a track record as a trail-blazer in the employment of women. It had had good opportunities for women for many years and equal pay since 1956. The GPO employed tens of thousands of women, including a number in senior positions in management. Their male colleagues accepted them as unquestioned equals. What would be the attitude of a nationalized board towards women?

The small group of Civil Service administrators at the centre of the department faced their own dilemma. Logic, pay and promotion prospects all pointed to staying with the new Corporation. On the other hand they had chosen careers as Civil Service administrators, not as nationalised utility managers. What would it really be like? 'Management' was a word in a balloon hanging over a bit of territory still largely unexplored; they could not know if they would find their way around it for real. Whitehall was a seductive place. There was no substitute for the satisfaction of contributing to even small tugs on the levers of political power. Telecommunications itself was technological and obviously going to become more so. How would humanists survive?

Benn's original proposal had been that five distinct nationalized corporations should be formed out of the GPO, concerned respectively with posts, telecommunications, savings, Giro and data processing, the latter two new conceptions.

The idea of subdividing the monster in this way was very unwelcome to the largest single union, the Union of Post Office Workers (UPW) which represented postal staff and telephone operators. Both its bargaining power and its standing within the TUC depended on the number of members it had. The idea that it might have to face five separate independent managements, each of which could be expected to develop its own industrial relations philosophy and its own approach to Union recognition, was unthinkable. The UPW exerted a great deal of influence with Ministers and others to keep all five divisions together under a single statutory Board. In its evidence to the Select Committee it said:

> The view of the Union is that the proposed Post Office Corporation should be a single body charged with directing an integrated system of communications, responsible

to Parliament and aiming to provide good service at fair prices but with due regard to the maintenance of non-commercial services of a social character.[6]

The POEU took a different view. Its evidence said:

> It has, for some time, been the Post Office Engineering Union's conviction that the two industries comprised in the existing Post Office would be capable of more fully developing their services under a structure which would allow them to pursue their development separately.[7]

The basic decision to change the status of the Post Office was recognized by everyone as a political matter for which only Ministers could answer on the floor of the House. The question of the internal organization of the new Corporation was, however, a different matter. The Select Committee on Nationalised Industries had a rare formal opportunity genuinely to influence this in advance.

The consultants McKinsey were already developing a reputation in Britain. It was decided to commission them to assist in the development of the new internal structure. This began an association between PO telecommunications and McKinsey which was to last into the 1980s. One important question on which McKinsey were asked to advise concerned the organization of the Regions. If the businesses were genuinely to be separate under a single board, the Regions would clearly have to be split.

Ronald German, representing the Post Office itself, gave oral evidence to the Committee on the question of internal organization on 9 August 1966. He said:

> It seems to me that it would be almost impossible to have an organization in any way similar to that of the gas industry with separate internal units for various reasons. One reason which immediately comes to mind is that certainly on the postal side it would be virtually impossible in a country like ours to run a system with different charges in different parts of the country. The same consideration would not apply so much to the telephone service, but in a small country such as ours completely autonomous regional boards would not have much attraction. We have from time to time thought – indeed the view has been expressed publicly by all sorts of people – that something might have been said for a complete separation of telephones from posts with completely separate boards and organizations . . . the Postmaster General's statement on this is clear: that there is to be one Corporation . . . It would for instance be very difficult indeed to give complete autonomy to separate executives below a policy forming board.[8]

In this single answer lie a series of issues profoundly affecting internal organization, some of which are live to this day.

In its Report issued in February 1967 the Select Committee itself said:

> The third solution – and the one favoured by your Committee is, broadly, a recreation in the form of a corporation of the power and authority structure of the present Post Office (with one or two amendments). This, in itself, may have merits. It is a well-tried pattern, and one that has on the whole worked well; it is understood by those who work in the organization; and it would ease the transformation from Government department to public corporation.
>
> Your Committee believe that the Corporation should be governed by a small, powerful executive Board. All major decisions, including all tariff questions, investment

policy, expenditure planning, pay questions, procurement policy, manufacturing policy, research and development policy and management staffing policy should be taken at Board level.[9]

Parliament was getting the Post Office it had decided it wanted. The question was whether it could be made to work.

Preparatory work had continued inside government while the Select Committee was deliberating. The government's decisions were announced in March 1967 in the White Paper *Reorganization of the Post Office*. It said:

> Posts and telecommunications are vast businesses in themselves, with different characteristics and meeting different needs. But they have been run jointly by the Post Office in the past and are complementary in some respects and interdependent in others. Many of their supporting functions are effectively and economically organized on a common service basis. There are thus real advantages in the continued overall direction of their affairs by a single body. The bill will therefore create a single statutory Corporation which will be headed by a single small largely executive Board.
>
> At the same time, if the two businesses are to develop successfully in their different ways and seize their different opportunities, they must be managed separately within this single overall framework. The Government consider that the managerial structure of the Corporation should provide for this at all levels – national, regional and local.[10]

Inside the GPO, a Reorganization Department (ROD) had been established to carry the changes through. Maurice Tinniswood was appointed Director of Reorganization (Under-Secretary). I was appointed as the Assistant Secretary reporting to him.

The first priorities were managerial. Half the Civil Service, providing services absolutely essential to the community, had to be extracted from Whitehall as a going concern. It was vital to preserve the confidence of the staff.

It soon became clear that special attention was needed to pensions. The most important single term of employment distinguishing Civil Servants from the rest of the community was their pension status. This did not rest on contract, like that of everyone else, but on a typically British formula. The entitlement to a pension was not a right but a privilege granted by the Crown. A series of Superannuation Acts defined the terms of the pension when granted. It was non-contributory. The task facing Tinniswood and Nobby Clark, who joined him to work on pensions, was to organize the transition from this curious situation to that of a funded contractual scheme combining employee and employer contributions, and to do so while preserving complete staff confidence that their pensions were secure.

The fact that the Civil Service scheme was not funded added special complications. Civil Servants' pensions were paid out of the Consolidated Fund like any other government expense. The Treasury and the GPO came to the conclusion that to get the logic of the process right they had to do a calculation of the finances of a completely notional fund reflecting the accumulated rights of past and present GPO employees on vesting day. The calculation showed a large deficit. Fall-out from this problem and the formula used in the Act to resolve it was to continue for many years to come.

The problem was made worse by the intention of the Treasury at that time to raise the general male retiring age to sixty-five. The Post Office was a natural test case on which to seek to make this stick. It was bitterly resisted by the unions. Tinniswood loyally held the pass for the Treasury. Feeling became so intense that in the end the General Secretary of the POEU, Charles (later Lord Delacourt-)Smith made a direct approach to Ministers. Tinniswood was relieved of direct responsibility for staff matters in the reorganization, though he continued as Director of the Department. In the event the male retirement age remained at sixty. Other problems with pensions on the union front persisted after the new Corporation came into being.

This episode and the treatment of the structural difficulty were important pointers to the problems of the managers of the PO as a nationalized industry in dealing with unions under a Labour government, problems which were to become more and more apparent as the 1970s wore on.

Ministers and staff were anxious to get on and complete the process as soon as possible. But they could not do so until the Bill had been drafted, considered by Parliament and received the Royal Assent.

Sir John Ricks, the Solicitor to the GPO, had written the official commentary on the PO Acts in Halsbury's *Statutes of England*. The Bill itself was so important that it was allocated to Second Parliamentary Counsel, Harold Chorley, to draft.

The central provisions of the Bill were built round the common form model of the earlier nationalization Acts. The Post Office was to have powers and duties appropriate to its services, centring on Sections 7 and 9 in what became the PO Act 1969. The government's powers of direction are incorporated in Sections 12 and 13. They looked impressive; but with the exception of certain specific powers they would be treated in practice as reserved powers only, in the background in case things went catastrophically wrong but most unlikely to be used in real life. The provisions that mattered were the Minister's powers to appoint and dismiss the members of the Board (Section 6) and to approve the capital programme (Section 11 (8)), the Corporation's general duty to make the books balance (Section 31 (1)) and its power to borrow from the Minister (that is in reality the Treasury) (Section 35). Between them these embodied the essence of nationalized industry status.

To replace the function of Parliament and MPs in day-to-day matters to do with the services the Bill provided for creation of a national Post Office Users Council (POUNC), with supporting Councils in Scotland, Wales and Northern Ireland. Government took no express statutory power in relation to changes in charges or conditions, but POUNC had the right to be consulted about them and government had limited statutory functions in this respect in support of POUNC.

The decision was taken early on that the Bill would not be used as a vehicle for new policy or law about the services themselves except where absolutely necessary. The task of conversion was too formidable in itself.

The exception was the monopoly of carrier telecommunications. The wording of the existing monopoly provisions had been framed by Victorian lawyers and administrators, who had had had to use dead reckoning in lieu of experience. Its actual words related to telegrams, which by 1969 were as near defunct as made no difference. It had been extended to telephonic messages only by a court ruling in 1876. It was quite spectacularly out of date. It was so central to the position of the new Corporation that it simply had to be recast in 1969 terms.

In the spring of 1968 Ricks and I went down to Chorley's office overlooking Horse Guards Parade to discuss his first draft of the new monopoly provisions. The key words read: 'the exclusive privilege of operating systems for the conveyance of signals'. Ricks and I were unhappy with 'operating'. As rehearsals for Trooping the

Colour went on outside I said, 'What we do is something related to "What a way to run a railway".' Counsel stared at me and walked across to the bookcase. He got down the *Oxford English Dictionary* and read out the definition of the meaning of *run* (no. 17 in the concise *OED*) which says 'of . . . business, person etc . . . . keep them going, conduct, manage their operations'. He said, 'You've got it, boy.' Today Section 5 (1) of the 1984 Act reads, inter alia, 'a person who runs a telecommunications system within the United Kingdom shall be guilty of an offence unless he is authorised to run a system by a licence'.

The 'exclusive privilege' conferred by the 1869 Act had been of the conveyance of telegrams. It had been framed specifically to exclude telegrams conveyed internally within organizations, largely at the insistence of the railways who of course used telegraphic communication very extensively for internal purposes. In framing the new monopoly Ricks, Chorley and I went to a great deal of trouble to make sure that it excluded systems run by companies for internal purposes. The words we devised were carried forward into the licensing powers in the 1984 Act.

To restate and emphasize the point in the language of 1996, neither the PO monopoly nor the Secretary of State's licensing powers have ever extended to networks used solely to carry companies' internal traffic. The whole business of acquiring private (leased) circuits (or virtual private networks), having them assembled into internal private networks and operating and using them has never come within the ambit of the monopoly and does not require licences today. It has always been open to private companies to commission independent operators to construct private networks for them. Put another way, British telecommunications law has always recognized that public and private telecommunications are distinct markets and has provided for competition in the latter. The significance of this point in considering future policy is brought out in Part VI.

The 1869 Act formed part of the family of nineteenth- and early twentieth-century legislation known in the trade as the Telegraph Acts. They were in a truly awful mess, riddled with partial repeals and amendments and saddled with decades of complex case law. Work had been in hand to replace them completely for some years. But it was a task of formidable complexity and it was not yet complete. The decision was taken to transfer the main mass of these Acts to the Corporation by adaptation, leaving the task of modernizing them properly to later. (It was finally completed for the 1984 Act. The Telecommunications Code in Schedule 2 to that Act is the successor to the relevant provisions of the Telegraph Acts.)

The biggest single technical legal problem concerned the loss of Crown privilege and of the status of the Post Office as a government department. Effect could be and was given to this as a general matter by a straightforward provision in the legislation (the eventual Section 6 (5)). But it was nowhere near as simple as that. Over hundreds of years the practice had grown up of including explicit protections and provisions about details of GPO activity in almost every imaginable kind of British, Scottish, Northern Irish and even Channel Islands and Manx legislation. Both common sense and legal logic required all these to be traced and repealed or amended. The mess that would otherwise have been created for the courts and for the law generally would have been absolutely intolerable. Each one therefore had to be found and checked for later repeals or amendments and from the point of view of policy; and a decision taken about it. Some of the provisions themselves had long and complicated histories due to repeals and interactions in later legislation; just tracing them was a major undertaking in its own right.

The law of the Post Office services themselves presented another formidable problem, even though apart from the monopoly it was not to be recast. There was no avoiding scrutiny of it to make sure simply that it would work in the new circumstances and would not create legal or practical nonsenses. It was encrusted with the attitudes and approaches of generation after generation of postal and telegraph administrators, lawyers and legislators, and much of the encrustation had never been rationalized. One annoying set of difficulties arose from the nineteenth-century practice of including in primary legislation (Acts themselves) details of tariffing and other operational arrangements which in later years would have been included in statutory instruments or orders made under them, and which today would be in contracts. A good deal of the resulting mass of detail still stood on the statute book in a highly confused way. There was no alternative but to wade through it and sort it out.

Other legal problems had immediate practical force. Planning and road traffic law were typical. Both had buried in them key provisions affecting Post Office operations. In some cases there were issues of policy with significant implications, for example on the working of planning law on Post Office plant and on national exemption for postal vehicles from parking restrictions. It took many iterations to tease such matters out.

There were other areas where the problems of reorganizing the PO were a microcosm of more general muddles. It was decided that the provisions of the Official Secrets Acts should apply to PO staff as if they were Civil Servants. The Secrets Acts themselves were a tangle of overlaps and amendments which took months to bring into the necessary focus. Again, the PO was an extremely important ratepayer. Its future position under rating law had to be argued out, even though the old national rating system was already the subject of the highly uncomfortable debate which in the end would give birth to the poll tax and the Council Tax.

The favourite experience of the Reorganization Department concerned dog licences. With the determination of cleaners of Augean stables, David Savill and Henry Tilling set out to clear the dog licence decks for the Corporation, which would have actually to issue the licences. Their innocent enthusiasm faltered and died in face of the discovery of one of the hoariest of all the King Charles's heads of Whitehall. Everyone knew that the licences and the fee were anachronistic anomalies. But five departments were involved; none of them would admit to definitive responsibility; and Ministers emphatically did not want to know. Section 12 (2) (which authorizes directions on the issue of dog and game licences) stands to this day as a memorial to a gallant attempt which failed.

This mass of legal detail turned out to be the critical path for the reorganization operation as a whole. Ministers wanted to introduce the Bill in the 1967-8 session of Parliament. But to their lasting credit they accepted that the work on the statutes could not responsibly be short-circuited. Ricks's advice that the Bill would have to await the 1968-9 session for this reason was reluctantly accepted. (The contrast with the attitude of Ministers on the 1984 Act could not have been more marked – see Chapter 15.) The Bill was finally introduced in the autumn of 1969.

Although many of the policy provisions of the 1969 Act ceased to apply to BT as a consequence of the 1984 Act and of privatization, the enormous task of rationalization and refocusing of British statute law in its bearing on the PO carried out between 1966 and 1969 was an essential step in the creation of the modern regime. It was carried out by a handful of people, at whose centre Ricks carried an extraordinary personal burden. The 1969 Act and its content were the principal achievement of his career.

Although the two main parties were in agreement on the principle of the Bill, Parliament was not disposed to take lying down an event as large as the extraction of half the Civil Service from Whitehall. The GPO and GPO services bulked large in the daily concerns of most MPs, and they were determined to make their mark in the debates on the Bill. The Committee stage lasted several months. Report and Third Reading were the scene of something approaching a filibuster. Royal Assent was finally granted on 25 July 1969.

While the Bill proceeded on its way, work had been in hand on the actual creation of the Corporation and on reorganization as such. It had been decided after much heart-searching that the new Corporation should be called 'The Post Office'. Her Majesty the Queen had agreed to the continued use of 'Royal Mail' and of the Crown on kiosks and pillar boxes. Sir John Wall had earlier been selected as Chief Executive designate of the new Corporation. There was an organ called the PO Board, made up of officials under the chairmanship of the PMG, although it had no real power and served little real purpose. Wall had been appointed Deputy Chairman of this Board; but he had left the PO again by the time the Bill reached its final stages in Parliament.

The Bill provided for a single statutory Board with a maximum of twelve members plus the Chairman, which would take over the PMG's responsibilities for the services. The Corporation and its Board were to come into existence following Royal Assent, so that the Board would be up and running by Vesting Day on 31 October 1969. The Board was now appointed (see Chapter 4). Maurice Tinniswood was appointed as the first Secretary and the rump of RoD formed the nucleus of the Secretary's Office. Lord Peddie was appointed as the first Chairman of POUNC.

Vesting was set for midnight on 31 October 1969. At that moment four hundred years of PO services under the direct control of government came to an end and nearly half a million people left the Civil Service. From now on it was up to the statutory Corporation.

Notes

1. Tony Benn, *Out of the Wilderness* (Arrow Books, London, 1987), p. 265.
2. *Ibid.*, p. 217.
3. *Hansard*, 3 August 1966, cols 467–8.
4. *Ibid.*, col. 468.
5. *Ibid.*, col. 468.
6. First Report from the Select Committee on Nationalised Industries – The Post Office, HC Paper 340–I (HMSO, London, 1967), p. 620.
7. *Ibid.*, p. 618.
8. *Ibid.*, p. 767.
9. *Ibid.*, paras XVII.65, 66.
10. Reorganization of the Post Office, Cmnd 3233 (HMSO, London, 1967), paras 33, 34.

Part II
The PO Corporation

4 The New Organization

The Post Office . . . is bursting out with new ideas and is making serious efforts to think of its customers as people who must be wooed rather than the 'public' who must occasionally be thrown a Civil Service titbit.

The Sunday Times Magazine, 20 June 1971

Lord Hall, the new Chairman, had been a senior official of the International Finance Corporation, an offshoot of the International Bank for Reconstruction and Development. Ryland was appointed Deputy Chairman and Chief Executive. Fennessy, the Managing Director Telecommunications, was a successful private sector manager and a telecommunications engineer who had played a major role in building Britain's radar defences during the war and subsequently founded the Decca Radar company. Prior to joining the Board he had been Managing Director of the Plessey Electronics Group. Ashton, Board Member for Finance and Corporate Planning, had been Finance Director of Esso Petroleum UK. The Board Member for Personnel, Sir Richard Hayward, had been a Post Office and Civil Service trade unionist. He had been Chairman of the Civil Service Whitley Council National Staff Side. Merriman, Board Member for Technology, was a career PO engineer. Laver, Member for Data Processing, had started in the PO and gone on to a career in computing. On the postal side the Managing Director Posts was Geoffrey Vieler.

Ryland had already done much to shake off the Edwardian mould of the GPO before Vesting Day. In addition to the organizational changes described in the preceding chapter, telecommunications had a well-developed management-by-objectives system and well-established mechanisms for improvement of staff productivity. But there was a very long way to go yet. The situation which the new Board faced on the operating side of telecommunications was daunting.

The absolute basics of customer service were unacceptable. There was a large and growing waiting list for service. The international service, on which the City and exporters were coming more and more to depend, was inadequate and deteriorating. The performance of the inland network was also deteriorating and the supply industry had been shown to be seriously unreliable. The business was still seriously undermanaged. There was no satisfactory structure of command and control and no meaningful management accounting system. Labour efficiencies had been improved but there was still a long way to go. There were no controls on non-labour current account spending or on the efficiency of use of capital or the execution of projects. The confidence of the staff had been affected by the change, despite all the efforts. An industrial relations climate needed to be forged of a kind which would restore this confidence and permit the carrying through of many different kinds of change.

At the start the omens on the industrial relations front looked favourable. As Bryan Stanley, by now General Secretary of the POEU, says:

> When the Corporation was established there was an entirely different [industrial relations] approach. There was a Board appointed and Lord Hall became our chairman, and for a short time the Secretary of the Whitley Council [Hayward] became the personnel Board member and so on. So there was a total change in atmosphere. We [POEU] had been moderately successful in our pay negotiations in the period leading up to that time. And there was a new approach. At the time Lord Hall became very deeply involved in staff matters. He was the sort of guy who when he went out into the field wanted to meet the staff; he did not want to meet the managers, he did not want to be on a conducted tour, he wanted the staff to be brought together and he wanted to go right into the middle of them. So he used to address them over the heads as it were of the local managers. He would say things that were quite astounding, things that he wanted to do to improve the position and then he would say to them, 'Right, now I want you to tell me what you think – never mind about these ★★★ managers that are all around – you tell me – I believe in calling a spade a bloody shovel.'
>
> So this was a new era in negotiations. Flowing from that came things like the superannuation scheme, which was a wonderful improvement; the abolition of the over-riding maxima, which had been a thorn in our side for years; the changing attitude that Civil Service need not necessarily dominate everything in the PO.
>
> Hall was the most remarkable, refreshing experience to us. He was astounded at the things that we were doing because of tradition. But [it was] for a very short time.

Stanley catches the atmosphere of detailed work in industrial relations in these early days:

> We set up this joint Council of unions working towards the Corporation. It was a very good job we did because at a very early stage we began to examine and re-examine in minute detail all the conditions of service, all the arrangements that applied to staff. It was almost like a total renegotiation. To be fair, management in the end did not damage us and in many respects were prepared to go further than they had ever gone before in the establishment of conditions in the new Corporation. The negotiations started quite badly [before 1969] from the bullish position that some top managers were taking – that was 'Well of course we have no real responsibility to perpetuate or continue anything and anyway we can't commit the new Board that is going to be appointed'. We started from a very weak position because everything was going in the melting pot. But step by step by step it emerged, as we met each group of negotiators from the various divisions of the PO, that that was not going to be the problem that originally we had anticipated.

In 1971 the Conservatives took over from Labour. Lord Hall left the PO (see page 106). Ryland took over as Chairman. What happened inside the PO at the time has had no parallel, before or since. Stanley again:

> On the day that it was announced that [Christopher] Chataway [Minister of Posts and Telecommunications in the Heath government] had removed [Lord Hall], the

demonstrations that took place were totally and absolutely spontaneous. And it wasn't only on the telecoms side. When the the news came through on both postal and telecommunications sides people were so disgusted that they just walked out of their jobs into the street; and spontaneously criticized and condemned what was happening. Because in the short time he was there Hall had made an impact on the staff.

In 1971 the postal workers' union, the UPW, became involved in a very damaging strike over postal pay. The union lost. Hayward resigned soon after as Board Member for Personnel and was replaced by Kenneth Young, who had a distinguished record in personnel in the GEC group.

Ryland was a very different and very much more Post Office kettle of fish than Hall. He had himself been a POEU member and was later lead pay negotiator for the GPO as Director of Establishments and Organization. He was the architect of a revolution in managerial methods, and scarred up to the armpits with battles with Treasury, suppliers and unions. He represented the PO establishment. Under him things were to take quite a different tone from that set by Hall.

Ryland was now a dominant figure. Peter Shaw of the POEU says: 'The reputation was that he was a very strong, powerful, nothing-moved-without-his-permission kind of person.' The highest priority of all those facing the Board in 1969 had been the establishment of a new identity distinct from Whitehall. A new relationship had to be forged with the government machine from which the Corporation had so recently been born.

Legally, the relationship between the Corporation and the government was set by the Act. Ministers could be questioned on the floor of the House about the working of its provisions. But, apart from the requirement in Section 14 for reference of proposals for tariff increases to POUNC, there was no statutory machinery governing the relationship on charges and prices; or the requirements for the target return on capital under Cmnd 1461. These key matters were left to be determined informally behind the scenes.

'Government' for this purpose meant the newly constituted Ministry of Posts and Telecommunications (MPT). The first Minister was John Stonehouse. The Permanent Secretary (in rank only a Deputy Secretary because of the small size of the unit) was Frank (later Sir Frank) Wood. Many of the original staff of MPT were ex-GPO people, including Dennis Lawrence, the Under-Secretary responsible for telecommunications. The big issues were dealt with day to day by the Chairman, the Board Members for Finance and Personnel and their staffs, dealing with the Minister when appropriate and otherwise with officials. Stonehouse had been the last PMG and had steered the Bill successfully through the Commons. As the first Minister of Posts and Telecommunications he understood the importance of leaving the PO free to manage its affairs to the greatest possible extent. He recognized that the day-to-day handling of Parliamentary Questions and MPs' letters would set a pattern which would be formative when it came to bigger issues.

At the level immediately below the Board the PO had advantages which other nationalized industries did not share. Its senior staff had very recently been part themselves of the government machine, and they understood how it worked. They were united in determination to protect their freedom now they had won it. They were equipped to put and argue their case in a way Whitehall officials could understand and to which they could relate. The PO had the advantages of specialist knowledge, large staff resources to support its submissions and above all the initiative in the topics raised in the first place. The tactic the PO people used was to supply fact, encourage DoI officials to test it and leave them free to make up their minds on their own terms without trying to force the process. Once officials had reached a set of conclusions of their own they could be relied on to put them and to defend them to Ministers. The art lay in ensuring that these conclusions were correct.

Telecommunications had one other advantage which posts did not share. Apart from short periods when inflation caused costs to rise before prices caught up, telecommunications was consistently profitable throughout the period. It was never in the situation where it had to be subsidized; and therefore never subject to the law of administration which says that if you accept government subsidy you have to accept being told how to spend it. Telecommunications was a natural subject for independence.

Inside the Corporation, as 1 November 1969 dawned, every procedure, every record, every rule book and every form the staff used was an artefact of Civil Service practice. The pressing nature of the task of change was obvious. The Post Office had been part of government for four hundred years. Despite the advances of the Bridgeman Committee and those accomplished by Ryland in the later 1960s, the way it went about things was still basically that formed by the Ministers, Permanent Secretaries and Engineers-in-Chief of Victorian and Edwardian times, working by the lights of the Whitehall process, not by those of business.

With the exception of Lord Hall, Fennessy and Ashton the team which had to address this task had all been career Civil Servants; or in the case of Richard Hayward had grown up in PO and Civil Service trade unionism. It had been the wish of GPO officials ever since the final nationalization of telecommunications and the institution of formally published 'Commercial Accounts' in 1912 to find a place of respect alongside the business community. The hazard was that despite this they would fail to grasp how completely different the environment they now faced actually was. They could be relied on to try very hard indeed to comply with the new mould. It was after all the wish of Ministers, and Ministers' word was law. But that did not mean they would succeed. Presented with a concrete problem like changing the personnel structures, they would still address it with their traditional way of doing things. Many operating problems would be solved, and many solved very well, in the next ten years. But the telecommunications machine would fail to change itself. It was perhaps asking too much of human nature to expect it to do so.

A number of significant changes followed automatically from the loss of the privileges of a Crown department. In matters like planning and highway law and compulsory purchase of land PO staff were accustomed to the direct powers and privileges of government. They now had to learn to live with a status in such respects just like that of the other nationalized industries. Some pretty bizarre things happened in the months around Vesting Day. PO cable ships had never been subject to the Merchant Shipping Acts. On Vesting Day they suddenly became subject to them; and Acts of Parliament had to be obeyed. Registration numbers had to be burnt into the ships' timbers. Much more seriously, the ships became subject to merchant shipping construction and upkeep rules. The marine surveyors found to their horror that steelwork on one of the older ships had become so corroded that they could put a hand through it.

But, as we have seen, most of the legal provisions specific to the services had been carried forward for lack of time. The most important remaining element of the Telegraph Acts were the powers of the PO and BT to place plant on other people's land and in highways (the 'wayleave powers'). These had not been affected by the loss of Crown privilege. They still embodied an advantage unique among street utilities. Appeal against their exercise was still through legal channels to the High Court, not through administrative channels to a separate Minister. The experience of a hundred years was that few people had chosen to challenge the GPO in these circumstances. By 1969 it was rare for people even to contemplate doing so and the GPO had almost absolute power to take wayleaves. The privileged wayleave powers continued to be exercised daily by a considerable number of junior staff in fifty Area offices throughout the country. The Post Office was still 'the GPO' to wayleave takers and grantors.

A lot of change in organization had already been accomplished by Vesting Day. Under the single Board of the Corporation the separation of telecommunications from posts and the creation of separate business headquarters were both complete. So far as telecommunications was concerned the most serious single defect of the old headquarters organization had been the hierarchy-based division of functions between the Inland Telecommunications Department (ITD) in the administrative headquarters and the Engineering Department (ED). It was mirrored in the Regions in the division between the Telecommunications Branches and the Engineering Branches. The new organization eliminated these divisions.

A completely new structure had been formed out of a comprehensive merger of the ITD and the ED. A number of new functional Departments had been created. They included Operational Programming Department (OPD) under John Whyte, concerned with oversight of and investment programming for the main core of plant operations in the Regions and with the corresponding central engineering functions, and Network Planning Department (NPD) under Frank Thomas, with both executive and engineering responsibility for the inland long-distance network, using the Regions as agents for activities on the ground like maintenance. They also included Telecommunications Development Department, concerned with application development of all new technology; Research Department; Telecommunications Marketing Department; Service Department, concerned with service and with operator services; Telecommunications Finance and Personnel Departments; and Management Services Department.

A new Purchasing and Supply Department (P&SD) had already been created by combining the old Contracts Department, the old Supplies Department (concerned with provisioning and warehousing supplies and stores) and the old Factories Department and quality and materials functions from the old E-in-C's Office. It was recognized that procurement was a critical area and that it had been one of the weakest of all in the old structure. It needed full-time attention at high level. Kenneth Cadbury, whose final appointment in the Civil Service structure had been the key post of Director [Under-Secretary] Inland Telecommunications (Planning), was appointed as the first Director Purchasing and Supply.

The new headquarters structure was a success. It soon became clear just how much energy and enthusiasm had been there to be liberated once the tensions and frustrations due to the old structure were removed.

The same approach based on the merging of engineering and non-engineering was applied in regional headquarters as at national level. The Regional Directors themselves were a mixture of engineers and non-engineers. With one exception (Hughie Holmes in North-East Region) the Planning Controllers at the heads of the Planning Divisions were all professional engineers. A number of them had been Chief Regional Engineers in the old structure. The Service Controllers were a mixture of engineers and non-engineers. People from the Executive Class were appointed to most of the Finance and Personnel Controller posts.

The old regional structure had been distinguished by some classic feuds between Engineering and Telecommunications Branches. As in headquarters, the new regional headquarters structure worked remarkably well from day one and demonstrated how much talent and energy had been locked up in unprofitable disputes.

Telephone Areas were of course already purely telecommunications units. There was no inherent need to change their organization. It was recognized that the existing structure was unsatisfactory. But changing it was a very much bigger and more difficult undertaking than remodelling national or regional headquarters. It was linked to the hierarchical structure inherited from the Civil Service for the main mass of staff. These questions were left to be addressed later. They were in fact never to be addressed effectively right up to privatization.

The next priority was to recast the ranking and pay structures. The logical place to start was with management. The continuing unification of the Post Office was seen as calling for a common management structure across all the businesses. It was taken for granted that this structure would include pay scales up to the level immediately below the Board, just like the Civil Service structure. Viewed with the eyes of someone like Lord Hall, one of the most urgent objectives was to detach middle and senior management from the long tradition of unionization and of uniform pay scales with no immediate rewards for success. In the Civil Service even some Under-Secretaries belonged to their union, the First Division Association. Its chairperson was often an Assistant Secretary – that is, only four levels down from the very top. The senior managers needed to be encouraged to think as individuals identified completely with the Corporation. To do this it was essential to introduce a relatively generous pay system, with a proper stick and carrot element bearing on individual performance.

As soon as work started, the differences in the character of the businesses made themselves felt. The qualities required of postal managers were concerned with personnel management, leadership and the basic skills of business. Telecommunications managers had to have these qualities also; but they had to exercise them and produce results in a capital-intensive environment, with a highly specialized technology which was advancing all the time. The practical demands on the two sides in terms of relative skills and responsibilities at superficially similar organizational levels were quite different. A Head Postmaster with a staff of perhaps five hundred and a territory ten miles in radius might well be headquartered in the same town as a Telephone Manager with a staff of two thousand, a territorial radius of thirty miles and operating responsibility for several hundred million pounds' worth of plant. Yet both would see themselves and be seen by the local civic authorities as ranking equally as representatives of their respective services. Analogous situations were common throughout posts and telecommunications. In what had so recently been a Civil Service environment, obsessed with levels and relativities, and with everyone still to be employed on pay scales published for all to see, such situations were bound to create problems.

It was decided to call the new structure the Senior Salary Structure. One of the most important questions involved its lower limit. The crucial question was whether or not to include the staff at the second line of supervision. In the traditional Civil Service structure each second-line group had had its place in its own hierarchy, as Executive Engineers, Higher Executive Officers and so on. Many of them had highly responsible jobs. In the engineering and commercial structures in the field they bore much of the responsibility for actually making things happen. By the standards of outside business they were important people, often controlling substantial groups of staff. The new approach to management pay was likely to lead to substantially higher pay levels. The cost of including the second-line supervision would be very high. There was also a more subtle dimension. Among Board members only Bill Ryland, Merriman, Laver and Richard Hayward had served in the ranks of the PO; and only Ryland had personal experience of second-line supervision work. The gap of understanding between Hall as Chairman, most of the Board and the supervision in the field was just too great to be bridged. To the Chairman, coming from the very special background of international finance, managers were powerful and influential people in elegant offices in city centres. It was asking the impossible to expect someone like him to appreciate the status and self-image of second-line supervisors in an organization like the Post Office; and in particular the store they set by being considered part of management.

In the event, despite serious misgivings among more senior management and warnings from many of them, the second-line staff were excluded from the Senior Salary Structure. However much their immediate bosses might try to reassure them and to draw them along, from now on they saw themselves as positively excluded from management and almost pushed into the arms of first-line supervision and the rank-and-file.

The designers of the internal detail of the Structure were heavily influenced by current fashions. The most important was job evaluation, resting on the assumption that a detailed line-by-line analysis of what managers and professionals did would provide an objective basis for ranking their jobs for pay purposes. The results of such analysis applied to Civil Service psychology were predictable. A series of furious rows developed about vertical and horizontal relativities, all starting from the implicit assumption that the relationships before Vesting Day had been right. The rows were determined by decisions which again were seen as imposed from above. The loyalty of senior managers was never in doubt; but a sense that it had been uncomfortably strained was left in many minds.

When it was finished (after Hall left the PO) the Structure turned out to include considerably more pay bands even than the Civil Service structure at the same levels. A complicated mechanism was introduced of bonuses and additional or withheld increments, based on an elaborate annual reporting system. The reports themselves were redesigned. At Fennessy's insistence they gave prominence to identifiable and measurable results achieved. To make things even more complicated, a new organizational structure was introduced across the Corporation at the same time. There were fewer organizational levels than pay bands. The result was that some organizational levels included posts graded for pay purposes at two different levels, to accommodate differences emerging from job evaluation.

Seen as a piece of abstract personnel engineering, the new arrangements had the attraction of a complex piece of machinery devised to solve a very complex problem.

What no one perceived at the time was that as a mechanism for moving the psychology of management away from the Civil Service they were a recipe for disaster. The ritualization of differences of rank, with the scope it offered for invidious comparison of relativities of pay and status, appealed to all that was backward-looking in the Corporation. It out-Civil-Serviced the Civil Service. Equally if not more seriously, in face of the immense vested interest of the unions in the status quo no move was made to restructure below management level at all. At this level the Civil Service hierarchies, the grading structures within them and the attitudes that went with them were to remain basically unchanged right up to privatization.

The Senior Salary Structure arrangements also typified the effects of the handicaps imposed by the continued coupling of the businesses. The quite different requirements of posts and telecommunications had had to be accommodated by a cumbersome compromise worked out centrally which was not optimized for either. The combined effects of all this were among the most important handicaps with which the operational side of the business was to have to wrestle during the fifteen years that followed.

In a highly significant perpetuation of Civil Service practice the personnel function remained a world on its own, whose priorities were driven as much by the tactical requirements of contention with the unions, especially on pay, as by the operational requirements of the business.

Against this background the Corporation and its Board now turned to the future.

5 1975 and After

When we first examined the nationalized British Telecom we discovered that, in true east European style, the corporation had not the faintest idea which of its activities were profitable and which were not, let alone any finer points of management accounting.

Nigel Lawson, *The View from No. 11*[1]

It is not clear where Mr Lawson got this particular impression. PO telecommunications had been publishing separate financial results for its main services since the 1960s. And by the early 1980s the business had accomplished much more by way of reform to its management procedures than the Ministers of the time were likely to give it credit for. But that is not to say that there were not continuing grounds for exasperation with its finance systems. There were.

As we have seen, the saga of PO finance reform had begun in the 1930s. In all, between 1955 and 1984 the line managers of telecommunications found themselves required to grasp and produce results under no fewer than five different accounting systems. These were the original Parliamentary appropriation system; the distinctive GPO system introduced following the 1961 Act; the adaptation of this system used in the early nationalized industry days, from 1969 to 1975; the mixture of outside and inside practices followed from 1975 to 1981; and the normal system of private business, the introduction of which had begun in the pre-privatization period. Between 1969 and 1984 five different Board Members for Finance, all but one recruited from outside the Corporation, were to wrestle with the financial systems of the business. The story was still to be unfinished at the moment of privatization.

The situation in 1969 was extraordinary, given the scale of the trading operations of the PO and their significance in the economy. The most immediately striking difference between PO arrangements and those outside was in the staff. In outside business financial matters were always the responsibility of qualified accountants. The PO had about thirty chartered accountants on its staff, but they were employed exclusively on procurement work. The whole of the financial and accounting operation of the PO was conducted by people who had been general service staff in the Civil Service. Many of them were able people with a high degree of expertise in the specialism of public and PO finances. But none of them had professional accountancy qualifications.

The systems themselves were spectacularly unsuited to the job they had to do. In one of the largest organizations in the country, with a turnover and a conglomerate structure which towered over all but the very largest private companies, there was no mechanism for financial accounting for any unit smaller in scope than the complete businesses – posts, telecommunications, Giro and NDPS – and therefore no machinery to provide any financial basis for devolution of line responsibility within them. Management accounting in any proper sense was unknown. Capital investment was effectively managed outside the finance function.

The accounting system had hardly altered since Edwardian times. There was a Whitehall dictum that 'administration is finance'. Some of the best brains in the country had been devoted to the Civil Service financial procedures which the GPO followed. But they had been perfected to serve the purposes of the Parliamentary machine and the wishes of governments and MPs. They had almost nothing to do with managing a modern telecommunications business.

The problems were well illustrated where the real money was collected and spent, in field operations. Great numbers of basic working expense and stores consumption vouchers were generated by something like a hundred thousand engineers and processed along with millions of bills by thousands of clerical staff. But the potential of the information buried in these bills and vouchers as a management tool was left completely to go to waste. To the managers on the ground they were simply paper flowing in and out of an incomprehensible central system. Again, the accounting system made a distinction between current account and capital. But the rules for this distinction and the significance of the allocation were an arcane subject of concern only to a handful of accounting specialists at headquarters. In a business turning over billions a year there was nothing to bring the significance of the money they were collecting and spending home to line managers in real terms; and they had nothing to give them a grasp of something as basic as the distinction between capital and current account.

At national level current account expenditure was treated as something which the services had to incur to operate. It was a handle-turning matter. The money required was applied for each year through estimates laid before Parliament and authorised through appropriation procedures in the Commons. The House had set up the Public Accounts Committee in the nineteenth century to root out maladministration by enquiry after the event. The Committee was heartily feared and respected in the GPO. In consequence there was a heavy emphasis on the safeguarding of funds, cash and stocks against dishonesty. But there was only token attention to the efficency with which the money was spent; and even the arithmetic behind price changes worked on a by-guess-and-by-God basis. The ideas that financial systems existed to serve the purposes of management, or that there should be attention to financial results and the bottom-line of profit for their own sake, were basically foreign to the system.

This did not mean that wage increases or staff numbers had gone undisciplined or uncontrolled. Far from it. Wage negotiation was a prestige activity; and wage claims were often acutely contested. GPO negotiators were regarded with respect in other parts of Whitehall and by the unions. There were also elaborate procedures for controlling the number of posts and for inspection of establishments to eliminate waste at a detailed level. But this work was done at arm's length from its financial consequences and from the financial organization. The implicit assumption was that if inputs like wage levels or staff numbers were optimized in their own terms the finances of the service would look after themselves.

Important changes were made following the 1961 Act. The officials concerned did their genuine and considerable best to understand the new world they were moving into, but they were working inside a government department, in a climate of administration rather than management. The mechanisms remained heavily focused on financial and cash accounting and the preparation of the global accounts of the business. The set-up met its Waterloo in 1975.

During 1974 the country had gone through the oil price shock, the three-day week and their aftermath. The PO had survived as it was bound to, though its suppliers had suffered along with the rest of British industry. The country now moved into a combination of recession and seriously mounting inflation. During the preceding year or two, PO prices had been held back for the usual political reasons. During the summer of 1975 it became clear that PO telecommunications was running so seriously into the red that something simply had to be done. Ministers had reluctantly to accept one of the most dramatic price increases in PO history (Figure A2.2). As evidence of the inadequacy of the financial systems, this increase actually turned out later to be overstated.

Hurried arbitrary cuts were made in spending. Recruitment was stopped, even of apprentices who represented the seed corn of the future high-tech operations of the business. Damaging effects on service soon became apparent.

It was painfully obvious that things could not go on like this. Bill Ryland saw that the way of working had to be reformed drastically and in a hurry. Bill Kember had been recruited from Coopers & Lybrand to a senior position in Central Finance. He now transferred to THQ as Senior Director Finance and Management services. Working under successive Board Members for Finance he began a task of reform in telecommunications accounting systems which was to occupy him for the best years of his life.

The most urgent requirement was a proper system of management accounting control. A system of Telecommunications Monthly Reports (TMRs) was set up which was considered each month by the Managing Director's Committee. But that was only the barest of beginnings. The real problem was the basic accounting system. What was really needed was a completely new one. But to introduce it in one operation would have imposed a discontinuity of gargantuan proportions from which it would have taken years to recover. The business of telecommunications was not going to stand still while a new accounting system was introduced and run in. There was no real option but to set out to convert the existing system on the job. It was to prove an almost incomprehensibly difficult undertaking, which was still uncompleted in 1984. It was not helped by the fact that PO salaries simply would not attract professionally trained accountants, who could make much more money outside.

One of the most intractable problems of all, and one of the most basic, was to prove to be the proper recording of capital assets. These included tens of millions of discrete elements of plant, from thermionic valves and exchange switches to cables, ducts and street cabinets, all installed at different dates, all having individual histories, and all being added to daily. Even recording on big mainframe computers it was a task of almost unmanageable proportions to keep track.

With the TMRs in place the line managers at the top of the business had a proper tool of control for the first time. They now had to learn how to use it. The first priority for this obviously had to be field operations.

Repeated attempts over the next few years to draw the finance function into its proper role in the control of the field and to institute a true financially based control system were to fail. A great deal of important managerial information was buried in the stream of engineering vouchers inputting to the financial accounting system. The system generated outputs which to the untrained eye might seem to correspond to managerial variables. But managers who tried to use them for real decisions, say about recruitment or improving the cost-effectiveness of operations, were foolhardy. The experienced among them had learnt the hard way that they could never use such outputs with confidence. Not only might the figures themselves be wrong; there were often serious mismatches between the accounting categorizations and those needed for management purposes, which might only be apparent to experts; and more likely than not some indecipherable financial accounting rule would be at work which would result in a completely false picture. To be sure of what was actually happening managers had to rely on records of physical variables like hours worked, telephones installed and so on.

Knowing the problem, Ryland had caused an elaborate system of non-financial controls to be set up. Service performance and productivity measured in working hour terms were monitored and targeted in detail through an elaborate system of management-by-objectives called the Telecommunications Improvement Programmes (TIPs). By 1975 these controls had been biting steadily into field performance for six or seven years. Personnel productivity improvement in particular had made important advances. In the energetic Regions on the eastern side of England it had been elevated almost to the status of a religion, with David Blair, the head of the specialist Productivity Improvement Division at THQ, as its relentless high priest.

The PO already had a long and successful record of matching staff to work and of handling the consequences for employment of decline in workload and the consequences of change in technology. As a result of the automation of local and trunk services, the number of operating staff had had to be reduced by a whole order since the Second World War. Thousands of manual local exchanges and a considerable number of centres handling trunk traffic manually had had to be closed, with the loss of tens of thousands of operating jobs. In a remarkable example of good workforce management and of responsible union co-operation, the whole programme had been handled successfully, with no significant industrial action or opposition.

In recent years the business had learnt that engineering productivity improvement was hard work for managers. The PO had learnt in the 1960s that to get real gains in engineering staff productivity it had to lead with a constant programme of improvements in work practices and organization. But it was no use inventing a mechanical aid which would cut the time taken to pull cable through duct by eighty per cent if the saved time was wasted on the ground by people standing around waiting for instructions or simply making tea by the roadside. The quality of supervision was crucial. But a great deal also depended on the staff themselves. The great majority were responsible people. But there was no way the second or third largest employer in the country was going to be insulated from the characteristics of the working population as a whole. Some areas like the West Riding of Yorkshire had a long tradition of a fair day's work for a fair day's pay, just as much in the PO as outside. Provided they thought they were being fairly treated, staff in these areas would co-operate energetically in any new development and indeed get pleasure out of it. Others had a more leisurely approach to life, or were caught up in deteriorating national attitudes to work.

Under the system of productivity pay bargaining which had grown up, the POEU entered into regular undertakings on behalf of the staff to contribute to productivity improvement. The union expected consultation in advance on changes of organization and practice. Provided it was forthcoming, the approach of union headquarters was usually constructive. There were exceptions when co-operation might be withdrawn in the context of a national dispute, as a form of industrial action; or in other situations of tension. Unofficial local disputes occurred from time to time. A good deal of the time of senior people at RHQs was taken up firefighting complaints by the union side about lack of consultation in Areas; and the same was true, *mutatis mutandis*, in THQ in relation to Regions. But on the other side of the coin it was not unknown for union specialists actually to contribute improvements to management proposals. They would often support the position of management in internal debates within the union. But they were in the end the servants of their members. The real brunt of the drive for productivity had to be borne by management.

In 1975 it was urgent to get costs generally under control. I concluded that the only thing to do was to try to use the existing patchwork of controls. The inadequacy of the financial systems was a real handicap. But, properly and vigorously used, the Ryland mechanisms and particularly the TIPs system ought to provide a reasonable substitute. With all its faults the Senior Salary Structure included useful stick and carrot mechanisms, in the shape of procedures for awarding and withholding annual increments on salary and bonuses for good performance. Coupled with the annual appraisement system, with its emphasis on results, these provided a mechanism asking to be used down the line of field operations. I decided to use it; and with it to use the practice of open reporting. Managers would see and have the chance to comment on the actual reports I was making on them to my superiors.

Under the 1979 reorganization (see Chapter 9) I became Deputy Managing Director (Operations), with my own operations support staff in THQ. To my regret the finance function still remained basically aloof from the line machinery, with a mindset directed to financial accounting and the overall finances of the business. Control of field costs remained uphill work not least because the essential ingredient of the real bottom-line profit of subordinate units was still missing from the mechanism.

Ever since the Bridgeman Committee everyone who encountered the problem for the first time had seen Areas and Regions as natural candidates to become profit centres in their own right. If this could be done it would make the money they spent real in a way that nothing else could do. In the early days of the nationalized Board under Lord Hall, all the talk had been of Regions as autonomous units with their own published accounts in proper commercial format. I myself had wanted to see profit centre arrangements introduced in the field ever since the Hall days, when I was myself a Regional Director. The consultants McKinsey made a thoroughgoing study in a report called 'the Red Book' at the end of the 1970s which proposed the idea of 'contribution' by the field units, as a form of profit fitting the circumstances. It was an attractive concept. George Jefferson was later to make his own determined effort to implement such thinking in the early days of his regime. But the idea could not be made to stick. It was not just a question of the limitations of the accounting system, serious though they were. The inherent characteristics of telecommunications posed (and pose) obstacles to internal accounting separation within operating companies which will never be overcome (see Chapter 17).

Control of the size of the headquarters itself proved an intractable problem. Merriman had introduced an effective system for R&D budgeting back in the early 1970s. But otherwise the expenditures on central staff and overheads were never brought under satisfactory control before privatization. When BT was originally formed out of the PO in 1981 the telecommunications share of the CHQ staff was transferred to BT, swelling the central numbers even more. At that time THQ accounted for some 16 per cent of the total staff of the business.

Despite these difficulties, spending was brought under control. Appendix 3 plots total current account expenditure and shows that by the end of the 1970s it was coming under proper discipline. Given that THQ was at this time by common consent overstaffed, the field contribution to the savings in cost per line visible in Figure A3.4 deserves recognition it has never had.

Investment and its funding posed an important set of problems of their own. Under the GPO, capital financing and the arcane capital accounting system had been the preserve of the Accountant General's Department. The business of compiling the investment programme and securing government authority for it on the other hand had traditionally been responsibilities of the administrators in the Inland Telecommunications Department. This division of functions continued after 1975. Capital financing and accounting became a matter for the central finance staff in Howland Street under the successive Board Members for Finance, with Bill Kember and his people as their outstation in the business. But investment budgeting remained a matter for the business planners and operating specialists under me in Gresham Street.

So far as the statutory rules for investment were concerned, Section 11 (8) of the 1969 Act said:

> The PO, in carrying out any such work of development as involves substantial outlay on capital account, and, if it has subsidiaries, in securing the carrying out by them of any such work, shall act in accordance with a general programme settled from time to time with the approval of the Minister.

This was directed to the investment programme as a consumer of national resources. The clear concern behind it was as much to ensure that enough was spent as to ensure that not too much was. Telecommunications investment was very big business indeed. Quite apart from service to the public for many years to come, the livelihoods of many thousands of people and the fortunes of a large number of firms in the private sector depended on it.

Up to the late 1970s investment programme work was conducted entirely in constant prices, related to a point in time specified centrally for each financial year by the Treasury. There was no mechanism for assessing the actual money cost of what was planned for or being done until after the event, when the formal accounts for any given year were published. Management was in the extraordinary position of having to operate without any way of finding out the likely cash cost of the programme or of individual projects in advance. Everyone thought and acted as if the planning and budgeting system worked in real money, but in fact it did not.

There was a high premium on the accuracy of bidding and forecasting in constant price terms. From the point of view of central government, unexpended resources were culpable because they could have been spent on some other politically desirable application. Overspending was equally culpable for the obvious reason that the resources to support it had to be found from central sources after the event. From the PO point of view what mattered above all was credibility. If in a given year the PO could preserve its reputation for submitting bids close to actual consumption, it stood a very good chance of getting most of what it asked for the following year. If it was tempted to overbid this would soon become apparent to Treasury, who would under-allocate in following years as a matter of course. If it underbid it could be in the obvious trouble of running out of investment authority before year end and would again lose credibility in next year's round of discussions.

Sophisticated tactics were required. All Treasury administration has to be run as a matter of bids and reductions, as the aggregate ambitions of departments are balanced against the political scope for raising money. There is no other way to play the game, with the cards of the actual negotiators held close to their chests. Both sides knew that it was up to them to apply the correct tactics so as to try to get an end result which was a fair balance between need and the national ability to provide funds, just as prosecuting and defending counsel in court are both trying to contribute to a fair verdict.

The planners in THQ observed two guiding principles – first, always to maintain an atmosphere of capital stringency internally; and second, never to yield to the temptation to overbid to DTI and Treasury. The art was to pitch each year's bid sufficiently above irreducible need to be able to give a bit of ground when Treasury pressure came on but not so far above it that if Treasury played fair there would be significant underspending. There was no mechanical way of working out what the bid ought to be. It had to be learnt by each generation in the hot seat and communicated by seat-of-pants to the next.

This sort of situation was and is common to all big-spending authorities. What made the telecommunications game peculiarly difficult was first the existence of two intervening levels between THQ and Treasury, in CHQ and in DTI as sponsoring Department, each with a legitimate role in the process and with its own standpoint; and second the number of very interested spectators shouting on the touchline. The supplying industry, POUNC and the PO and industry unions all had a legitimate interest and a right and a desire to know what was going on and to express views, not least to the media. With the best will in the world it was all too easy for them to do more harm than good.

But the most difficult flank from THQ's point of view was the field. The exact balance of impressions in the mind of Treasury officials and Ministers could be decisive. It required only one chance encounter between, say, the Minister concerned in DTI and a local Telephone Manager or Regional Director who happened to be their constituent as an MP complaining about one deferred extension to an engineering training school, or in the other direction between a Treasury official in a pub and a local PO engineering manager boasting about having funds to spare at year end, for the whole delicate balance to be upset.

In terms of investment results, by and large the Gresham Street planners made the system work with remarkable success. Bids for peripheral investment on optional or semi-optional projects like training schools were from time to time deferred during the negotiating process, to bring the global bid down to levels acceptable to Treasury. But only once – as a consequence of the oil price crisis in December 1973

– did the main network investment programme have to be cut because the government cut authority to invest under Section 11 (8).

The funding and borrowing game was another matter altogether, however. The funding arrangements were prescribed in Section 35 (2) of the 1969 Act, which said, inter alia:

> The PO may borrow from the Minister . . . such sums in sterling as it may require for . . .
>
> (a) provision of money for meeting any expenses incurred in connection with any works the cost of which is properly chargeable to capital account
>
> (b) provision of working capital required by it . . .

This bore on overall borrowing of actual money by the Corporation for all purposes – posts, Giro and NDPS as well as telecommunications and working as well as investment capital.

Each year's Corporation borrowing requirement was made up of a whole string of cash components, some up, some down and some of which might cancel one another out. The telecommunications component was made up of requirements to fund changes in working capital due to changes in debtors or creditors (which could be very substantial) or in inventory holdings; and of any difference between investment capital requirements and the internally generated funds available from the business.

When the cash limit system was introduced by Labour towards the end of the 1970s, PO Corporation borrowing figures acquired a significance which from the point of view of the telecommunications business and its finances was quite unnatural.

In the telecommunications case the cash limit procedures themselves were creaky and drawn out almost to the point of farce. The government expenditure planning system required the first estimates of cash requirements for a given financial year to be made about August of the preceding calendar year. Final predictions had to be made in the later autumn. The THQ capital planners were expected to make a precise forecast of the out-turn of cash spending in an individual year nearly two years ahead on some thousands of contracts, many of which might have two or three years still to run; and of the working hour cost of some thousands of direct labour construction staff, some of whom might not even have been recruited; and all this with highly uncertain forecasts of capital price and wage inflation. This then had to be related to a finance function forecast of the funds likely to be generated internally, which also could not possibly be other than uncertain, to produce a figure for the external funding requirements of the investment programme if any. This in turn had to be combined with forecasts of cash requirements for working capital to produce a single external funding requirement for telecommunications. That then had to be merged with those for the other businesses to give a global external funding requirement for the whole Corporation. It was this latter figure which was incorporated in the central Treasury calculations leading to the PSBR.

The THQ business planners soon discovered that they could never win at this one. Even if, as one year they did, they produced an estimate of investment cash flow requirement in aggregate which was within £10m of the final money out-turn (on a programme of over £2bn and in circumstances of high and volatile inflation), that estimate was absorbed and re-absorbed so many times in other higher-level estimates that the end product external financing figure had a million to one chance, if that, of being right and never actually was. On the other hand when it was wrong everyone looked for the biggest single expenditure block, which was of course telecommunications investment, and blamed them for being wrong.

Cash limits on borrowing fitted purely spending organizations like central and local departments of government. But they were quite inappropriate to a commercial undertaking like telecommunications, especially one which was now funding its investment from internal sources. The amounts involved in each year's borrowing requirement were marginal to the main finances of the Corporation, and they had little or nothing to do with the real running of telecommunications, yet the cash limit procedures took up an alarming amount of senior line management time just to make them work. No private firm would have dreamed of working under such a system, nor would it have been expected to.

Returning to investment as such, the actual record over the period from 1972 to 1995 is summarized in Figure 5.1. Investment at constant 1990 prices is set against productive activity measured in terms of working lines added to the system and modernized.

As will be seen, the 1970s had begun with an enormous hump of spending out of all proportion to its useful products. Ministers and Treasury had met the investment demands of the GPO in the late 1960s with something like generosity. But as the situation in the early years of the graph began to become apparent they began to grumble with increasing loudness about extravagance and lack of control in what was being done with the money. They were justified. The telecommunications programme represented something of the order of 0.7 of one per cent of total national GDP. The way it was managed had a significant influence on the whole inflationary process. And the finances of the business, and the prices the public had to pay, were going to suffer seriously if large amounts of capital were spent without earning their keep.

Before 1975 the business had had no recognized system of capital project control. It was obvious that one was needed but it was not easy to design. In most businesses the capital programme is made up of a small number of projects which are often large or very large in the perspective of normal activity. Boards and top management take a close interest in them and project monitoring flows from that. The telecommunications capital programmes in the 1970s were made up of several hundred projects running from anything from £1m to £10m in value, plus a very large number indeed of lesser projects, for example local cable schemes. It was a physical impossibility for all of these to be monitored centrally on an individual basis. What was needed was a devolved system of project authorization and control which would guarantee that spending on individual projects was properly authorized after due scrutiny by the finance function and by management; and that any later departures from estimate were properly brought to account. THQ and CHQ were instructed to co-operate to devise one, and successfully did so.

The engineering project controllers knew that departures from estimate thrown up by the new financial project control procedures would have to be approved. The only alternative would be to bring the project concerned to a grinding halt; and in a monopoly there is no way a project providing capacity can be stopped without serious effects on service. Coupled with their basic cynicism about the financial systems of the business, they were an unpromising constituency to have to ask to operate the new system. But they were well-drilled ex-Civil-Servants, and conscientiously they set out to do so.

The other big question was better matching of spending to need. There was an urgent requirement for a system for the global assessment of existing capacity and that planned to be created by new projects; and for relating both to existing and forecast need.

The existing situation was a matter of the faults of virtue. In late 1971 Holmes and I, then respectively Planning Controller and Regional Director of North-East Telecommunications Region, had visited Scarborough exchange on the trail of over-provision. Scarborough was in the territory of York Area, run by one of the best Telephone Managers in Britain. It was obvious at a glance that the exchange was over-equipped with capacity for calls – it later turned out to have roughly twice as much as it needed. The reason was equally obvious – conscientious response by good managers to top management emphasis on delivering good service had resulted in extensive over-provision.

It was a complicated problem. The point at which control needed most to be exerted was the moment of decision-taking by local or regional planners on the detailed plans, exchange-by-exchange and cable-scheme-by-cable-scheme. At any point in time well over half of all larger exchanges were at some point in the cycle of planning and execution of expansion. The problem was to devise a system which would measure the global effect of all these thousands of individual planning decisions in a way which could be brought to account for complete Areas and Regions so that proper line management pressures could be exerted. It was made more complex by the fact that the project design processes were concerned with meeting need up to seven years out. Design quantities therefore required to be related both to existing capacity and to forecast requirement seven years ahead.

The problem was solved, though it took time to implement the solution. Ratios called asset utilization factors were devised, designed scientifically to relate capacity existing and planned in exchanges to the present and forecast requirement. The same techniques could be applied to the plant used for inter-exchange links. Control of capacity in local (customer distribution) cables posed a special problem, which is discussed in the next chapter.

Figure 5.1 shows that as a result of these measures the relationship between spending and its products improved dramatically. An important contribution was made to the financial performance of the business; the need for price increases was reduced; and the hand of telecommunications was strengthened in bidding to government for authority for investment. OPD under Keith Hannant could be proud of the system. As Part III will show, the flow of investment into the network was now hampered in any serious way only by the performance of the manufacturers.

The final area where disaster struck in 1975 was in procurement. We have already seen that new organizational arrangements had been hammered out in the late 1960s. Purchasing and Supply Department had been set up, first under Cadbury, then under Jack Baldry and under me from 1972 to 1975. Whyte replaced me in March of the latter year on my promotion to Senior Director Planning and Purchasing. New rules for purchasing had been set up to replace the Bulk Supplies Agreements. In March 1975 these new arrangements began seriously to come apart. This story is taken up in Part III.

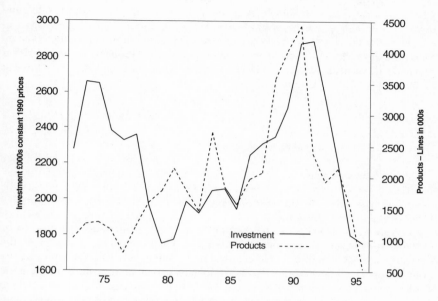

Figure 5.1   Investment and products (lines added or modernized) 1972–95

The postal business had serious difficulties of its own at this time. On 12 November 1975 the Secretary of State for Industry announced that C. F. Carter, Vice-Chancellor of Lancaster University, was to be chairman of a Committee to review the PO with the following terms of reference:

> To examine the performance and main features of the PO and its use of its resources and assets; and to consider whether any changes would better enable it to perform its functions under the PO Act 1969; to assess the policies, prospects and social significance of the Postal Business, including methods of financing it as a self-supporting public service; to consider whether the PO Act 1969 places undue restrictions on the activities of the PO; and to make recommendations.[2]

The Committee's Report was published in July 1977. In paragraph 1.8 it said:

> The efficiency of telecommunications services has considerably improved in recent years, though (for reasons suggested in Chapter 12) it is not yet up to the standard in some other countries, particularly the United States. The cost to the user is currently high, the last price increase having proved in retrospect to be more than was needed to enable the telecommunications business to meet its financial targets. The cost of supply is also higher than it should be, Britain having fallen behind in the installation of systems which are economical in maintenance. *However, there is now a possibility of an extended period in which the 'real' price of telecommunications will be falling, and in which a greatly increased volume of traffic can be handled by a static or declining labour force* [italics added]. The PO record in telecommunications deserves responsible criticism, but not the exercise of our national habit of condemning all things British as though they were the worst in the world.[3]

The analysis in this paragraph bites accurately on fundamentals which still apply today. The sentence in italics looks forward in an important way to the analysis in Chapter 16 of the reasons for real price reductions since privatization. Carter correctly foresaw that real prices were likely to fall and that the labour force would either remain static or decrease (see Figure 16.1 and Appendices 2 and 3).

Paragraph 12.26 of Chapter 12 says:

A consequence of introducing System X [see Chapter 12 of the present book] will be a substantially reduced requirement for technical staff per subscriber. The experience of the Bell telephone system in the USA indicates that the introduction of SPC alone has halved the maintenance manpower, and the new ESS4 exchanges will require less than one-third of the manpower. Fortunately the United Kingdom telephone service is expanding at the rate of 5 per cent to 7 per cent per year, and this should greatly ease the redundancy problem. The faster the expansion of existing services, the less will be the need to reduce the manpower; the quicker new services are introduced the easier it will be to re-deploy staff rather than to reduce job opportunities. It is therefore in the best interests of the PO, its staff and its customers that the service should expand at the fastest possible rate, and tariff policy is the key to this. However, tariff policy has both short and long term aspects. In the short-term the aim should be to stimulate greater use of the telephone, thereby seeking to make more efficient use of the capital invested in the existing network. In the long term the aim should be to increase the range of services which attract subscribers and to make them as efficient, reliable and easy to use as possible. *Indeed the PO has an impressive list of new services in development and we welcome this demonstration of initiative on its part* [italics added].[4]

Read with hindsight, the latter part of paragraph 12.26 has an almost prophetic ring for the 1980s and indeed for the 1990s. What the Committee says about maintenance staffing was justified; but it had fallen into the common trap of assuming that engineering staffing was dominated by the exchange maintenance requirement. In fact exchange and repeater station maintenance staff accounted for only 14 per cent of the total engineering labour force.

Paragraph 12.27 of Carter says:

The quality of the telephone service has improved substantially with the near completion of STD . . . The number of failed calls due to plant defects has steadily decreased, and can be expected to continue decreasing, but by far the principal cause of failures to make a call is wrong dialling or the absence of a response at the called number. Congestion of the network accounts for only a very small number of failures. In spite of this progress in eliminating the causes of defects there is still a long way to go before the British telephone system can claim to give the standard of service enjoyed by subscribers to the Bell telephone system. One must be careful in comparing performance in different telephone services in view of the different types and ages of equipment, but from evidence we have received we conclude that maintenance in the PO is not as effective as it could be in spite of widespread use of automatic test equipment. We recommend therefore that maintenance operations be reviewed with the object of matching our performance more nearly to that of the Bell system.[5]

Taken together these paragraphs from the Carter Report accurately catch much of the self-perception of Gresham Street in 1977 and the problems and prospects of the day.

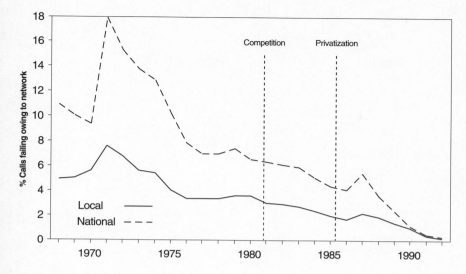

Figure 5.2   Quality of network service 1968–92

Soon after the Report was published the PO took an important step forward in procedures for monitoring network performance. Computer-based Measurement and Analysis Centres (MACs) were established to take over from the old manual service observations. This provided for the first time the basis for a properly targeted approach to network quality and maintenance. With MAC to guide it, Service Department under Ron Back began a renewed drive to improve network service even within the limitations of the existing electro-mechanical switching and copper distribution plant. Figure 5.2 plots network performance over the whole twenty-five-year period.[6]

As later chapters will also show, whatever the Ministers of Lady Thatcher's successive administrations might have thought, by 1981 PO telecommunications had been running itself as a business operation for more than half a decade.

Notes

1. Nigel Lawson, *The View from No. 11* (Corgi Books, London, 1992), p. 222.
2. Report of the Post Office Review Committee, Cmnd 6859 (HMSO, London, 1977), p. 1.
3. *Ibid.*, p. 4.
4. *Ibid.*, p. 104.
5. *Ibid.*, p. 105.
6. The MACs soon showed that the percentage of calls failing because of defects in the network had been seriously understated by the old service observation procedures, which could not allow properly for the varying load on the network throughout the day. The results for the earlier years in Figure 5.2 have been adjusted to make them comparable with MAC results in later years.

6 A Task with No Precedent

When the Corporation took over in 1969, PO telecommunications was heading for what was to prove the period of maximum rate of growth of lines in the whole of the history of the British system before and after privatization (Figure 6.1).

The Macmillan boom of the 1960s had finally woken the British public to the value of the telephone. The stop–go of the British economy between 1973 and 1983 was to add its own dimension of difficulty. There were to be two severe recessions in the space of six years, with a boom in between, which were to cause an extraordinary oscillation of spending power in the economy (Figure 6.2). Without realizing what it was getting into, the business was embarked upon one of the most remarkable exercises in logistic expansion in peacetime British history in a roller-coaster economic environment.

The way of doing business which had been inherited from the GPO in 1969 was by common consent unequal to the task the PO now faced. The Select Committee had said in 1967:

> The rapid expansion of the telephone system would in any event have created many problems for the Post Office. Even if forecasts had been accurate the Post Office believe that there would have been difficulties in obtaining all the required equipment. With forecasts for recent years proving consistently too low the supply problem became more acute. In addition the length of notice that the Post Office were able to give industry of their precise requirements was, at least until 1961, too short. Your Committee fear therefore that, at a time of rapid expansion in telephone demand, inaccurate forecasts and inadequate warning of requirements to industry have been the root causes of the shortages of exchange equipment. For this damaging shortage of vital equipment the Post Office must accept responsibility, except to the extent to which it was due, up till 1961, to the consequences of the Government control of public investment that then applied to the Post Office.[1]

There was more than a grain of truth in this, although the Committee had fallen into the usual practice of criticizing forecasts with hindsight. The only fair criticism of any forecast is that it failed to take account of circumstances and data which should have been known at the time it was made. The Committee had also fallen into the difficulty facing all outside inquiries of the sheer number of ramifications to any telecommunications situation. The relationship with the telecommunications supplying industry had attracted attention because the industry itself had a voice and used it. But there were many other dimensions to the problem which the business now faced, to which the Select Committee had not directed its attention. It was no good adding new capacity for lines and calls if the existing plant did not work properly; it was no good

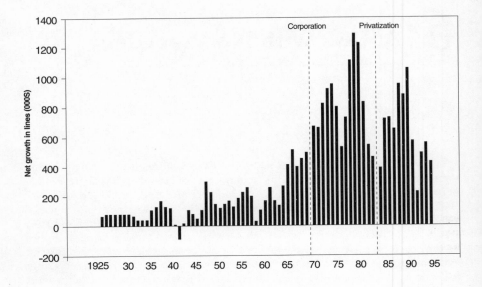

Figure 6.1   Net growth in lines 1925–95

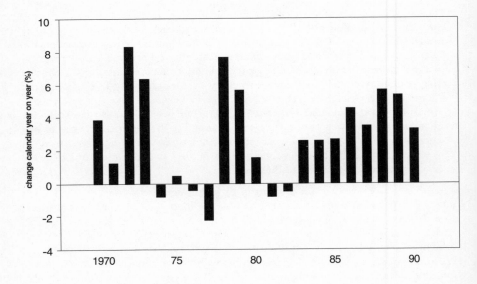

Figure 6.2   Real personal disposable income 1970–90

ordering new exchanges if there were no buildings to put them in; it was no good constructing buildings and installing exchanges if there were no engineers to run them and operators and directories to help people use them; it was no good having thousands of engineering recruits if there were no stores for them to use, no schools to train them or no vehicles for them to drive; and so on.

The complete programme was to require investment of well over £30bn at present-day prices between 1971 and 1984. Managing it and keeping all the elements in step was as formidable a task as any British organization has ever undertaken in peacetime. It was a whole order bigger than most private businesses would ever contemplate.

At the same time the two hundred thousand staff of the business, scattered right across Britain, were faced with their first experience of managerial priorities. So many things were happening at once; in what only a year or two before had been a Civil Service environment they were bound to have unexpected effects. Formally, the first priority of the organization right up to midnight on 31 October 1969 had been support of the PMG in discharging his political obligations. It was accustomed to being told of a particular political priority like getting rid of a waiting list, and to all hands being called to the pumps to support the image of responding, until the next one came along. A managerial drive from the top, concentrated on balanced objectives over time, was a completely new experience.

Perhaps not surprisingly, the momentum created in the field turned out to be difficult to steer. Steering it certainly needed. There was a serious risk of a downside as well as an upside to what was going on, as the asset provision experience recounted in Chapter 5 showed. The proper object of the exercise, after all, was not service at any price but balance between service and cost. In ordinary business managers grow up facing the pressures of the bottom line in a competitive environment. This automatically forces them to find such a balance. Civil Service psychology is geared primarily to doing the will of the Minister. If that will is seen as pointing to growth and service, growth and service is what you get without regard to cost. Guiding a huge organization with such a mindset towards a commercial balance was a formidable undertaking in itself. And it all had to be handled with unsatisfactory personnel practices, some of which, like the Senior Salary Structure, were actually moving in the wrong direction; with financial and accounting systems which were equally unsatisfactory and were moving only painfully slowly in the direction of improvement; and with a weak supplying industry still heavily geared to obsolete technology.

In the ten years after 1970 the machine lived under constant and conflicting pressures. In the boom years the pressure from customers, government and Board to uplift the capability to handle growth was intense. In the upswing years up to 1980 not just the number of lines but the growth in the number of lines was to increase annually by an amount quite out of scale with any previous experience. Growth in calls was to behave in a similar way. But on the two occasions when the economy swung into recession the priorities abruptly reversed. Suddenly the pressure was on tailoring purchases, capacity and working power back to diminished demand so as not to waste money and to hold prices down.

As any truthful economist, Treasury Minister or official will tell you, genuinely accurate forecasting is impossible in the real world. The telecommunications planning of the 1970s (and for that matter of the 1990s) had (and has) to be built round this reality. The only way to do it is to get hold of the best forecasts that the state of the art will produce and then to use them with one's eyes open to the certainty of error.

An ideal mechanism would accommodate the effects of forecast errors without wasting money or risking outputs like service. The task of real-life planners is to get as close to this ideal as they can and hope that their inevitable errors do not do too much damage.

In PO telecommunications in the 1970s the effects of departures from forecast were magnified in ways no normal business would ever encounter. In the period of peak growth around 1979–80 a ten per cent error upwards in a national lines forecast would mean capacity over-provided for perhaps 180,000 lines in a given year. This meant £22m under- or over-expended on plant to meet demand in that year, and approaching £3m added to annual operating costs. Ten per cent shortfall leading to ten per cent fewer lines in service meant a revenue loss for as long as it lasted at the rate of £6m a year. Such sums were big enough to be significant in the overall finances even of PO telecommunications. And forecasts accurate to ten per cent would be accounted good by most people with any experience of the work. Bigger errors are common in many fields. Perhaps the worst thing of all was the way the risk of error increased the further out the forecasts had to be made. Repeated studies had shown that it was uneconomic to revisit particular exchanges or sections of the cable network to expand them more than about once every seven years. This was a very long time over which to have to make forecasts with such a loading in real money. The money riding on the combined risks would have turned the hair of most private business people of the day white overnight, monopoly or no monopoly.

In addition to the problems of growth, the programme for modernization of the network (discussed in detail in Part III) was just beginning to get off the ground. It was under its own conflict of forces. On the one side was pressure from Board level to go faster. Sir William Barlow, who joined the Corporation as Chairman from private industry in late 1977:

> The great trouble you had then was to decide how fast you could afford to go on with the modernization of switching. The British system was based on Strowger. They had had an abortive attempt to get into electronic telephone switching ahead of their time which had frightened them all because it didn't work and was abandoned. They had not really embraced crossbar. They had an early version of electronic exchange which turned out to be very good in practice called TXE4.
>
> I well remember us trying to get to grips with what rate we could afford to change over at, assuming industry could supply. John Harper made a presentation in the main Board room about this. I don't know whether he said 1994 or 1993 [I actually said 1992]. Whatever he said I said it was too long. I wanted to get on and get it done very quickly. The grouse was very simple. It is very interesting now that the dates we were talking about then were the dates that have actually been realized.

On the other side was the ever-present worry about the weakness of the supplying industry, especially in new technology. There could be nothing worse than a growth and modernization programme which went wrong. If the PO pressed the industry to go faster than the agreed rate with reed electronic systems, it could well repeat its failings on crossbar in the late 1960s. Also, the programme as it stood had been planned and proved in using thorough discounted cash flow procedure (see Chapter 11). This was supposed to guarantee that it was correct from the point of view of the future financial health of the organization. If the business was to sustain its claim to observance of proper business discipline, it must stick to the programme proved by

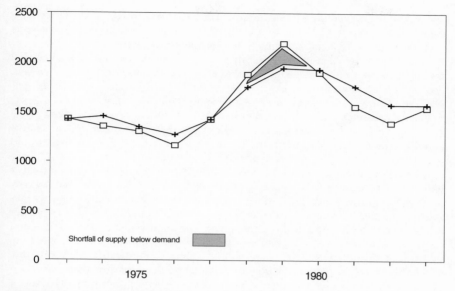

Figure 6.3   PO demand and supply for lines 1973–83

the original studies to be economic and not spend faster. As Gresham Street saw it there was nothing for it but to grit the collective teeth and plough on with the planned programme unless and until actually ordered to change it.

All these threads came together on the desks of the planners in Gresham Street. They had no past experience to guide them except the disastrous record of the late 1960s. The GPO had learnt then the hard way a lot of ways not to do things; and just how weak its suppliers were. It had learnt precious little which could guide its successor in the situation it now faced. There was only one thing to do, which was to try to hammer out a better way of doing things on the hoof; and to pray.

The business girded itself to do just that and it came very close to complete success. In its fifteen years of life it was to create nearly three-fifths of the network inherited by BT plc in 1984 and to replace Strowger equipment with modern systems in exchanges serving fifty per cent of its lines. It added nearly twelve million additional lines to a network which in 1969 was inadequate to serve eight million; and the capacity to handle thirteen thousand million additional calls a year to a network which in 1969 was inadequate to carry nine thousand million.

The bottom line of service for any business is how far it succeeds in matching demand to supply for its basic product – in this case telephone lines. Figure 6.3 shows just how far the telecommunications business succeeded in this in the period of maximum growth.

The first real peak of demand and growth had started at the very end of the 1960s and run on into the early 1970s. The waiting list, defined as people who were having to wait because of shortages of plant, reached a peak in 1972 of 450,000, equivalent to more than a year's growth of the network a year or two before. The country and the economy then dropped into the trough of 1973–74 and the 1975 recession.

The heat came off and the waiting list dropped. By 1976–7 the Report and Accounts was saying: 'The waiting list fell for the fifth successive year, and at 38,000 represents seven working days average supply, the lowest post-war figure.'[2]

The sharp contraction in the economy faced the business planners with a new and testing problem. On the one hand it was essential if costs and prices were to be held down that the amount of idle plant in the network was minimized. At 0.7 per cent of GDP the investment programme had a significant place in national economic performance. Investment-generated capital charges and telecommunications prices were a component of overall inflation in their own right. The economic imperative could not be gainsaid. On the other hand too big a reduction in capacity would pose serious risks to service in face of a future upswing.

The asset control procedures described in the previous chapter now came into their own. The business at last had a reasonably defensible way of tailoring provision of new plant to forecast demand. The problem of course was that although the procedures allowed margins for forecast errors to be built in, they could do nothing to protect against such errors if they passed a certain point. The improvements made to provision contract lead times described in Chapter 10 helped where exchanges were concerned; but you could not provide service without cables to connect customers to the exchanges, and these presented particular planning problems of their own.

There were only 23.9 exchange connections per 100 population in 1976; and at such a relatively low level of penetration it was beyond a certain point impossible to plan distribution cable layouts which would be economic over time and still have reserves of capacity to cater for unexpected excursions in demand. The basic difficulty was that each customer required a dedicated pair of wires back to the exchange; and that at this low penetration level individual requests for service were inevitably dotted around in a random and unpredictable way anywhere in the country, so that it was impossible to have reserves of plant in the ground to meet all of them instantaneously and still preserve the economics of the network. (By the early 1980s the problem was to go away as penetration rose and the density of existing lines increased.)

The business had had techniques for detailed study of prospective demand on the ground and for liaison with local authority planners and others since the 1930s. But repeated experience had shown that there was a limit to what this sort of thing could achieve. It remained basically impossible to plan expansion of distribution cable networks in a way which would guarantee that they would meet any level of demand without impossibly high margins of spare pairs. Traditionally, the overall margin of spare pairs had been supposed to be kept in the region of 26 to 29 per cent. But this was quite empirical, and nobody really knew if it was right or wrong. With so much money being invested in this sector as in others, there was an urgent need for a more scientific system which would give a better guarantee against both over- and under-provision. With considerable effort such a system was now devised by Gresham Street. The case for its introduction on grounds of business economics was unanswerable and I sanctioned it. I did so knowing that it depended crucially on the demand forecasts which would be used. If they turned out to be too far wrong, demand could go spectacularly over the top of supply in a matter of months; and it would take eighteen months or so to retrieve things.

It was just my luck that the economy now went into one of the most remarkable oscillations ever. As Figure 6.2 shows, in 1977 the business was trying to make a judgement about exactly how much capacity to create for the future after four years of declining personal income growth ending with a reduction in the current year of 2.2 per cent, with all the effects that had had on demand for telephone service. Just twelve months later it was facing nearly 8 per cent increase in disposable income in one year. It was a bold man who in the depths of 1977 would have forecast the upswing of the year 1978, let alone predicted a precise numeric value for it.

William Barlow's experience when he began looking round the business in 1978 illustrates vividly the sort of problems to which this gave rise on the ground:

> Whenever I used to go out on a Regional visit I used to get down and meet a selection of workers. One of the main complaints was the inadequate provision of absolutely essential stores. Almost without exception in my early days the complaints were shortage of telephones – that's in a telephone company – shortage of ladders, and shortage of brackets 22. The bracket 22 is the bracket that goes on the outside of a house or a building and you put the dropwire through. If you don't have a bracket 22 you can't do the job and if you don't have a ladder you can't get up.
>
> I was astounded about this. I thought, 'That's something simple. Even I can settle the supply of ladders or brackets 22.' I found out the ladders were carefully specified – safety regulations and so on – you couldn't go out and buy any old ladder. But bracket 22 was the simplest piece of ironmongery.
>
> I don't know what happened about brackets 22, but so far as telephones were concerned I got on to my old friends in industry and said, 'You are not going to believe this but they are short of telephones.' 'Short of telephones? But you so-and-sos never ordered them.' So I said, 'I'll get you the orders, can you do the production?.' They promised faithfully they would make a lot of telephones. So we gave them the orders and they increased their rate of production. The end of the story is obvious. We finished up with so many telephones in stock we did not know what to do with them. And yet when I started there was a sort of black market in telephones. The only telephones you could be sure of getting were the ones someone had hoarded under the front seat of his van.
>
> The end of the ladder story is equally interesting. When I left the PO I joined the board of Thorn-EMI. One company made ladders. I went on a visit and I found an enormous store in Lancaster full of ladders. So I said what on earth are we doing having this enormous stock of work in progress. 'Oh it all belongs to the the PO. They are their ladders and they have paid for them. They draw them off as required.' So that I had some impact on ladders.

As Figure 6.3 shows, the PO machine coped remarkably well until 1979. By then the country had been through the Callaghan 'winter of discontent' and pay settlements nationally had gone through the roof. The cumulative effects on disposable income and demand for telephone service were more than any system could have stood, especially given the then current policy of not increasing tariffs. The reserves of capacity in the network and especially in the distribution cable network finally ran out. The waiting list peaked again to 252,000. But the work done in improving forecasting had paid off. With an increase in connection charge to check demand ruled out by the tariffing policies of the time (see Chapter 8), the forecasters and planners still got within 1.6 per cent of the total requirement for working lines at the peak of the demand upswing – a quite amazing achievement. This time the total of orders on the waiting list at its peak represented only some two and a half months' supply; and the situation was rapidly restored. By March 1980 demand once again matched supply and the business soon made up the lost ground.

The bogey of the plant waiting list had been tamed. But service, in terms of the number of days it took to get a line installed routinely where plant was available, was still not good enough. A visit I made with Harry Tomlinson and Colin Davis to the USA in the summer of 1980 confirmed that there was still some way to go in this respect. On the other hand this visit showed that the steadily improving call failure performance of the UK network was on track to match US standards; and fault service was within the North American ballpark. The visit confirmed that otherwise the least satisfactory area in UK service was the provision of private circuits.

Our team studied the customer experience sampling system which had recently been introduced at the request of the US regulators. Each month a random sample of customers who had experienced call service, fault service and/or the provision process was rung up by an independent agency and asked for their experience. Global statistics have severe limitations as a measure of performance. It is the unfortunate cases that matter. The sampling system went a long way to crack this problem. I set up in BT a corresponding system, called Telcare, which still operates today.

Otherwise service generally was under control, except for central London. A Mori poll in 1982 found that the public generally saw telecommunications service as acceptable. The main complaint was about noise on calls. This was being addressed by the modernization programme.

By 1982–3, just before privatization, the Report and Accounts was saying with some pride:

> the number of customers waiting for telephone service because of shortage of equipment was cut during the year from 20,000 to 2,560. Provision of service where equipment was available was appreciably speeded up and by year end 73.6% of residential orders for service were being met within 12 working days and 78.4% of smaller orders from business customers in 8 working days.[3]

In 1969 the organization had started more or less from scratch with unscrambling a quite extraordinary mess. It had had to work out from first principles techniques for balancing risk to service against risk of wasting money; and then to apply them in a roller-coaster economic environment where its errors were calibrated in hundreds of thousands of dissatisfied customers and tens of millions of pounds of investment. It had very nearly come through unscathed. When it had come unstuck it had retrieved its error in months rather than years. Its managers could hold their heads as high as any private business. And next time round, if there was a next time round, they should do better still.

In fact there would never be anything quite like the years 1976 to 1980 again. BT plc was to face its own lesser growth problem and run into its own service difficulties in 1987. But the real hothouse growth of telephone service in Britain had peaked out around 1979.

Notes

1. First Report from the Select Committee on Nationalised Industries – The Post Office, HC Paper 340 (HMSO, London, 1967), para. VIII. 24.
2. PO Report and Accounts 1976/77 (HMSO, London, 1977), p. 15.
3. PO Report and Accounts 1982/83 (HMSO, London, 1983), p. 14.

7 Corporation, Staff and Unions

Sir William Barlow joined the PO Board as Chairman in the autumn of 1977. He had had a distinguished career in the electrical and electronic industry. In his last appointment he had been Chairman of Ransome Hoffman Pollard Ltd.

His first encounters with the PO had a quality of their own. In his words:

> I found that the amount of paper flowing across my desk and in the higher reaches of the PO was enormous. The amount of paper going to the Board was outrageous. I introduced the theme that under no circumstances were the papers to the Board to exceed half an inch in thickness.

On his second day he addressed the whole senior management:

> I did not realize when I spoke that that address would contain some quite shattering messages to people. I followed it up by writing a piece for the magazine which reverberated around because I put in a very simple message to say that as far as I was concerned I was running a business; and all business starts in the marketplace. The customer comes first. That aroused enormous adverse comment around union circles, who felt that I was not sufficiently interested in 'What's in it for us'. I was quite surprised to find that such an innocuous statement aroused such discussion.

Again:

> The first telecommunications visit I made was to South-Eastern Regional headquarters in Brighton. I had lunch with the Telephone Managers. They did not know what to make of this strange animal from outside – almost like a man who had come from outer Siberia or something. I started off on the tack that we had to get out and sell the telecommunications service – get more traffic, get more people on the telephone. I said I would not be satisfied until there was a hundred per cent penetration. The spokesman read me a lecture on how if you got telephones in houses that were not going to use them very much they would be an ornament in the hall which was nothing but a nuisance. They were bound to be delinquent in paying their bills; and they did not want that sort of customer. I went back to the office and dictated a note to Cadbury, then acting Managing Director, saying that I could not believe what I had heard.

How did the PO organism he now presided over operate after nearly ten years as a nationalized industry?

The Carter Report had said:

> the structure [of the complete PO] lends itself all too easily to a style of management

which is strongly centralised, and which thus continues the traditions of the former Government Department. We have received ample evidence of the great range of decisions which go up to the central Board, and of the powerful control exercised within that Board by its Chairman.[1]

Perhaps because it had taken only limited evidence from the businesses themselves, the Committee had got this a bit wrong. It had failed to perceive the division of function that had developed internally. The businesses under their respective Managing Directors had come to function largely as independent units, with their Managing Directors' Committees working much like the boards of major subsidiaries of a conglomerate. In the words of Peter Benton, Managing Director Telecommunications and a Member of the main Board from early 1978:

> The sort of issues that had to go to the PO Board were those which involved relationships with the unions, because it was quite obvious that one business could take an initiative with the unions which could have repercussions for the others. But broadly the only significant reason for other decisions to go up to the PO Board was that Bill Barlow, who was a very able engineer, very much enjoyed the technology of telecommunications. Issues such as the modernization programme and so on went to the Board but there was not much the Board could contribute, except the sort of contributions that any set of able non-executive directors can make. The formation of the policy was within the business.

The Board sat in Central Headquarters (CHQ) in Howland Street. The CHQ departments had little involvement with practical operations. Many people in Central Personnel Department had personal roots in one or other of the main services but their work was not specially identified with any one of them. With certain distinguished exceptions the senior people in Central Finance Department came from outside business. Their attitudes and their value systems were those of the finance sector and the City. They had no personal links with any of the services and no special reason to identify with them. Public Relations looked upwards to the Chairman and the Board and outwards to the worlds of the media and advertising. Barlow and the Board Members for Finance and Personnel lived and worked in this environment.

Peter Benton had his office two miles away, in Telecommunications Headquarters (THQ) in Gresham Street in the City. THQ was the line headquarters of one of the largest businesses in the country. Its job was to run the business and the field operations. Its priorities had to do with its own absorbing world. Engineering was important in the telecommunications of the 1970s, and the value system of Gresham Street reflected this. Work took up all the hours THQ had in its day. It was a busy, preoccupied place and it had little time to spare for the intricacies of Whitehall or the City. Apart from the people concerned with the special business of negotiating levels of investment with DTI and Treasury, it was happy to leave such matters to Howland Street.

Gresham Street might run a monopoly service but it had two natural internal targets of rivalry – Howland Street and posts. A large part of its effort was consumed in contention with two outside groups with highly symmetrical interests – its own unions and its industry suppliers. Human nature makes a group which has to contend with powerful opposite numbers of this kind close ranks internally. Gresham Street was no exception. Personal differences and rivalries were suppressed in a collective effort to get the better of its various opponents.

With half a million people spread over thousands of outstations throughout the country, it was a physical impossibility for top management personally to meet or talk to more than a minority of middle or junior management, let alone the main body of the staff. In a normal firm an office or factory meeting could catch a large proportion of a company's staff in one audience. This could not be done in the PO. The fact that the top leaders were so isolated was a fundamental handicap. The case for devolution gained force from the idea that managers in line charge of local units small enough for them to be known personally to their staff could help with the communication problem. A typical provincial Area might have two or three thousand staff stationed in thirty or forty places over a radius of thirty miles. It was physically easy for the general manager to visit the field units regularly. In many cases the staff developed a genuine loyalty to their manager as a result.

Both CHQ and THQ spent a great deal of effort on sophisticated techniques of communication. Generations of outside experts and consultants were employed by generations of top management, but none of them succeeded. 'Headquarters' remained remote. It was all too easy for them to become villains of the piece. Area Managers would not have been human if they had not sometimes have been tempted to encourage this. The soft option was to blame headquarters or Treasury for shortage of money, rather than to accept blame for oneself and one's managers for not spending what one had efficiently. Many an otherwise difficult meeting with local unions was defused by doing just this.

All levels of management up and down the business were drilled and redrilled in the need to communicate. People in national headquarters were taught from the youth up that every important development must be formally communicated to the Regional Directors, to the unions and to the customer consultative organs of the day. It was recognized as a legitimate complaint for Area Managers to tell their Region that they had heard a development first from the press or, most damagingly, from the unions at local level. Much effort was expended to get across to junior management and to supervision that they had their own responsibilities of communication, and the system gave emphasis to bottom-up communication as well as to top-down. But despite all this effort top management communication with the mass of staff was at best patchy; and at worst honoured in the breach rather than the observance.

All staff have a natural desire to know what the final boss at the top thinks of them. In a very big organization like PO telecommunications the one set of pointers with guaranteed effect were pay, conditions of work, ranking systems and promotion structures. Top management were judged above all by their actions in these fields. One pay settlement or other measure which was viewed as seriously unjust, however unfairly, could set staff attitudes back for years. The Senior Salary Structure episode and its effect on morale among second-line management was a classic case in point.

First-line supervision is a key part of any organization. There were special problems in this respect on the engineering side. Inside exchanges and repeater stations the engineering first-line supervisors suffered by comparison with their immediate subordinates, the Technical Officers (TOs) who did the hands-on construction and maintenance of the real technology. Much TO work was intellectually demanding, and virtually all of it was responsible. If supervisors are to hold authority in an engineering environment they must be able to demonstrate superiority in grasp of the technology itself over their subordinates. The technology was becoming more and more specialized; and all TOs were soaked in their own specialisms in fine detail. Many of them were people capable of the work of first-line supervision or higher who had forgone promotion because they did not want managerial responsibility or simply because in take-home terms it did not pay as well. Take-home pay relativities sometimes took TOs up into overlap with management. In such circumstances it was hard work for the supervisors to be fully effective, and many were not.

Supervision of outdoor staff posed another set of problems. Most telecommunications outdoor construction staff work in small gangs scattered throughout the territory, tightly knit under foremen equivalent to non-commissioned officers. Some construction staff and most outdoor maintenance staff work at most in pairs and often on their own. It is an exacting task to supervise them properly, involving a great deal of driving around, getting in and out of cars and telephoning. With all the pressures of statistical returns and other paperwork to contend with, it was all too easy for supervisors to become desk-bound. When they did, the efficiency with which the actual work was conducted was bound to lose its edge, even in the best units. In the worst it could be lost completely, not necessarily because the staff were slacking so much as because of a lack of drive which the staff themselves could not supply, in work organization or in dealing with matters like shortages of stores or defective mechanical aids.

The Civil Service system, geared as it was essentially to office work, had never grasped that so far as engineering work is concerned the efficiency with which day-to-day work is conducted depends more on first-line supervisors than on any other single group of staff. In their turn the Corporation and especially its personnel policy-makers were too slow to learn this lesson and to act upon it. The engineering supervisors remained the weakest link in the whole chain of command, and performance suffered accordingly.

There were fewer problems of the kind in respect of exchange operators, whose supervision and management was traditionally tightly geared and had a pioneering history in work study. The problems of supervision of clerical staff were no different in the PO from those in other big organizations.

The big battalions and the big costs were on the engineering side. The need to overcome the weaknesses in this area lay at the core of the task of the higher line structure in raising operating efficiency overall. THQ, with the ultimate responsibility, had reacted over the years by setting up an elaborate hierarchy of statistical targets and controls. As we shall see, these could and did do a lot. But the units where the highest efficiency was achieved were still those where it happened spontaneously under self-starting first- and second-line managers.

It all added up to an open invitation to the unions to exploit the situation in their own interest, and not just on the engineering side. Because the union channels of communication were more direct than those of management, and because unions of their nature run on grapevine communication and leaks, they often succeeded. Year after year the need to outdo unions in the speed and authority of communication would be on the agenda of management conferences; year after year managers would try very hard to achieve it; and year after year they would know that they had failed. The natural advantages of the unions were simply too great.

The most important single union in the telecommunications business was the POEU. Within this union the TOs formed a particularly important group. The vast majority were responsible and conscientious people, but they were well aware of their key role in the business and of the power it gave them. The confidence born of the progress they had made with their campaign to raise their pay and status (discussed in Chapter 2) had gained force with time. Bryan Stanley, now General Secretary, himself came from this section of the union membership. There had earlier been moves to form a breakaway union to represent TOs' special interests. In the complex internal politics of the union the leadership had constantly to balance these pressures from the TOs against the pressures from the left, which were strong in London in particular.

In the nature of things it was much harder for the UPW and the Management Services Association (MSA), which between them represented telephone operators and their supervisors, to find the rallying points for a forward position in telecommunications. But what the UPW had got in the combined PO Corporation was industrial muscle. Even if the union had lost the big strike in 1971, there was no way the postal service could operate without its members.

The POEU position as regards industrial action was more complicated. A withdrawal of labour could halt installation and fault repair work, which as events were to show could cause serious embarrassment to management. But as network automation and modernization proceeded, the service itself was becoming less and less vulnerable to industrial action. Management was to discover in the later 1970s that, sabotage apart, the network would run for a surprisingly long time with only minimum attention to failures, of a kind which could be given by a handful of third-line managers; and the time for which it would do so was increasing.

In the early 1970s PO clerical and ex-Civil-Service executive staff still worked in an atmosphere redolent of the Civil Service. Their unions were by tradition docile. But as the decade wore on they became more and more restless about the way their pay relativities with the POEU and STE grades were developing. This was to prove a breeding ground for militancy.

The telecommunications business had staff everywhere, including the worst industrial relations blackspots in the country. It knew all there was to know about awkward trade unionists and the eternal management choice between hawk-like and dove-like approaches. Management at every level was never backward in coming forward if the unions overstepped the mark; and the unions were adept at creating controlled pressures in the opposite direction. There were local units with really bad relations, as there were in any national organization of the time. Gresham Street had an essential service to keep running. The essence of its philosophy was to feel all the time for a balance of forces which would keep relations somewhere about the middle of the scale; and to pray that Howland Street and Ministers, whether Labour or Conservative, would know better than to upset it. Sometimes its prayers were answered. At other times they were not.

At the interface between management and unions there were much-fought-over distinctions between matters appropriate for negotiation, those for consultation and those which were for management to decide and notify. So far as management was concerned, negotiation covered pay and conditions; consultation covered working practices and matters affecting the interest of the staff as people, like safety, catering and accommodation; and the management decision area covered everything else. The boundary between the area for negotiation and the rest might be contested by the unions in the no-holds-barred context of a particular dispute; but otherwise it was rarely challenged. On the other hand the union representatives waged a ceaseless war to move topics from the area of management decision followed by notification into that of formal consultation and union influence.

One of the most important target areas in this war concerned decision-taking about staffing levels, recruitment and overtime. From the staff representatives' point of view it would be an important trophy to take to annual conference if they could claim or even legitimately imply that management had officially consulted them in advance on the number of people it intended to employ. It would bolster their position with the membership by demonstrating the influence they exerted. But there was a lot more to it than that. The majority of the union membership were highly responsible people; and some of them actually voted Conservative. But the paid union officials had to reckon with strong left-wing feeling among some of the members, especially in the big cities. There were union members who went as far as a determined belief in workers' control and who maintained continuous pressure on their officials to seek to move towards it; and staffing was an obvious battleground.

The union officials had to work hard just to balance all these forces. But management for its part had to manage. Four hundred years of practice had taught it which ground to give and which to hold; and woe betide a weak or inexperienced manager who stepped out of line. The battle never stopped.

In essentials Fennessy had continued the industrial relations approach which went right back to Alexander Little in 1950, holding the management line with determination but looking all the time for a constructive atmosphere rather than conflict. But by the 1970s the unions were coming at things in a much more hardheaded way. Kenneth Glynn, since 1960 General Secretary of the STE: 'Samuel Gompers defined it many years ago. The employer tries to buy his labour as cheaply as possible. The employee through his union tries to sell it as dearly as possible.'

The engineering unions had been building up their collective strength for some time. Bryan Stanley, by then General Secretary of the POEU:

> These were very heady days, because we (the POEU) were strongly organized. [STE] were strongly organized. Kenneth Glynn and I had a good friendship and a mutual bond. We worked together – the first time that had happened [between the two unions]. I found sympathy with Kenneth's view. We formed an alliance which lasted right the way through until he retired. That was admittedly a pretty powerful alliance, when staff and management are acting together.

The later 1960s and the 1970s were the era of productivity bargaining. Stanley describes the way the unions saw themselves as coming to it and going at it:

> When we came to the middle sixties the situation arose that pay was going to be restricted not just by the Macmillan approach but when Wilson won the '64 election he endeavoured to put some detailed consideration of the basis of pay claims which had to be agreed by bodies whose names kept changing. At that stage we recognized that it needed different tactics, so we seconded Ted Webb to the [government] pay organization and brought in some different research staff, including Bill Jones who later became the personnel assistant to the Board in the steel industry.
>
> Michael Foot was the Minister responsible at that time for pay questions. He laid down at Wilson's command that to justify pay increases there had to be proof that

productivity was improved. Well, OK, so there were practices that management had introduced over the years like six-man gangs that were not as productive as they might be. So in discussion between the two sides we agreed after consulting our members and for a fair share of the benefits flowing the reduction of the size of these.

[Such changes] meant tremendous disturbance and upheaval in the way in which the work was organized and meant that a number of people were redeployed and retrained. Because if we were going to achieve the greater efficiency then less staff would be required. [The resulting payments] were not a pay increase – the pay was quite separate from the productivity. Go back over the records. We have never accepted that pay and productivity payments were part of the same negotiation – we always had separate negotiations. They might be at the same meeting, but we were always very careful to say, 'Having dealt with pay now let us deal with productivity.'

We quite specifically sought to persuade management to join with us in improving the efficiency and effectiveness of the work in return for a share of the benefits that were received. Management would not have achieved the smooth change and the effective change unless there had been the goodwill and total co-operation of the entire workforce. This co-operation depended on there being no compulsory redundancy, a position maintained even to the present day.

In any other organization outside the PO these would have been traumatic changes. It was the days of the demarcation disputes, when you had only to move somebody in the car manufacturing world from one job to another and you had got a strike on your hands. We were co-operating fully, totally, at a time when the general atmosphere in other industries, other unions was one of conflict and strife. We had none.

Management of course saw the situation quite differently. But with the unions taking such a position a pattern developed under which the telecommunications basic grade unions expected annual increases in two parts, made up of a more or less automatic increase to reflect the increase in the cost of living and an increase related to the measured gain in their members' productivity. The labour productivity measurement system had been developed in the late 1960s purely for management purposes; but it was inevitable that it would be drawn on for pay purposes. Each year's pay round became a technical encounter between experienced specialists on both sides to determine the theoretical productivity gain due to the various groups of staff, followed by top-level negotiation to determine the actual pay settlement. There were detailed monitoring procedures. Stanley says:

> The system of verification was so thorough that in fact we had to prove every bit of productivity gain before we could have a share of it. That was a very good system, particularly at that time when there was so much productivity improvement needed.

The contribution which the staff were making to productivity improvement in this period has to be set alongside the continuous efforts of management. The workload was rising all the time and the more the ground that was gained through improvements in work practices and organization the harder it became for management to find new ones. But they continued to be found.

The field force of some two hundred thousand was there not because of a sinister 'compact' with the unions or because of Nigel Lawson's vision of Eastern European incompetence, but because such numbers had to be there to handle the ever-rising investment activity and the growth in lines (see Figure 16.1). Natural wastage due to retirement and so on from the overwhelmingly male engineering labour force, numbering 124,000 in 1980, amounted to about 5 per cent per annum. The corresponding natural female wastage rate was about 14 per cent. Faced with the constant pressure from Board and Ministers to hold down price increases, it was open to the business to take advantage of this wastage to run numbers down at any time, simply by suspending recruitment. But the experience in 1975 had shown the damaging effects which arbitrary action of this kind could have on service in face of the ever-mounting workload and the complex skill-mix demands of the technology.

Against this background the twin aims of the THQ budgetary controllers in the later 1970s were to hold staff numbers constant in face of ever-expanding workload but to do so without damaging either the service or the autonomy of the Regions. It was a delicate business. It would have been easy to impose a rigid ceiling on each Region, and the temptation to do so was great with some. But the Bridgeman doctrine of devolution had proved its worth over the years. Most of us directly concerned in THQ had worked in Regions, and the 1975 experience had underlined the dangers to service of pre-empting the power of field managers to take their own short-term recruitment decisions. The approach we adopted was to preserve the power of Regional Directors to take actual recruitment decisions within expenditure budgets and targets for improvement in labour productivity set annually.

As Figure 16.1 shows, the approach worked. Hard work though it was, the amalgam of conflict, co-operation and management initiatives over which we presided from the upper floors in Gresham Street accomplished steady improvement. By 1982 field staff overall were three thousand fewer than they had been in 1970, where the network and the annual growth of the network had both more than doubled in size, and investment activity had risen by even more.

Central headquarters staffing was a different story. In 1982 central staff numbered 38,000 or 16 per cent of total staff. This included research, factories, supplies and data processing staff. The rest were THQ staff and some 12,000 catering, medical and administrative staff taken over from the old CHQ. The staffing of the central headquarters itself was undoubtedly excessive at this time.

As the acquisitive society formed round them – inflationary effect or no inflationary effect – it seemed from outside the union movement that the union General Secretaries came more and more to depend for their personal survival on their ability to deliver increases in pay in line with their members' expectations. They became more and more bullish in their approach and more and more disposed to use their political influence to union ends.

But that was not at all how it looked from inside the movement. The outlook of the responsible core of the POEU and the effect of the hierarchical structure on attitudes are put by Bryan Stanley with great eloquence:

> The two major grades were the Technician 2A (T2A) and the TO, and they were by far the majority of the people we represented. Therefore we based our case on the best arguments. Everyone else in the business was either assisting them or working with them or related to them in some way. Apprentices and trainees working up to that level, T1s and Senior Technicians acting as foremen to groups of T2As, the Supplies, Motor Transport and ancillary grades were all contributing to the overall success and therefore should be sharing in the benefits that were obtained. Therefore, by a single entity argument we were able to achieve very good results for the lower paid, but only

reasonable – fair perhaps – results for the people with the highest skills. But by bringing all those people into one negotiation we did something else. We created peace amongst the grades. How many problems did you get from the arguments over one group having better pay than others among our grades? None.

When PRU began to be belittled and began to fade in its significance we recognized that we had got to perpetuate the same approach, but to do the work ourselves. So we further expanded the Research Department. Of course it is true that the further we got away from the last actual PRU report the more management were attempting to belittle the results that were being obtained. But they found that very difficult because we were able to establish evidence to prove the points we were making. Therefore it was not an unjustified advance that we were making, it was an entirely justified advance. The fact of the matter is that the TOs on the floor of the exchanges were holding together an antiquated system which should have been changed to crossbar and better systems much earlier; and their skill and technical ability had to be recognized by adequate returns.

In the case of the T2As they were our front line of contact with the customer. To be quite honest they were the ones that were keeping goodwill with the customers going, because the management at that time were seeking to economize on maintenance and service and we really thought our front line troops were maintaining goodwill and service to the customer in spite of management reluctance to improve service. Here we have the people that were essential to the running of the business. Surely the key role that they were playing in the whole PO was worthy of recognition.

It [was not] our responsibility either to drive or not to drive inflation. The members that we represented were not responsible for the inflation of the day. They were contributing a very, very significant increase in productivity year after year after year; which if other workers had been doing the same we would have had little or no inflation. Our argument was that workers who are increasing productivity and are actually producing the wealth from which their pay increases can be met are not contributing to inflation; that they are worthy of the repayment of part of their efforts – not the full amount. About one-third for the staff, about one-third for the improvement of investment and about one-third to give the customer better service at a lower price. That's how we saw the situation.

The last paragraph was of course not how management saw it.

In the first place, the actual source of gains in productivity could only be the efforts of management in introducing new technology and changing working practices; and management skill in matching staff to workload. So far as the staff were concerned their obligation to do a fair day's work for a fair day's pay did not alter just because the content of the work changed. What the staff and the union were really contributing was willing co-operation and acceptance of change without resistance or dispute. Stanley is right that this was of real value and in contrast to the approach of unions in other industries. It is a pity that he pushes this highly creditable point into second place.

Second, the suggestion was in fact belied by the actions of the union's own negotiators. As the 1970s wore on, the PO found itself fighting an increasingly bitter battle to stop the whole of the gains being passed on to the staff, with government standing not far behind the unions' shoulder, albeit nominally on management's side.

The drive of the POEU for advancement had a momentum all its own. Stanley again:

> We started this whole thing massively underpaid. We were engineers and technicians; and the supremos in the Civil Service atmosphere in which we were living did not recognize us – many years before if you could push a pen and keep a piece of paper clean you were recognized more fully than if you were an engineer or technician, never mind all the training that had to go into being an engineer or a technician. We came into a culture in which the Executive Officer class was supreme in the Civil Service and for a fraction of the skills and responsibilities of a TO they got considerably more pay. That was a driving force that was utterly unstoppable. As long as we were being confined to the Civil Service straitjacket and lagging behind the EO class then there was a driving force that did not need politics, did not need class warfare, did not need the Communist Party. Every reasonable TO knew that we [union officers] had got to be instructed and driven forward to get better pay relativities with the EO class.
>
> The next thing about this was that we were in a situation where there were tremendous changes taking place, particularly in telecommunications technology. And what was becoming ever more apparent was that just ahead was an even greater revolution in technology which was going to demand complete changes in thinking and attitudes of our members and that it would also lead, as indeed the changes in work practice had led, to less people being needed to do the same job. Expansion was taking place and we were driving it because we constantly argued for more marketing, better publicity, faster expansion of the telephone service. We coined the phrase 'a phone in every home' and management and Ministers ridiculed us. We sought to get a better marketing organization because we said that we were losing many opportunities to sell better equipment, up-to-date equipment, a wider range of equipment.

It would be difficult to find a better illustration of the self-assurance of the unions at this time. Paradoxically enough, there is more than a trace of Thatcherism in the POEU's confident and relentless pursuit of its members' aspirations.

Unstoppable this momentum certainly proved to be, until it finally went over the top in 1978 and 1979. In the closing stages POEU pay increased by over twenty per cent in a single year, ruthlessly fuelling national inflation and imposing strains which tested even telecommunications' cash flow.

The momentum created by the POEU did a lot more than just trickle back up to the professional engineers and engineering managers. As the leaders of their unions saw it, in earlier years the PO had systematically underpaid the key engineering graduate entry grade of Executive Engineer, with serious consequences. Kenneth Glynn says:

> The PO was paying Executive Engineers so badly, because it was looking sideways to the Civil Service, that it had to lower the qualifications on entry from honours to pass degree from 1958 to 1978. I think that dilution may well have damaged the PO R&D and technological change in the seventies in particular. What we were saying was, 'Here is a business which has got to recruit good quality people, with all that means; and it must pay the price. When we had pay research we demonstrated that the PO was not paying the price.'

As we saw in Chapter 2, whatever their outside relativities, the engineering management had held an internal pay lead in earlier years. But now their leaders were happy to jump on the bandwagon being driven with such force by the POEU. Glynn again:

> Subsequently what we did was to use productivity bargaining. The POEU certainly pioneered it. We jumped in as quickly as possible. We secured our share from the same date by arbitration. In 1980 we cited at arbitration the authoritative Finniston Report on the poor status of engineers in Britain.

The skill and success with which the engineering management union pressed its case and exploited arbitration machinery for the raising of its members' pay began to have its own consequences, and not just as a contribution to national wage inflation. As the 1970s wore on, top levels in the supplying industry began to complain that the PO engineering managers were unduly well paid relative to their peers in the manufacturers. The PO found itself with something like a glut of able engineering graduate entrants for whom there was not sufficient demanding work on the technology to go round. Morale suffered in consequence.

Caught in a complicated sandwich between the determined expansionism of the Chairman and the various unions in their respective ways, a conservative and largely unreformed field management, a weak supplying industry (see Part III) and the hard realities described in preceding chapters, Gresham Street was fated to look like a pedestrian pig-in-the-middle. But someone had to keep the whole thing on track, try to preserve the fundamental balance between service and cost, and to go on hauling the organization up the slope towards genuine efficency of operation.

THQ was inhibited from putting its case in the terms it might have wished. As a subsidiary of a public board whose members were government employees (and unlike BT plc today) it could not mount an independent public case in its own defence. Again as a public body it had a responsibility not to knock the share prices of its private sector suppliers by a public exposition of their failings. It was in unending adversarial conflict with powerful unions who would pounce on every tiny opening for attack. With all these forces to reckon with it could never come out from cover and take the fully free and open line which it might wish. It had to hold a low profile and grin and bear its frustrations with equanimity.

Against this background the PO and PO telecommunications within it were now to become the laboratory for a major experiment in industrial democracy, which is dealt with in the next chapter.

Note

1. Report of the Post Office Review Committee, Cmnd 6859 (HMSO, London, 1977), para. 1.26.

8 Industrial Tension and Industrial Democracy

the British trade union movement has always been more anxious to screw the highest possible wages out of hostile employers than to share managerial power and the responsibilities that go with it.

David Marquand, *Independent*, 15 January 1996

Up to the mid–1970s serious industrial disputes were unknown in telecommunications. The real stuff of PO industrial relations was made from good-humoured but unending conflict between management and union officials. Outside observers would comment that each side deserved the other, and in a sense they did. Apart from a few professional trade unionists virtually everyone in every room in which consultation or negotiation took place either was or had been a PO employee. But there was nothing remotely resembling a 'compact', except perhaps a common desire to consume as much of the smoke of day-to-day conflict as possible within the telecommunications business. Neither side enjoyed what happened if ordinary disputes got even to Howland Street.

Once Labour gained power, however, it rapidly became clear that a basic problem of management was that government was always standing just behind the shoulder of the unions, even though nominally on the management side. So far as the PO was concerned, every major confrontation became an exercise in testing how far a hard line would go before the unions pulled the plug and went to Ministers. The art lay in keeping the battles inside the business. When the POEU abused its direct access to Ministers in this way, the union people would avoid the gaze of management at the next working meeting. They had broken faith and they knew it. But so far as they were concerned, the end justified the means.

The same problem afflicted the Board in Howland Street. As William Barlow says:

The thing I did not enjoy enjoy under the Labour government was the easy access the trade unions had to them. They had better access than I did to Ministers and they were listened to. It got to be serious when I decided that the PO should be split. When I was first approached to take the job on, the theme was, 'You've done a lot of mergers. The government has been looking at splitting the PO. We think that anyone who has done a merger might do the unmerger.' That was in everybody's mind at the time I accepted the job. I said, 'Well, we'll see.' When I got into the organization it was clear to me that there was every conceivable reason for splitting. When I said, 'Right, we'll see about splitting it', the unions ran for cover, ran to the Labour politicians and persuaded them not to do it. So there was no way of splitting at that time.

During 1977 new thinking began to emerge on the industrial relations front at political level. Barlow again:

> In between accepting the job and actually taking it up Eric Varley, who was the Secretary of State, sent for me. He said, 'Things are changing a bit and you may not wish to go on with this job. The Lib/Lab pact which we have done with David Steel had one point concerning the Bullock report on industrial democracy. It had a requirement from the Liberals that there should be an experiment carried out in one of the large nationalized industries. The PM has decided that it is going to be done in the PO because the PO has such good industrial relations for a start that it seems to be a good place to do it. Would you still go on being Chairman if you have to chair an industrial democracy board?'
>
> That board was going to consist of seven executive members, seven trade-union-nominated people and five outsiders. At that time I had been involved in industrial disputes with unions for twenty or twenty-five years. I was getting very tired of it, as most people in industry were. I thought, 'Well, why not give it a try – it's an interesting idea.' So I agreed to do that. When I really could have done with more time getting to grips with the job I had to take time organizing the industrial democracy Board.

Industrial democracy was viewed in Gresham Street with sceptical detachment. It was hard for people whose lives were spent in real confrontation with powerful unions to believe that the presence of union people on the Board would in some way transform the situation. That kind of magic just did not exist. THQ knew well the people who were going to represent telecommunications staff. It respected them as individuals. But it could see from the outset that they were going to face an impossible conflict of loyalty. It simply was asking too much to expect them to cast off their roots.

There were doubts among some people on the union side about the desirability of industrial democracy in principle. Some of the unions, as we saw in Chapter 7, had a tradition of lecturing management on issues like system growth and marketing, which might get them to first base in favour of a system of industrial democracy. Kenneth Glynn's position in STE was much more pure-blooded trade unionist:

> I believe [the staff can be caused to identify with the employing organization] by a realistic negotiating set-up. I said to your people, 'Any form of co-operation you want on productivity, on reorganization, on how the show is run, provided the conditions of the staff are not adversely affected and provided the staff share in the benefits, and that of course includes no compulsory redundancy. But within that no sacred cows – whatever you want we will talk about. I believe that it was for management to clarify its own ideas on that. It was not for the unions to make proposals on how the outfit should be run.

Peter Shaw, now POEU Research Officer and shortly to be appointed as a union nominee to the industrial democracy Board, says:

> [Industrial democracy] was fashionable, it had TUC support, Labour Party support. Bryan Stanley was very interested in the concept, and certainly from the union's point of view he was the main pusher. He really drove things along. He believed in the idea. He wanted to see it realized and he directed quite a lot of the union's resources into seeing that something was achieved, politically and down through the union. I

did most of the leg work for this at the time, without actually being terribly enthusiastic about it, to tell you the truth. I thought we were going off in a wrong direction and there were much more important things the union ought to be spending its time and money on.

Barlow had to bear the full weight of the problems of the experiment:

> Some unions wanted to have elections, some wanted to appoint people who worked in the PO, some wanted to have full-time officials. All that had to be done. The whole thing coincided with the appointment of new non-executive directors, so in the event I started with a brand-new Board in February 1978. The big unions were entitled to two members, so that the UPW had two and the POEU had two. There were in all seven unions, so that the other five unions had to be content with three members between them. I arranged for training of those people in the work of a Board to try and make it possible for them to participate in the work of the Board right from the beginning.
>
> When I faced that new Board I suddenly realized that, unlike any other Board I had chaired, the directors were not all facing in the same direction. If you are the chairman of a publicly quoted company and you go to a Board meeting the executive directors work in the firm and the non-executive directors are trying to help. You are all pointing in the same direction, although there may be arguments about how you get there. I found with this PO Board that that wasn't the case. You could easily have thought, not exactly that we were working in two separate organizations, but the objectives were not the same. It was quite obvious soon that when we came to the big capital subjects, which had been well prepared – the quality of papers coming to the Board was always high, with the investment return shown and so on – you would have quite a good meeting on them. But then when you thought it was all settled the union members would say, 'Ah, but there is nothing in that paper about what's in it for us, in terms of conditions or pay and so on.' To answer that with a general theme that if we a run a better PO we will all be better off never cut any ice at all.
>
> The minutes of the Management Board always went to the main Board. The union members on the main Board always complained that we deliberately dealt with things on the Management Board in such a way that they never got a look in when it came to the main Board. This actually was not correct, although without the Management Board we could not have run the organization at all.

Peter Shaw on how it worked in practice from his point of view:

> I must say I enjoyed the two years immensely. I learnt an enormous amount. I enjoyed the experience. So far as the experiment itself was concerned, two years was never enough to run an experiment like that and hope to get something sensible about it. But I think conceptually there were faults in the design of the thing which were bound to cause it to hiccup and fail eventually. The union simply wasn't prepared either itself to take responsibility for managerial-type decisions or for its representatives – whatever the rules were we were none the less representatives – to take that kind of decision. I don't believe that anything like that can work until those involved really have the guts to say, 'Yes we are prepared to take this or that kind of hard decision which temporarily or even on a longer term basis affects the conditions of service of the people who are paying their [union] subscriptions.'

The combined effects of the separation of the Board and CHQ from the business and of the industrial democracy experiment were to have important consequences in the next two or three years. But with one crucial exception the experiment with industrial democracy had remarkably little practical impact on the day-to-day work of the telecommunications business. CHQ, the personnel side of THQ and the unions became involved in a long and extremely tortuous dispute about arrangements for industrial democracy in the field, which was never properly resolved. But otherwise the ordinary processes of consultation and negotiation continued as if nothing had happened.

The exception involved one of the most serious industrial disputes in the history of telecommunications. During the summer of 1977, on the instructions of its annual conference, the POEU had put in a claim for a reduction of five hours in the working week with no loss of pay. The background was a growing groundswell of opinion in TUC and Labour circles generally that the employment implications of automation and of modern technology generally could only be, and should be, contained by changes of this kind. The claim also had two rather less altruistic objectives. A shorter basic week meant more overtime for the same hours actually worked. And the attractions of more genuine leisure were considerable for staff on high pay like the POEU; it would give them a chance to spend their surplus income.

The PO reaction was one of deep concern. It was impossible to see how a negotiated settlement could possibly be reached over such an expensive claim, which could be seen as the equivalent of a claim for a pay increase of 5/42 hours, or 11.9 per cent, on top of the normal pay round. To make the situation even more difficult, Fennessy and Merriman had just retired and Bill Ryland was on the point of retirement himself. The claim had to be faced up to at the outset in complete uncertainty about who would be the new Chairman and Managing Director Telecommunications. Cadbury was 'acting in the place of Managing Director' and I was 'acting in the place of Assistant Managing Director'. Both of us were temporarily appointed to the Management Board of the Corporation. As one of Ryland's last acts he caused me to be put in charge of the Shorter Working Week negotiations at the Gresham Street end.

The claim faced the new experimental main Board with a test which would have been exacting if it had been running successfully for a decade. From the national point of view it was a full-blown test case for reductions in working hours generally. Labour was in power. Experience, not least with the two earlier episodes concerning Corporation structure and the retirement age, gave cause for serious doubt about the likely attitude of government once the chips began really to come down. Equally seriously, discussions on the Board had to be conducted in the presence of staff members who, however much their integrity might be respected as individuals, were still very clearly linked to the unions. Peter Shaw was in an exceptionally difficult position as a Board member who was also a member of the union negotiating team. Barlow himself was new to the PO and its idiosyncrasies but he had no option but to try to fight his way through the maze.

Discussions between the two sides started in the autumn of 1977 and continued through the winter. The union's officials knew that a claim for a reduction of five hours really was unrealistic. They decided they could gain an advantage by voluntarily reducing the claim at the outset to two and a half hours, and this they persuaded the union to do.

The problem on the management side was quite stark. The only defensible basis for any concession at all on working hours would be to find gains in productivity which would pay for it. There really was no other course but to sit down with the union and see if they could be found. The first problem was that all the justifiable productivity gains available from conventional changes in working practice had been used up in the ordinary pay settlement. The main place from which productivity gains to justify a concession on hours had to come was from changes in attendance patterns themselves. It was an unpromising brief. Even by scraping the barrel the largest reduction the management side could find to offer was nine-tenths of an hour.

The negotiators on both sides made a great effort just before Christmas 1977 to construct a formula around this. The union's officers made a determined attempt to sell it at a special conference of the union at the start of the New Year. But the membership would have none of it. Their original claim had been for five hours. Half of it had already been conceded. No way would they give up most of the rest.

The special conference had given the union executive a mandate for industrial action. The officers were reluctant to take it up. The POEU had a record as a responsible union and official national action was practically unknown. But it became apparent that some action to satisfy the membership was unavoidable. There were various limited measures available short of full withdrawal of labour. The union executive issued instructions for a mix of these to be applied.

Barlow:

> I said to the Board that this matter was grave enough to have it on the Board table. I invited the two POEU members to withdraw from the Board meeting, because they had a conflict of interest. They refused to go, on the grounds that they had been appointed by the government and that I couldn't force them to leave and that if they stayed they could probably help to determine the dispute. So I was forced to go on with the discussion with them being privy to everything that was going on at Board level. By the time it got to the next Board meeting the dispute had got a lot worse. I was in the frame of mind that if there was any industrial action started we would take retaliatory action, suspend people and so on. Of course it was not very convenient to disclose my tactics to the union. The union members obviously could not dissuade their union from any strong action.

After over six months of dour negotiation the dispute was at a stalemate. The industrial action bit mainly on installation of new lines and equipment. The City was particularly affected and becoming more and more impatient. Growing numbers of staff were being sent home for refusing to do work they were given. The service situation was becoming intolerable.

There was one element of the otherwise threadbare negotiating agenda which offered the chance of worthwhile productivity gains arising directly from a change in attendance patterns. It concerned the work of external cable and construction gangs. Once these staff were on a given site there was clear benefit to be gained from extending their working day on that site. The process of getting work going in the morning and of packing up in the evening on an outdoor site involves unavoidable and significant loss of effective time. If the working day could be lengthened so that jobs of this kind could be completed in one day less — say four days rather than five — there would be a real gain in output. Detailed studies in the field showed that an actual gain could be achieved in productivity if 18 per cent of the engineering field force moved to a nine-day fortnight. With one or two other changes which had been on the table for some time it was at last feasible to assemble an operationally acceptable proposition for a two-and-a-half hour reduction for the complete engineering staff.

THQ negotiated a detailed formula built around the 18 per cent limit subject to approval by higher authority and submitted it up the line. But the separation between Gresham Street and Howland Street fatally bedevilled the course of events. The two were on completely different wavelengths – the former worried about the service, the latter wrestling with the relationship with government and the politics of the industrial democracy experiment. The formula was rejected. In the early summer the dispute was referred to Lord McCarthy for resolution. He found for a settlement very similar to that embodied in the *ad referendum* formula, but with a more generous limit for the number of nine-day fortnights. The dispute at last ended. Bryan Stanley, the union General Secretary, said at the time, 'This is a very good agreement but the union had offered to settle the claim on a very similar basis even before industrial action began.'

Right at the start the PO had announced its intention to give responsibility for the detailed implementation of any settlement to Area General Managers, as a concrete exercise in devolution. This was done. The central question was the proportion of the staff who would be allowed nine-day fortnights. The THQ assumption was that Regional Directors would ensure their General Managers drove the necessary hard bargains. Some did; but unfortunately some did not. In some areas the proportion was allowed to rise to as much as 70 per cent. The POEU branches concerned had failed to keep the word given so often on their behalf by the union officers that they would offset the cost of the settlement by their own efforts. There could not have been more telling demonstrations of the risks of devolution without a proper mechanism of answerability; or of the downside of industrial democracy.

In all, the Shorter Working Week dispute and its settlement took a year, from the autumn of 1977 to the autumn of 1978. It was one of the most obdurate in British utility history. As we shall see, it left behind it the seeds of two further bouts of industrial action by the engineering staff, one before and one after privatization. It was also in a very real sense the rock on which the national experiment in industrial democracy foundered.

At the same time industrial relations problems were increasing among the rest of the staff. Barlow says:

> The worst dispute for me came in 1979, when the computer workers, who were in a senior staff union, went on strike. We could operate a few computers with management but not many.
>
> The result of this computer strike was that we could not send out telephone bills and we could not account for stores. This meant that we were having to borrow money. In the middle of 1979 the Conservative government came into office. I had an early conversation with Keith Joseph and with Geoffrey Howe, the new Chancellor, and said, 'I had better tell you we have got a computer strike on and we can't send out telephone bills. It's going to have a negative cash flow of enormous proportions. Already it's about £300m and I can't see any end to it. Nor can I give in on it. I've got to win this strike; and I am prepared to stick it out *ad infinitum*, because the system

actually works but you can't account for it.' Before that ended at the end of that year the PO had borrowed £1,000m extra and it was so big as to affect the whole national situation, interest rates and so on. But I will give that government credit for standing by me.

The aftermath of the computer strike was that the PO and its successor made a number of provisions to avoid ever getting caught again. Another thing that came out of the computer strike is that the accounts for the following year could not give an accurate view of the stocks, work in progress and so on; and the accounts were qualified very heavily indeed.

On top of all this the chickens of the Senior Salary Structure decision now began to come home to roost with a vengeance. There were various forms of minor industrial action among junior management. Even the loyalty of third-line management began to be debated. In the space of two or three years the good industrial relations record of the telecommunications business had become a thing of the past. The country was heading for the 'winter of discontent' and the rampant pay inflation of 1980. The PO was in line for a large and thoroughly unwelcome piece of the action.

Putting it all together it would be difficult to imagine anything less like Lord Howe's 'malign unspoken compact between state ownership and monopoly trade unionism in Britain's bloated public sector'. Elsewhere maybe, but not in PO telecommunications. The industrial democracy experiment was doing less than nothing to resolve the growing real industrial relations problems of the business.

In the real world of THQ, Regions and Areas, the everlasting battles between management and unions, especially that about the staffing of field operations, went on unabated. Headquarters and field management continued to hold the pass. In the event, and despite the unsatisfactory character of the arrangements in some Areas, even the effects of the engineering shorter working week were absorbed with remarkably little effect on field staffing levels overall (Figure 16.1).

Amid all the comings and goings in Howland Street Gresham Street had to keep up the momentum of improvement as best it could. After such a prolonged dispute the obvious priority was to restore morale among the engineering staff. In Peter Benton's words:

> The task I saw – and I must say I found Bryan Stanley very good on this – was that we had to take the fear out of the minds of the general workforce. Because there undoubtedly was a fear that somehow technology was going to throw them out of work. They had not worked out for themselves that while technology created less need for employment in old tasks it also made possible quite different ways of creating wealth and new employment which had not yet been thought of. So there was a fear in that workforce that had been played upon by the union in the thirty-five-hour-week campaign, that somehow something was happening in that technology that would be destructive to their personal jobs and career prospects.

It was a daunting problem but the potential rewards for success were great. If management could gain the confidence and allegiance of the staff as individuals the business would gain a huge advantage for the future. If the new environment was be handled successfully it was essential for management to be able to redeploy and retrain staff rapidly. The work of THQ manpower planners showed that even on cautious assumptions it would be possible to trade a constrained promise of no compulsory redundancy against suitable undertakings by the union on redeployment. Such a package was offered and an agreement was negotiated. At the same time Benton, Stanley, Back and I between us recorded an audio-visual programme seen by all engineering staff which was designed to pose the combined opportunity and challenge of the future.

The positive approach was more than justified by the potential benefits. But there was an obvious risk that it might misfire. As Benton says: 'As I said rather sardonically to Bryan Stanley when [the audio-visual exercise] was over and he said how successful it had been, "Yes, the fear has gone, now all that remains is the greed".' We shall see in Part IV how things turned out.

The rest of the story of this period is best told by Barlow himself:

In 1979, when the Conservatives came in, in my first big session with Keith Joseph I said, 'It is my considered opinion that [the PO] should be split. It is also my opinion that the monopoly should be removed and that the industrial democracy experiment should be canned because it is not successful. The organization should be made into a company operating with shares under the Stock Exchange Yellow Book rules.'

The government was very quick to react on some of these things. They embraced the idea of split and the removal or reduction of the monopoly. And just before the recess Keith Joseph stood up in the House and said that the organization was going to be split and the monopoly was going to be reviewed and reduced. On the basis of that Ministerial statement I then set about organizing the split.

The government did not want to give up the industrial democracy experiment, and they refused steadily. By December 1979 the matter was urgent because it was a two-year experiment. Just before Christmas 1979 I had a session with Keith Joseph and Jim Prior. I said that in my view it had become essential to drop the experiment and I could not understand why they were delaying. Jim Prior's view was that they had offended the trade union movement and the TUC particularly over something to do with Neddy [the National Economic Development Council] and they did not want to offend them again by doing away with this experiment. Would I go along with it for a further period of months? I refused point blank. I said, 'You had better make your minds up. I am going on holiday and if you don't give me an affirmative reply by telex before Christmas I am not coming back and I am having a long holiday.' I absolutely made it a point that I just wasn't going on with that experiment.

I explained that I had made proposals to the unions that in my view would have given them a great deal and I was disappointed that they had not taken it up. I was prepared to give the unions the Board papers and to meet them either monthly or bi-monthly – the General Secretaries, not the nominated people, the men with the power – and discuss with them our Board papers so they could tell me what they believed and I would tell them what I believed and then both parties could go away and make their own decisions based on the absolute same facts. We did operate for a few months on that basis but it petered out.

The government did not like the idea of Telecom being made into a company on Stock Exchange rules. I was not proposing that shares in the company be sold to the public as was done later. I was saying, 'You government can own a hundred per cent if you like, but leave me to run the company by the rules I understand for running a business, which mean I can go and raise money anywhere on the basis of the strength of the company. This business of only having one banker, the Treasury, who own it as an expenditure and are not interested in the business is no way to run a modern business to the requirements of the country. I am not prepared to be responsible for it.'

I should say that where this talk of split was concerned it was assumed by the government and by me and later it was said to me that I would go on to be chairman of Telecom. I was interested in that because of the technology of telecoms. I certainly would not have gone on to be chairman of the PO. I set off in July 1979 with that as my intention, so I set about the split.

The announcement on the monopoly immediately made people think a bit harder about being competitive [see the next chapter]. But [the government] always refused to make it into a company. They always listened to Treasury and Bank of England doctrine that if you borrowed anything for an organization owned by the government it was a charge against the National Debt.

I had a lot of trouble during that year – the computer strike and the aftermath of industrial democracy – and I was also getting more intervention from government on matters that I considered detail. I was really getting tired of interference and dependence on the government machine, particularly the Treasury. I said in April 1980 that unless the government would make it into a private company and release it from the Treasury yoke I would finish the split, which was what I came in to do, and go off into the private sector. They said they could not do that. It was not part of their policy or their wish. So I went to see Keith Joseph one evening and said that that was it and there was my letter of resignation.

It was announced the next day. It took people by surprise. There wasn't any great row around. People were generally mystified that I had decided to leave and do something else.

I felt also that unless you could get it run as a business the power of the unions was still too strong. Union power in a monopoly is an unequal balance of power between unions and management; and management can never win. Because if management in a monopoly situation gets into a strike first of all the public say, 'Jolly good, you are teaching the unions a lesson.' After a month they say there must be something wrong with the organization. After two months they are saying, 'The chairman must be an idiot to go on with a dispute like that.' After three months they are saying, 'Off with his head.' There is no way you can win these disputes. There has got to be something to counter-balance that and competition is the only way I can think of. I would actually have torn the monopoly up.

We started to organize the split. We took each [common] department and decided what to to do with it. The unions were consulted. It went very smoothly. The one thing that was not done when I left was how to split the pension fund.

The emphasis Barlow places in this account on his resentment of Treasury oversight illuminates a basic difference between public and private sector psychologies. The PO officials had all grown up in a world where the Treasury was by definition the overlord. Particular Treasury actions might be bitterly resented; but the institution itself and its power were an inescapable part of life, there to be outwitted but also there to be lived with. Barlow was a private businessman. He repudiated the whole idea of Treasury paramountcy in principle and could not live with it.

The announcement of Barlow's departure came as a real blow to Gresham Street and to me personally. The business had been ready to give him of its best. Geography and organization had prevented us making our case properly to him. I for one hoped things would be different if he became chairman of an independent BT with his office on the spot. But it was not to be. A community of ex-Civil-Servants was accustomed to disconcerting changes at the top. The organization girded its loins to await his successor. After an interregnum during which Sir Henry Chilver served as temporary Chairman of the combined PO, the first independent telecommunications Chairman was to be Sir George Jefferson (see Chapter 13).

9 A Ferment of Activity

The PO record in telecommunications deserves responsible criticism, but not the exercise of our national habit of condemning all things British as though they were the worst in the world.

The Carter Committee

Peter Benton joined the business as Managing Director in the early part of 1978. He had had a career so far with the consultants McKinsey, where he had led the studies preparing the British gas industry for North Sea gas ten years earlier, and in private industry. In his last appointment he had been Chairman of the engineering companies Saunders Valve and Mono Pumps, and with Barlow a Vice-President of the British Mechanical Engineering Confederation.

In Benton's own words:

What one saw when one got there was a monolith – well not quite a monolith but substantially a monolith – with a strong functional organization with strong functional barons at the top; and with most decisions requiring a balance between specialist requirements landing on the desk of the Chief Executive [i.e. the Managing Director]. It was also an organization that was quite noticeably introverted with its famous sixteen feet of Telecommunications Instructions. Excellence as perceived by the internal view was the criterion for most individual actions of over two hundred thousand people.

It was a business in which the technology had been moving quite slowly. It was in the final years of the Strowger technology which was perhaps ninety years old at that time, and of course it was an organization which had an unassailable and unassailed monopoly. All those features – deliberate decision-taking, strong functional baronies fighting for their functional interests, an introverted point of view – could all be compatible with survival because there was an impregnable monopoly. And of course the realization amongst almost everybody there that the monopoly at least during the Labour Party's time was impregnable meant there was always an absolute grand slam answer to any suggestion that life could be handled in a better way, which was 'Why do we need to?'

Asked the question directly, most of the people at the front line in Area offices in the 1970s would have replied without reservation that their object in life was to help their customers. Many of them would go to great pains to do just that. There was no one to touch some PO Sales Division Clerical Officers of the old school in helping deserving cases find their way round the rules. But as often as not they did it as fellow members of the world outside helping customers to beat a system of mind-boggling impersonality. The concept of active selling and customer relations was simply not in the rule book.

The idea that the public were customers and that top management actually *wanted* the staff to act in a human way had been articulated as long ago as Ernest Marples's *Friendly Telephone* initiative in the 1950s. But however hard later generations of top management tried, it never seemed really to get through. The system ruled and no one seemed able to break it. Staff worked day-in-day-out in an environment where rules were rules, where hierarchies were hierarchies, where union considerations were high on the agenda and where there was nowhere else for the public to go. No one could blame the staff in the offices as individuals if the public found the results discouraging, with a sense of take-it or leave-it, and with enquiries passed from pillar to post. The system was all. As Bryan Stanley observed in Chapter 7, the people best placed to escape from it and to act like human beings were often the engineers who went out to people's homes and offices. In consequence many of them actually had a better reputation with the public than their office colleagues.

By 1978, however, management, staff and unions were all beginning to be aware with varying degrees of uneasiness that the monopoly might not be going to last much longer. Benton set out to build on this awareness and to jolt the monolith into a new world.

The original Carterphone decision which had opened the way for customer apparatus competition in the USA dated back to 1967. Since then customer apparatus liberalization had gained considerable momentum in the USA. The Bell system was under heavy criticism for sluggish progress with new customer apparatus. Technical developments were having an important effect. Traditionally, the telephone instrument itself, the subscriber relay set in the exchange and the interconnecting pair of copper wires had formed a single integral unit of circuitry which could not be subdivided. The situation was rapidly changing now, however. New high-impedance calling telephones were being developed which were electrically distinct from the network and could be plugged and unplugged at will. The technical scene was being set for revolution.

For many years the most telling and hurtful criticism one could make of PO telecommunications had been that it was behind the Bell system. Whatever the recent perception of its failings, AT&T led the world in most people's estimation. Fennessy and Benton and their immediate colleagues had good reason to know how they were really judged. Their fellow members of the London establishment would go to the USA and bring back glowing stories of the quality of service and of the range of innovation. The resulting motivation ran from Board level right down into the organization. Developments in the USA provided at once the yardstick and the model for emulation. Technology with exceptional potential was coming out of the PO research laboratories. Monarch, which was to become one of the very first digital PABXs in the world, and Prestel, which was to be the trail-blazer of screen-based public information services, were both on the test bench. There was a chance not just to draw level with the USA but actually to get ahead. That would be a touchstone of real success.

It was an exciting period. As 1978 wore on, the electricity of possible competition began really to charge the atmosphere of Gresham Street.

Frank Lawson, Chris Rowlands and I set out for the USA to take the measure of what was happening. We reported that customer apparatus competition was coming with a rush. But there was much more to it than that. After many years of contention between the giants of telecommunications and mainframe computing – AT&T and IBM – the battle in the disputed area between the two disciplines was suddenly hotting up. At the same time the developments which would lead to the emergence of the personal computer as we know it today were gathering pace; and people were starting to sketch out a completely new family of terminals which would combine computing and telecommunications functions.

Archie McGill had been recruited by AT&T from IBM to be the grain of sand in the oyster of their response to all this. After a session with him it was obvious to me that a completely new marketplace was developing. It was impossible to say yet where it would lead but the potential was immense. This new world was going to be fiercely competitive; and like it or not it was going to shake the ordered world of telecommunications to its roots.

Carrier competition proper was also beginning to gain momentum. Past tariffing in the USA had created a situation in which AT&T Long Lines, the sitting tenant long-haul operator, had artificially high tariffs and a huge $12bn pool of profit. A number of entrepreneurs were trying to make money by leasing AT&T long-distance circuits, attaching multiplexers and reselling the resulting increased circuit capacity. The threat this posed to AT&T Long Lines revenue was very serious; and the company was doing all it could to make life difficult for the resellers. As a result a new kind of entrepreneur had emerged, led by the late Bill McGowan of MCI. MCI had evolved from very limited beginnings. It started in the late 1960s as a small company which had successfully challenged AT&T for the right to run its own chain of radio towers along the Chicago to Seattle route to allow truckers to call head office on mobile phones. By the end of the 1970s the new long-haul competitors like McGowan were creating and running their own facilities. Before long the US cable TV industry, whose facilities at local level had much in common with telecommunications distribution plant, would also begin to speculate about the possibilities of getting into local telecommunications. The idea of 'facilities-based' competition had been born.

It was obvious that in one form or another these various developments were going to jump the Atlantic before long. The prospect began really to exercise management, staff and unions, all in their different ways.

With a Labour government in power the unions were torn between apprehension about what it all meant and the temptations of using political clout to beat it off. The staff felt a similar apprehension but also growing fascination. Nothing like this had ever happened before. What would the newcomers look like? Who would gain the upper hand? What was it going to do to jobs and prospects?

Senior management and the marketing function had good reason actively to welcome competition. Running a monopoly is a peculiarly difficult task, with no parallel in ordinary business. Since there is no competitive spur, the senior management of telecommunications had not only to be self-motivating but also to inspire all the rest of the organization. The marketing people faced their own deeply rooted psychological obstacles. For thirty years or more since the war the sales organization of the GPO and the PO had lived in a world where a very large part of its work involved explaining to people why they could *not* have things. Rooting out such a dispiriting mindset was a difficult enough task in itself. The work of marketing was still slightly surreal, with no actual opposition to beat. But with every day that passed now it was becoming more and more obvious that this epoch was coming to an end. With actual competitors out there the task would become much more concrete, albeit more directly testing.

But the immediate challenge which management and marketing faced was if anything even more difficult than stimulating a monopoly. There was every reason to think competition was still some way off. But the professional consciences of the managers, not to mention the unions and the staff themselves, were crying out for a vigorous reaction *now*. Morale depended to a considerable extent on what management did. But no one had any idea what form the actual competition would take or who the competitors would be. How did one work out what to do?

So far as customer apparatus was concerned, the business had a good pragmatic reason to welcome competition. With the precedent of the USA to draw on, the customer apparatus suppliers in Britain had fought a dogged battle right through the 1970s for the ending of the 'monopoly' in their sector.[1] The PO position had always been that the integrity of the network must be preserved for engineering reasons. Existing telephones needed a substantial current to flow to ring the bell when the receiver was on the hook. This current had to be regulated within close limits, and to do this over a wide variety of types of telephone and lengths of line required the whole circuit including the telephone to be under a single technical control. Customers generally could use only telephones rented from the PO's standard range; and the categories of device supplied by people other than the PO which could be attached to public service lines were strictly limited to things like answering machines which were not in the actual chain of communication.

But by the late 1970s the writing had become increasingly visible on the wall that things were going to change. The development of high-impedance calling telephones and the linked development of plugs and sockets instead of fixed connections were rapidly eroding the theory of network integrity. The PO had fought a particularly dour dogfight with opponents led by IBM over the question of attachment of modems to its network. The policy had led to a quite anomalous situation in which British customers of IBM, which offered a range of modems integral to its mainframe computers, had to rent shelf after shelf of free-standing modems from the PO instead.

The pass had been held so far, but at the expense of a good deal of management time and lost goodwill. Things were made worse by the requirement for the engineering side of the PO to act as a technical judge and jury over disputes to which the business was itself a party. Whenever an application was made for a particular terminal or PABX to be connected to the network it had to be vetted from the technical point of view. If a product was turned down it was asking too much of human nature to expect the applicant to refrain from suspicion that this had been done for policy rather than technical reasons. People both in the PO and in the industry were heartily sick of the stresses and strains all this involved. It was not difficult to work out that once competition began the responsibility for approvals would simply have to pass to some kind of new agency independent of both operator and applicant. This could not happen too soon for the people directly involved on both sides.

Coming back to what the business now needed to do, a good bit of it could be worked out from first principles. The first thing was to get an organization suited to the situation. Peter Benton:

> I was certainly intrigued to come into this huge organization, very set in its ways, with very powerful systems, to try and work out what I could actually do to change it. I was concerned about how we could get the management in that enormous monolith acting in a much more flexible and responsive way to the changes which were bound to come.
>
> There were two or three major aspects to that. Aspect one was to alter the organization at the centre to a business unit or task force organization. I would like to have gone the whole way to profit-accountable business units but we did not have the basic accounting systems to do that, so it had to be done in two steps. The first step was to get task forces each of which was given objectives which were sometimes qualitative but often quantitative and at the same time to get the accounting system able to differentiate between the costs and revenues of particular aspects of operations.

Benton put in hand a complete reorganization of THQ under my direction. With McKinsey help the headquarters was re-structured into two main units, Network Executive under Ron Back responsible for all network matters, and Marketing Executive under Gordon Pocock responsible for the existing range of terminals and services and the development of new ones. A separate Procurement Executive under Sam Swallow was kept in being to handle the main procurement process, but for the first time Marketing Executive had its own development and procurement unit under command. AT&T was restructuring its headquarters on a generally similar basis but the PO was ahead even of Bell in this arrangement for products and services.

Whyte and I were appointed as Deputy Managing Directors with responsibility respectively for technology and for operations. Whyte had responsibility for oversight of technical matters throughout the business and line responsibility for research and development. The Regions reported to the Managing Director, but I exercised the Managing Director's functions in relation to budgetary and performance matters. I retained co-ordinating responsibility for the investment programme and for the business part in the negotiations on investment with DTI and Treasury. Personnel and finance remained as separate staff functions.

The business had been producing ten-year business plans since the early 1970s but little serious attention had been paid to them. Up to now it had been the five-year Medium Term Plan, concerned essentially with finance and investment and geared into the Treasury public expenditure system, which had carried all the real weight. Benton set out to turn the business planning process and the ten-year plan itself into active instruments of reform and innovation. In his words:

> One could see that it was highly necessary that that devolvement of decision–making should not degenerate into a fragmented approach to what were coherent problems. And so we put together a business plan for the next ten years. Contrary to previous practice, which had always treated it as a rather confidential document, we printed forty thousand copies in colour and every manager had his own copy.

In the marketing area there were real foundations to build on. Over the years since 1969 Ron Martin, Freddie Phillips, Frank Lawson and their colleagues in Telecommunications Marketing Department had built up a real momentum, despite the monopoly environment. Aside from the obvious job of promoting sales of terminals and specialized services, two elements of the situation of the business called particularly for marketing attention.

Income from calls dominated financial performance. We have seen the attention which the planning side of the business had learnt to give to tailoring plant capacity to requirements, but the capacity they provided had to cater for the busiest hours of the day. The contribution which marketing could make was to stimulate traffic in the off-peak periods and so improve the network load factor. At the same time, the distribution cables which connected customers to exchanges were conspicuously under-used and unprofitable. On overall average each customer used his or her telephone line for only nine minutes in each twenty-four hours. There was an obvious contribution for marketing to make in encouraging the use of lines, especially by residential customers.

The business had been working on these problems for many years. Efforts to stimulate off-peak traffic and improve the network load factor went back to before the war. Concern about the economics of the distribution plant went back to the 1955 White Paper. The obvious way to improve the load factor was to offer cheap rates for off-peak and especially evening calls. This had been a feature of tariffing for longer than anyone could now remember. Marketing effort after marketing effort had been made to put the idea across to maximum effect. In the late 1970s TMKD, working with its advertising advisers, starting from the idea that birds said 'Cheep, Cheep' had realized that this could be presented as 'Cheap, Cheap'. The line of thought was worked up into a little bird called Buzby who became something of a cult object to the British public – liked and disliked almost in equal measure. But there is no such thing as bad publicity. Buzby did his job of calling attention to use of the telephone as well as if not better than any marketing approach before or since.

The new ME could build on all this with real expectations of success; and it set out to do so. The obvious thing was to forestall competition by innovation. A veritable ferment of activity now developed. Gordon Pocock and his colleagues would appear at meeting after meeting of the Managing Director's Committee with a new project each time. The business had strict appraisal rules which projects did not always pass first time; but the flow of new projects was sustained month after month, and morale boomed.

The results were formidable. The years of ferment under Peter Benton's leadership produced Monarch, the first digital PABX in Europe and one of the very first in the world; Herald, the first modern call-connect system in Europe; two of the first telephones of the new high-impedance calling generation to go into volume production anywhere in the world (Viscount and Statesman); Prestel, which became the world leader of the new family of videotext services; a modern alarms-by-carrier system which was to become the basis of a flourishing separate business after privatization; one of the first new generation teleprinters in the world (Cheetah) and many other similar products. Pocock and Alex Reid, his business services Director, began also to lay the foundations of a PO venture into the completely new field of office automation, which was ahead of anyone else in Britain.

The BPO took a leading role in the creation of engineering standards for the new services in Europe, breaking ground in particular for the modern Integrated Services Digital Network (ISDN) service.

The coin-box population came in for attention also. The original 1958 design of

STD coin-box had seemed a brilliant concept in its time. But it had never been wholly satisfactory. It was unreliable, notoriously difficult to keep in working order and prone to vandalism. The modern 'Blue' coin payphone and the cardphone which today dominate BT's population of coin-boxes were now introduced.

In France these were the days of the Nora/Minc report and the birth of Minitel. The British and French state monopolies were competing to lead in product innovation and they were up with the best in the world. Emulating a similar initiative by the French PTT, I launched a pioneer internal electronic mail system serving headquarters and Regions which was designed to gain experience with this brand-new medium.

The products of these years were to be the backbone of the marketing armoury of BT plc in the years after privatization. The office automation venture was to develop into the BT plc presence in this area. There were many who thought the BPO had met its own touchstone of success by drawing ahead of the Bell system.

The other obvious area of attention was pricing. (The global pricing record over the whole period 1966 to 1995 is examined in Appendix 2.) William Barlow had a very definite view:

> I was very keen indeed in not putting in a price increase on the telecommunications side, because I felt modern technology would bring the prices down. I also felt there were far too many people. We were not efficient. We ought to get our efficency right and then we would make a profit and get the pricing right.
>
> The effect of keeping pricing down with inflation was of course tantamount to a price reduction and, as a result of that, traffic grew quite steadily. The Treasury in the annual arguments about things were always taking the other line – 'Put the prices up, restrict the demand, you won't need as much money' – and taking a totally unbusinesslike view of what I considered to be a business. I found the Treasury were stultifying people to deal with, and whilst I was ostensibly dealing with DTI there was always a Treasury man about two ranks lower pulling the strings and controlling what the DTI people said. Within twelve months of my leaving, the Conservative government pressured Telecom on pricing and they put up the prices 19 per cent. I thought it was an absolute disgrace.

Figure A2.2 shows that he was successful in holding prices down and that there was an abrupt increase after he left. But Gresham Street saw things differently from the Chairman. Decades of experience supported in recent years by sophisticated regression analysis had shown that demand for calls and lines was remarkably *in*elastic to price. The only increases which had really deterred demand had been those in the lump sum connection charge and then only for a short time. It was true that for some time there had been an understanding with the Treasury that the connection charge would be pitched to cover the irrecoverable cost of providing service. The idea was that this would ensure that growth in telephone lines took no more and no less than its fair share of the investment resources available in the general economy. But otherwise demand always went its own inexorable way; and the PO had long ago convinced the Treasury that this had to drive the telecommunications budget and the investment programme. It was a striking example of how Gresham Street failed to get its point of view across over the two-mile gap to Howland Street.

The way prices were fixed might not have been as sophisticated as the modern price cap sets out to be (see Chapter 17); but it none the less provided a considerable practical incentive to hold costs down. In practice the procedures closely resembled an informal version of the price cap, except that they had practical effect only on a year-by-year basis. Each year's budgetary process would generate forecasts of forward costs, corresponding returns on assets and price increases needed to achieve them allowing for forecast general inflation. The Chairman and Ministers, who after all were the Board's employers, would almost invariably require the increases to be held down. The business would then have no option but to re-scrutinize its costs in order to maintain the target return, which was taken seriously by all concerned. In this period control of telecommunications costs succeeded much more than it has had credit for (Appendix 3).

It was obvious that competition was going to require a fundamental rethink of pricing policy. In the past the balance of prices within the total envelope of revenue requiring to be raised by costs plus the target return had been dictated largely by political considerations. Business users were always much less vocal about the effect of increases than residential users. The effect which had built up over the years was inevitable and predictable. In 1980–1 the return on capital earned by rental charges was actually negative. Inland calls on the other hand earned a 10.5 per cent return and international calls the very high return of 19.7 per cent. Within the inland envelope trunk calls were much more profitable than local calls. In short the services used predominantly by business earned a very much higher return than those used predominantly by residential customers.

The parallel with the situation in the USA was obvious. It was not difficult to predict what would happen once carrier competition began to operate. It would come first in long-distance and international calls, where the real profits were concentrated. Theory said that the prices concerned would drop. If the business was to maintain its profitability, rentals and short-distance call prices would have to rise. The balance would be changed by *force majeure*. But big increases in prices for residential service were never going to be countenanced politically. Some hard thinking was going to be needed if profitability was to be maintained. But it did not need sophisticated analysis to see that the more costs could be held down the better.

The most pressing pricing problems of all arose in customer apparatus. Existing prices in this area had been set partly by costs plus profit set by return on capital, and for new products partly by experiment and experience with what the market would bear. ME set about a fundamental rethink of its approach.

Private (leased) circuits presented pressing problems of their own; and not just on pricing. The root of much of the difficulty was that the network had to be laid out to optimize the economics of the public switched telephone service. Private circuits almost by definition required routings which cut across this layout in awkward ways. Especially at local level, complicated and inefficient physical routings were often needed where the actual physical path through cables and exchange frames might be several times as long as the crowflight distance between the customer establishments. Several cross-connection points at intermediate exchanges or other points in the network were often required. It was usually comparatively easy to deal with the long-distance element of private circuits, but real problems arose frequently with the local ends. The priorities of exchange and repeater station staff and management had to be focused on the public service. The result was that private circuit costs were high and service was erratic. Lead times for provision and repair were sometimes very poor indeed.

Private circuit service was particularly poor in London, where the routeing problems were at their most difficult. The problem was made worse because of the militants in POEU branches in central London, who seized on the chance to aggravate the problems of management. A serious dispute was fomented around the handling of the requirements of Reuters, which was only resolved with great difficulty between THQ and POEU headquarters, who maintained a responsible approach throughout. A large part of the problem in London was organizational. The way the Region was organized, in Areas geared to the requirements of the public service, did not fit the requirements for private circuits, where the natural unit was the Region as a whole. Ken Ford, the Regional Director, set out to change the organization to make sense of the situation. A second major and heated dispute arose with the local union branches, which was finally more or less satisfactorily resolved by brinkmanship bargaining on a Saturday night before a POEU conference. Such confrontations were to turn out to be quite spectacularly misguided from the unions' own point of view, because of the reinforcement they gave to the campaign to introduce carrier competition.

Private circuit tariffs had their own political overtones which were peculiarly difficult to handle. Fleet Street and the media generally were among the largest users of private circuits. Any proposal to increase charges called forth a particularly influential storm of protest. The result was that private circuits were seriously underpriced.

As the prospect of competition in the private circuit area approached, ME and NE therefore faced a quite extraordinary situation. The existing service was both underpriced and unsatisfactory and efforts to rectify things seemed doomed to failure. Peter Benton took a personal hand in trying to rectify the difficulties. Fred Dell was appointed to specialize in private circuit matters at THQ, reporting direct to the Managing Director. The concept of a digital overlay on the London network was developed, designed to speed the process of digitalization generally and specifically to improve service to the City. But the basic problems of private circuit service were deeply rooted, in the orientation of field priorities to public switched service and in the plant layout. They were to persist through privatization and beyond. The long-run answer lay in the introduction of advanced technology tailored specifically to the needs of private network customers. Such technology did not exist in the 1970s.

Private circuits were an area where the business was on the defensive. There was one private service area where it could attack. Ever since the war the PO had been excluded from providing PABXs over a hundred extensions. Now in the late 1970s when it looked as though the rules of the game were going to be changed, it was fair game for the business to set out to compete in this lucrative market. The main existing competitors it would have to take on were its own three main suppliers and, following a decision taken by Stonehouse as a Labour PMG in his office in the House of Commons one snowy morning during the passage of the 1969 Act, L. M. Ericsson of Sweden. But it was not going to be long before other world league companies would be trying to enter the market. ME began to lay plans accordingly.

ME also set out to create something the PO had never had before. A completely new sales force was organized to handle the accounts of all larger customers. A system was instituted for them of rewards according to performance; and of company cars and expense accounts. A real revolution had begun. The unions were really worried. These new people would stand on their own feet far too much for the unions' liking.

A linked issue if anything exercised the unions even more. The first steps were beginning seriously to be taken towards a completely new range of products and services based on the techniques of computing rather than those of voice telephony. The question arose of how the work was going to be organized in the field. There was a choice between a new 'thick slice' of specialist staff to do the work, controlled from ME through a separate chain of command; or having the work done by the existing customer engineering field force, supported only by a 'thin slice' of specialists from ME to give advice and help. Gordon Pocock and ME wanted the former. The field management and the unions were determined to have the latter. In a way which was all too familiar Pocock and ME found themselves involved in a disproportionate amount of argument about these matters, at the expense of their real priorities. The leopard was anything but thirsting to change its spots. The dispute continued unresolved after BTE was created and *mutatis mutandis* after privatization. It was finally resolved in the BT plc Project Sovereign reorganization at the end of the 1980s.

For practical purposes we have reached the end of the story of telecommunications in its fifteen years in the nationalized sector. In this time a veritable legion of developments and influences had been wished on the business from outside. Four of them stood out in particular, all on the downside. Combined together, the Labour government's failure to stand up to the UPW in 1965 and to impose Benn's original formula for complete separation of the businesses, the Board decision to exclude second-line management from the Senior Salary Structure, the Corporation's failure to restructure the Civil Service hierarchies below that level and the constant disposition of Labour governments to give in to union pressure had had disproportionately negative effects. But what were the successes and failures of the business itself?

In 1969 the basics of telephone service had been unacceptable. There had been a large and growing waiting list for service. The international service had been inadequate and deteriorating. The performance of the inland network had also been deteriorating. The business had been seriously undermanaged. There had been no meaningful management accounting system and no real controls on current account spending. There had been no controls on the efficiency of use of capital or the execution of projects. In short the business inherited by the Corporation in 1969 had been unbusinesslike.

By 1983 Fennessy's priorities had been attained. Eleven and a half million lines had been added to the network, representing well over half the system which was to be inherited by BT plc at privatization. The international service had been revolutionized. The programme for network modernization had been running for ten years and the back had been broken of the problem of network quality of service. The main transmission network digitalization programme was up with any in the world and ahead of that in the United States. Revenue at constant prices had doubled. The number of inland calls had more than doubled. The number of international calls made by inland customers had risen by a factor of ten.

The quality of the service generally had improved dramatically. In 1982 I asked for a Mori poll to allow future effort to be concentrated where customers wanted it. It gave the service generally a fair bill of health. The only serious complaint was a justified one about continuing noise on calls, which was being tackled by the network modernization programme.

Benton had brought about his own revolution. By 1983 the range of terminals and services on offer to customers bore no resemblance to that of 1976. THQ had been reorganized, on a pattern remarkably similar to that to which the plc would return in the late 1980s.

Whatever the continuing failings of the basic accounting system by the late 1970s the business had introduced a proper system of management accounting control. Current account costs were being disciplined (see Appendix 3). The extravagant capital spending of the early 1970s had been brought under control; proper controls had been introduced on capital projects and on the efficiency of use of capital plant. Field labour productivity had been notably raised. To restate from earlier, by 1982 a system which had doubled in size since 1970 was being run, enlarged and renewed, with 3,000 fewer field staff.

As we shall see in Part III, the procurement record was a mixture of weakness and of strength. The PO had been less than fully resolute in dealing with its traditional British suppliers. But in establishing L. M. Ericsson from scratch as a substantive competing supplier on British soil it had a success to show for itself unique among the major operators of Europe, which was to pay dividends in later years.

With all this behind us, we Gresham Street people might feel a justified sense of achievement. We had shown ourselves world class at engineering, good at logistics and up at least to first-degree level in economic management. In product and service innovation we were up with any telecommunications operator on the globe. Yet we had only to read the newspapers to know that, viewed from outside, the business was still seen by many people as a lot less than impressive. Public expectations were rising all the time. People were looking for an altogether new improvement in service and in the way it was offered, not just by us but generally. They took what had been achieved by the PO since 1969 as no more than their due and demanded more.

London remained the Achilles' heel. Its problems and its industrial relations were the worst in the country. At the same time national opinion-formers were concentrated in the City, Fleet Street and Westminster. The poor service in the capital played to the worst possible grandstand.

The real problem was that the great monolith had hit the glass ceiling of its own inheritance. It was next to impossible to push it any further up the road of improvement as it stood, however hard people might try. If things were to go on getting better a bigger jolt was needed even than the traumas of 1975.

On this note I end the story of PO telecommunications itself. Part III tells the story of the supplying industry, the network technology and System X. Part IV picks up the story of BT, with Jefferson's arrival, competition and privatization.

Note

1. The powers of the PO in this respect derived from its power under Section 28 of the 1969 Act (charges schemes) to determine what could be attached to its network. Contrary to general belief this had nothing to do with the carrier monopoly under Section 12.

Part III
The Suppliers and the Technology

10 The Suppliers

In the early years of the twentieth century the core of the British telecommunications manufacturing industry originally comprised five firms – the Automatic Telephone Manufacturing Company Ltd (ATM, later AT&E); subsidiaries of the British General Electric Company (GEC) and of Siemens of Germany (later absorbed by the British Associated Electrical Industries – AEI); the British Ericsson Company, which lost its links with the Swedish group of the same name; and Standard Telephones and Cables Ltd (STC). STC was a majority holding subsidiary of International Telephone and Telegraph, the US international conglomerate formed out of the original overseas operations of AT&T following the anti-trust divestiture of 1927 (STC).

There was at that time no exchange technology native to Britain. ATM had links with Automatic Electric of Chicago, well established as the home of Strowger (step-by-step), the pioneer automatic switching technology.

Many other companies were involved. The Marconi Company had a notable tradition of working with the GPO in the radio area which went back to the origins of radio in the late nineteenth century. There were a number of suppliers of more specialized products. Hall Telephones, which made telephone coin-boxes, was typical. Telecommunications plant and equipment was of course only a part of the procurement picture. In all the GPO purchased from several thousand firms across the whole of British industry.

Even allowing for the different perspective of the 1920s, five firms making the principal categories of telecommunications equipment and exchange equipment in particular was a large number for a market in those days of at most perhaps two hundred thousand lines a year. The fragmented ownership of the exchange switching industry in its early years left its mark on its whole subsequent history. By the 1970s a total of seventeen production sites were involved in the production of some three million lines a year. By contrast the principal independent manufacturer in the USA, GTE, concentrated a throughput of one million lines under one factory roof.

It may be difficult to say which was cause and which was effect, but the fragmentation of the industry and its diverse ownership, coupled with the undoubted technical strength of the GPO, drew the GPO Engineering Department into a position of technical co-ordination and leadership right from the start. This was in contrast to the situation in many countries abroad. In Europe it was the major manufacturers like Bell Antwerp, an ITT subsidiary, or Siemens in Germany, not the operators, who made the running so far as technology was concerned. It was also in marked contrast for other reasons to the situation in the United States. Western

Electric, the world's largest telecommunications manufacturer, was an integral part of AT&T, the dominant operator; and GTE, the second largest operator, also had a manufacturing arm.

The central role of the GPO and later the PO was to persist and to influence the course of events right into the 1980s. It led inevitably to an emphasis on development of designs to GPO specification, with development activity funded in one way or another by the operator, rather than development of proprietary designs by the manufacturers at their own expense, as was the norm in other European countries.

The first automatic exchange in Britain was tested at Epsom in 1912. Serious introduction of automatic exchanges began in the 1920s. The GPO decided to purchase its exchanges through a system of bulk supplies agreements with the companies. GPO requirements were notified in bulk to an industry Bulk Contracts Committee, which apportioned the orders among the five firms. Prices were determined by investigation of industry's costs and hammering out of associated profit levels for successive five-year periods in arrears. The results were then used to determine the prices actually to be paid for matching periods of five years ahead, with negotiated allowances for efficiency gains and inflation.

The system amounted to a cartel. It undoubtedly represented something of a breakthrough in its day. The engineering community was beginning to learn the hard way the difficulties of using different proprietary designs in the same network and the corresponding attractions of standardization. As the PO was to find when it finally changed things in 1969, genuinely competitive procurement of electro-mechanical telephone exchanges was a very difficult thing to arrange. The bulk supplies system had the virtue of short-circuiting these problems and providing a framework for product standardization, but still providing a basis of pricing which looked defensible on paper. The system also provided security of supply for the GPO and security of ordering for the companies and therefore a basis on which they could confidently create capacity.

But it also had within it the seeds of weakness. Even in theory the system could be expected to work properly only for developed products. It provided no satisfactory mechanism for dealing with the development and procurement of new products. In an industry where advance in technology was to become so important this was a very serious failing. The costs subject to investigation included research work; but there was no rational basis for determining how much research work the companies should undertake, either at PO expense or at their own. The cost investigation processes which were the basis of pricing were to become more and more cumbersome, contentious and long-drawn-out in practice as the years went by. It became the norm for the industry to be well into a five-year forward period before the price levels to apply to it were determined. By the time the agreements ended in 1969 the pricing backlog was verging on the scandalous.

The most important effect was, however, to prove to be the way the bulk supplies system protected the firms and allowed the fragmentation to persist. When the system was first set up in the 1920s the firms dismantled their sales departments. Active selling was no longer needed, at any rate in the home market. In 1996 there is only one major UK-based telecommunications supplier left – GPT – and even that company is forty per cent owned by Siemens of Germany. L. M. Ericsson of Sweden, which has never had a big home market, and the Japanese suppliers, who are driven by the national imperative to export or die, have thriven where the UK industry has not. In the 1970s the Swedish and Japanese companies almost entirely took over the original British export markets in the Empire; and L. M. Ericsson became established as a substantive supplier in Britain. It is difficult to believe that the GPO bulk supplies system did not make a major contribution to the weakness of the native firms. Similar bulk supplies arrangements were made for transmission equipment, subscribers' (customer) apparatus and cable.

Turning to technology, again it is necessary to go back in time. In the late 1920s the GPO was considering the automation of the London telephone service. The original view of the Engineer-in-Chief, Colonel Purves, was that the best system would be the panel system, to be made by Western Electric, primarily in the Antwerp factories which it then owned. Sir Alexander Roger, Chairman of ATM, prevailed on Sir Evelyn Murray, the then (Permanent) Secretary to the Post Office, to adopt instead Strowger or step-by-step switching, which ATM would make in the UK, for employment reasons.

The GPO and the industry concentrated for four decades on Strowger and on trying to bring the British version as close to perfection as the technology and its limitations would allow. During the prewar period the GPO and the suppliers working together progressed towards a standard product which could be made efficiently in volume and which would minimize GPO training and stores stocking costs. From the engineering point of view the bulk supplies agreements provided a satisfactory framework for such work. The Post Office 2000-type Strowger design was eventually ratified as the standard.

In the meantime other technologies were making strides in other countries, mainly using common-control techniques.[1] The most important was crossbar, which was in widespread use in the USA and elsewhere by the mid-1950s.

The choice of switching technology in Britain was reviewed just after the war. John Flint, Plessey Marketing executive responsible for the PO interface in the 1970s, says:

> In 1946 the powers that then were, Sir Thomas Eades of AT&E and the others, met with the DG of the time [Sir Alexander Little] and the PO and they said, 'What are we going to do?' The industry said in one voice, 'We are going to make Strowger because our overseas customers in the colonies and the Empire will take Strowger.'
>
> That was the fundamental point, especially as AT&E had a crossbar licence and knew about crossbar. But then the PO would have had to suffer not just crossbar but common control signalling. Would it have done that? I think I am also saying that the bulk supplies agreements should have been stopped as well as part of that. But the PO was being bossy – 'we know best'.

The great achievement of the 1950s was the adaptation of Strowger to the requirements of Subscriber Trunk Dialling. By pushing the technology to its limit GPO and industry development engineers were able to make it perform the complete range of automatic routeing and charging functions required to enable customers to dial their own trunk and international calls. In doing so they used electronics for the first time in serious service. The STD control equipment for the five largest cities including London used magnetic drum register translators which embodied many basic concepts of computer control.

At that time Gordon Radley was GPO Engineer-in-Chief. The GPO Research Station at Dollis Hill had played a significant part in the wartime development of code-breaking machines which was to evolve into computing as we know it today. The more imaginative engineers at Dollis Hill were convinced that the embryo computing techniques and the associated technology could be applied to switch telephone calls electronically. Radley took responsibility for the decision to bypass the crossbar generation and to concentrate research effort on the development of a British electronic switching system.

This decision was to have profound effects. It is important to consider the environment in which it was taken. In addition to its association with the early stages of computing, the Dollis Hill Research Station already had a distinguished record in land and submarine transmission development. It was the natural partner of AT&T's Bell Laboratories in the design and development of the first transatlantic telephone cable, which entered service in 1957. Neither Strowger nor crossbar was a native technology and it was obvious that exports were going to play a major part in the future of the British economy. The GPO research engineers would have felt they were letting the side down if they had not set out to develop a new and distinctively British product in their own field.

All product-oriented research makes implicit assumptions about production and marketing. During the war British industry was felt to have demonstrated what it could do by way of both development and production, once the chips were really down and it had had time to organize itself. It had developed and produced radar, the jet engine, the Comet, the Land Rover, nuclear power and many other major advances. The British switching scientists of the 1950s made the assumption that if they could develop a viable product it would be effectively produced and sold by the British firms.

The GPO and the firms set out to create arrangements for development of electronic exchanges within the bulk supplies framework. But progress was slow until Radley became Director General in late 1955. It was one of his first priorities to breathe effective life into the negotiations. The Joint Electronic Research Agreement (JERA) was negotiated within the framework of the bulk supplies agreements and signed in August 1956, simultaneously with the first engineering testing of the first transatlantic telephone cable. British scientific and engineering prestige was high and optimism was in the air. JERA was to provide the framework for electronic switching development until the bulk supplies agreements themselves came to an end in 1969.

The development programme became centred on the construction of a trial public exchange, which it was decided to install alongside the existing Strowger exchange called Highgate Wood in north London. The unit was constructed and installed, but it proved impossible to make it function in an acceptable way. It was formally opened by the Postmaster General in 1960 and inaugural calls were passed over it, but only in a demonstration mode. It was very cautiously cut over into public service at midnight one night soon after. But it lasted only eight minutes in service before it had to be withdrawn. Despite this sad fate the research team learnt a very great deal from Highgate Wood. The first practical understanding had been gained of the problems of electronic switching and in that sense the project had succeeded.

In 1960 the GPO reviewed the possibility of adopting crossbar as the standard system rather than waiting for electronic switching. There was a strong school of thought on the practical side of the Engineer-in-Chief's Office which favoured crossbar. But the research axis was dominant, and with the experience they had gained they were confident that the electronic development programme would lead to a viable system. The PMG accepted officials' recommendation that crossbar should not be adopted and that the Post Office should stay with Strowger until electronic systems were available.

Proposals were made for a second 'Mark II' phase of electronic development, designed to test the relative merits of two time division technologies: high-speed Pulse Amplitude Modulation Time Division Multiplex (PAM TDM); low speed PAM TDM; and Space Division Multiplex.[2] The high-speed TDM (100 channel) project was an evolution of Highgate Wood. Low Speed TDM (30 channel) was a more advanced conception of the leader of the GPO team at the Dollis Hill research station, T. D. H. Flowers. Sites were selected for trial exchanges at Goring (high-speed TDM), Pembury (low-speed) and Leighton Buzzard (space division). Development work began; and the administrators in GPO headquarters became seized of the potential of computer control to provide new facilities. Study began at this time of the operating requirements for call-waiting, call diversion and other facilities which are nowadays part of the BT family of select services provided from System X exchanges.

Structural changes now began to affect the industry. Flint again:

About 1960 A. G. Clark (then head of the Plessey Company of Ilford) realized that Plessey, with its very small link into telecommunications through the telephone [instrument], was not going to make the grade in the next generation. The given wisdom at the time was that Plessey were strongly in the electronic components field and that A. G. Clark wanted to take them to the next stage and pick up the manufacture of those components into telecommunications items. This led to him chasing two of the then five telecommunications companies, AT&E in Liverpool and Ericssons in Beeston (Nottingham), which of course had nothing to do with Ericssons in Sweden. It was always said by Ericssons Nottingham that they joined the [Plessey] club voluntarily but AT&E really had no alternative but to succumb to the bid. Consequently by 1961 we were all part of the Plessey group.

Strowger was on the allocation basis. We (Plessey) had acquired two of the five companies so we got two-fifths of the results. Crossbar was a development of AT&E, which probably resulted in AT&E being taken over because they put so much money into it. They had had a licence from LME at the end of the war which ran out. They had had either to renew it or to develop a different sort of switch (the AT&E 5005 crossbar system). [But] the PO people said, 'No, we don't want it. We are going to go straight from Strowger to electronic.'

The electronic development engineers were beginning to get down the learning curve and into the problems of designing practical technology. David Leakey, Technical Director of GEC Telecommunications in the 1970s and BT Chief Scientist in the 1980s, says:

I became heavily involved with Flowers arguing the relative merits of 30 channel and 100 channel PAM systems. Although I was involved primarily with the 100 channel system, I also attempted to assist Flowers in promoting his 30 channel system by suggesting that a more credible appraisal of the probable complexity be undertaken. However, it soon became apparent that probably neither approach could meet the required transmission performance targets, particularly when deployed in a large exchange environment.

PAM was therefore unlikely to represent a viable way forward.

Mel Price, eventually Deputy Chairman of GEC Telecommunications and recently sadly deceased, described the general state of the industry at that time:

> I took over the public exchange division in GEC in 1964. One is not talking about 100 per cent and zero, but at that time the people that had the system ability were AT&E – 5005 was quite a clever crossbar system with the self-steering principle which they thought out – and AEI. STC in the UK context did not have system ability. GEC and Ericssons were good at the technology and making the components; they were the more efficient producers of other people's systems.
>
> You had five companies in varying degrees of disorder. We used to have these so-called Managing Directors' meetings [with the GPO] with five companies round the table, some old, some new. You also had five companies sitting round the [negotiating] table because for some reason that I never understood Ericssons were a party in their own right in the bulk supplies agreement and carried on that way and AT&E were [also] a party in their own right and carried on that way. After GEC took over AEI, when Dick Bayliss and I went to TEMA (the trade association), he was AEI and I was GEC. In 1969 we decided this charade had got to stop because it was just getting out of hand.
>
> All this was never going to produce the solution.

By now the British suppliers had a considerable export market in the old Empire, developed largely because many British possessions procured telecommunications through the Crown agents, who simply followed GPO practice and bought British – and therefore Strowger. Plessey were seriously concerned about their ability to hold these markets in face of competition, especially from L. M. Ericsson in Sweden, with their excellent crossbar system.

At home the rise in demand for lines was seriously embarrassing the GPO. The trunk (long-distance) service was also in trouble, with serious delays and congestion. The following extract is taken from the evidence given to the Select Committee on Nationalized Industries on 23 June 1966:

Mr Mikardo

In Command Paper 2211 of November 1963, 'The Inland Telephone Service in an Expanding Economy', and I hope I am not touching on any tender nerves by quoting this paper, in paragraph 5 and again in paragraph 15 you said that your then five year plan had amongst its objectives 'to install sufficient plant by March 1966 at the latest, to avoid telephone installations being delayed by shortage of plant and so to abolish the waiting list'. I have the impression that this objective was not achieved. To what extent was the failure to achieve it due to capital stringency; and if it was not due to that, what was it due to?

Sir Ronald German (the GPO Director General of the time)

You are quite right, Sir, in saying that we did not achieve our aim. We did in fact much more than we thought we were going to do; that is to say at March 1966 more telephones were working in the system than we had planned at the time the White Paper was written. Our achievement therefore did not fall below our expectation, but what had happened was that our forecast of demand fell a long way short of the actuality. Therefore I cannot honestly say that the failure to achieve the ambition was because of a shortage of capital; it was really a direct result of under-estimating the steep increase in demand which we have had in the last couple of years. It is fair to say that had we forecast more accurately it is still doubtful whether we would have been able to get the equipment we required in the quantity we required it in time to have overtaken the waiting list. It is also fair to say that for 75% of our exchanges there is at the moment no waiting list. I do not wish to claim too much from that, but it is a fact.

Mr Mikardo

As I understand it, Sir Ronald, you are saying that if you had not underestimated and if you had guessed the figures right, it would have been inability to get the equipment rather than inability to get the money which would have been the main cause of this.

Sir Ronald German

That is fair enough.[3]

The demand for exchange equipment far exceeded the capacity of the industry's Strowger factories. Flint says:

German called in the industry and said, 'Gentlemen, we are going to need a LOT more switching equipment.' John Clark with his cohorts said, 'You can have your switching equipment but you have got to take crossbar.' The PO said, 'If we give you crossbar orders you have got to share your 5005 technology with GEC.' STC did not get that privilege. They lobbied around trying to get the ITT crossbar system in.

Minds in the GPO were concentrated on local exchanges. But some people in the industry saw things differently. Mel Price:

At that time the explosion in demand took place. The GPO were obsessed with getting the waiting list down by connecting more and more subscribers. This was getting us [in GEC] more and more nervous that the day of reckoning would come that the network would not take the trunk traffic. [The GPO] got hooked on going from Strowger to electronic, whereas the real number one priority was to understand how they were going to build a four-wire *trunk* switched network.[4] But, as I would see it in GEC, it then developed as an obsession to go to electronic. The local networks needed modernizing but the thing where you were getting these awful delays was in the long-distance network. All right, they introduced motor uniselectors and things like this. But what they needed was a four-wire switch.

Within the electronic research programme, both Goring and Pembury and their system concepts were now dropped as too expensive and impractical. Attention was concentrated on space division and on the trial space division large exchange at Leighton Buzzard. It was to prove very difficult indeed to make this exchange work satisfactorily.

Decisions began to be taken which were to have important influence for the future. David Leakey again:

A result of the Goring exercise was that it exposed the problem of designing a control system when the precise requirements specification was not finalised until well towards the end of the scheduled design period. This led to the use of a rudimentary form of programme control involving the use of a large diode matrix where the positioning of the diodes determined the detailed functioning of the control. Largely for economic reasons, the diode matrix programming was soon replaced by a threaded ferrite core approach, where the programme was achieved by the selective threading of the driver wires through the matrix of cores. This gave rise to the so-called Mark IA stored programme control machine, a serious attempt to use computer control in a critical real-time environment where down-time requirements were far more stringent than was achievable using conventional computers of that era. The Mark IA machine was not destined to control an electronic exchange. Instead it provided a very successful approach to the register-translator function in an electro-mechanical switching environment, ultimately superseding earlier electronic approaches using cold cathode tubes and magnetic drum devices.

At about the same time, we became concerned that the proposed reed relay switching systems would probably take longer to come into general service than originally anticipated, which left a time gap where some form of improved electro-mechanical switch compared with Strowger would be needed. There was a discussion with the PO as to whether they would accept L. M. Ericsson crossbar made under licence. A negative response led to an agreement with Plessey for GEC also to adopt 5005 crossbar. The result was a successful marriage of the now heavily updated Mark IC register translator to control crossbar notably for the large Sector Switching Centres in London.

In parallel with the upgrading of the Mark I machines and with the increasing availability of inexpensive integrated circuits, a more powerful Mark II machine was developed using a multi-processor configuration to achieve the required downtime requirements. This machine was intended to take over the entire control function of an exchange. It is interesting to note how the estimated memory requirements increased over time. The original Mark IIA machine had a 64k RAM memory which was sufficient for basic exchange control, but was insufficient when the rapidly increasing requirements for fault diagnosis, reconfiguration, supervision and special service provision were added. As a result, memory capacity was increased first to 256K, then 1M and so on.

With the prospect of electro-mechanical switching having a limited life and PAM electronic switching being unsatisfactory, attention turned to the use of pure digital switching in a PCM form with possibly reed relay concentrators on the periphery. Combined with the flexibility of modern computer control using derivatives of the Mark II machine, an exchange design which could successfully replace electro-mechanical approaches appeared on the horizon. This led increasingly to closer collaboration with GPO and with other equipment suppliers which formed the start of the System X era. Needless to say, the path forward was not without its difficulties, particularly since other designs, some incorporating reed relays, were also on offer both from within the UK and also from abroad.

All this time Roy Harris and his team in the GPO had been pacing the work in the industry. Harris and Leakey were at the high point of British creativity in the switching area. Looking forward for a moment to the 1990s and to the argument in

Part VI, it is important to remember that this high point, which was the substantive foundation for the digitalization of switching in the BT network in the late 1980s, was reached in the circumstances of a monopoly operator purchasing through cartel arrangements.

Things continued to happen affecting the structure of the industry and its pre-digital products. Mel Price on the view from the production end:

> We had come to the conclusion by '66 against the background of the [trunk] network situation that something else had to be done, because there was nothing on the agenda beyond the concept of a large local. The one thing we were clear on in our minds was that if we were going to get something done on the trunk side we had to have electronic control. We put in hand the Mark I [processor] – 'SPC' we called it but it was a classic electronic register translator with the programming done by wires looped through ferrite cores. That was the product that was used for the Sector Switching Centres [see Chapter 11]. From that we went to what became the Mark II and the Mark II BL [the System X processor – see Chapter 12]. We had seen a way that we could start controlling [exchanges] and it was a question, if we were going to do this for the trunk network, what [switch] were we going to control. George Tomlin [MD of GEC Telecommunications] went to see Charles Calveley [GPO] and came back and said, 'No way will the PO have one little bit of crossbar in their network.'
>
> We in GEC were already involved with AEI on the large [reed] exchange. Having been encouraged by the IRC, we took over AEI in 1967. They had the TXE3 [large reed exchange] development, which we realized was not going to be economic. One of the big things in all electronic systems is the plug and socketry and what you decide you want to unplug and plug up again has a big part in determining the cost. AEI were developing REX 18 which was basically TXE3 but with all the reeds wired into the rack which got rid of the plug and socketry and that did bring the cost down.

And David Leakey:

> When GEC took control of AEI, I had the task of rationalizing the telecommunications research facilities. This involved the closing down of three research facilities and bringing them together on to one site. The problem was not that the various facilities were not carrying out good research, but rather that the work was not co-ordinated and focused in a viable commercial manner. At the same time the work on large reed relay exchanges was concentrated at STC by the closure of the work on the REX18 at AEI. Again, the technical merits of the REX 18 system were considerable, but the commercial prospects were poor.
>
> All of these changes left crossbar as a major interim system, although unfortunately many tried to suggest it should have a life span well beyond that which was likely to be achievable.

The pattern now emerging was to prove formative. GEC was identifying itself with the use of 5005 crossbar with SPC control for trunk exchanges (PO designation TXK2). Within the Plessey group the AT&E and Ericsson companies still retained their separate identities. AT&E was identified with Strowger and with 5005 crossbar in local applications (PO TXK1). Despite the reluctance of its research and development engineers, by the later 1960s the GPO had a large order book for 5005 and would continue to order it for a decade or more. Ericsson was beginning to make real progress with its reed system designed for small exchanges (PO TXE2).

The GEC Mark II BL processor was eventually adopted to form the heart of System X and is in extensive use in System X exchanges today (PO TXD).

STC remained slightly apart. It had been a party to JERA and continued to play a part in the System X development programme. Its UK development laboratory, STL, had a very distinguished record. It was the birthplace both of PCM in the form used today and of optical fibre. But, owned as it was predominantly by ITT, STC had an obvious motive to push the ITT product range; and it was viewed with unease by the British-owned companies. The PO was purchasing STC BXB 1100 crossbar (actually ITT Metaconta) for local exchanges in London (PO TXK3) and for the new high-speed four-wire trunk transit network (PO TXK4).

The Ericsson TXE2 development was the first success of the British electronic programme. It began to be ordered in quantity by the PO in the late 1960s and began to make export sales. Like all pioneering developments it had its weaknesses. With PO agreement the facilities it provided were stripped down to the minimum in the interest of cost. It was inflexible and expensive, it involved a number of compromises and its practical upper limit of application was for exchanges with an initial capacity of 1,000 lines, (though Plessey later attempted to increase the capacity to no less than 10,800 lines). But it worked acceptably and it offered the basic advantage of elimination of conventional electro-mechanical switches with all their maintenance problems. A large number of TXE2 exchanges were eventually installed in Britain and abroad.

So far as the GPO was concerned, the big question still remained unsolved in 1969 – could a practical electronic system be introduced for the main mass of large local exchanges? Bell Laboratories in the USA were making real progress with their reed system ESS1, which was designed to be used in units of up to 100,000 lines. Friendly rivalry with Bell Labs was a powerful motivator. The natural target for the UK was to develop its own equivalent to ESS1.

The experiments with time division for Highgate Wood, Goring and Pembury had used PAM, which as we have seen had been found to be unsatisfactory. PCM was to become the basis of modern digital telecommunications. It had been proposed by Reeves in STL as far back as 1937. The advances in semi-conductor technology in the mid-1960s made it possible for the first time to contemplate using PCM in practical applications. The first PCM transmission system was introduced into the GPO network in 1967. By 1969 PCM transmission systems were coming into extensive use.

Practical PCM technology was the final building block which had been needed for the conceptual grand design of System X. The GPO and the industry had now to turn to organizing the actual development. It was a taxing problem. The most basic difficulty was the fragmentation of effort in the industry, which was getting seriously out of hand. Mel Price:

> The thing where I had real nervousness about what was going on was the fact that five competitive systems [two crossbar, large and small reed and fully electronic] were being looked to and having a design competition in the 66–67 period, where in actual fact the whole of us would never produce *one*, with the resource we had got then.
>
> What we [just in GEC] ended up trying to do was (*a*) to satisfy local exchange demand with Strowger; (*b*) in our wisdom or otherwise we were trying to introduce a reed electronic exchange; (*c*) we were certainly trying to do the same on crossbar;

and (*d*) in the end getting ourselves geared up to produce what became System X. Nobody, but nobody, had ever tried to do that sort of thing in the past. Four different technologies with four different system concepts and four different production facilities.

Questions about the structure of the industry were not going to go away. Price again:

[Lord] Weinstock and some of us had a meeting with [Sir] John Clark about 1967 when we were going to take a licence for 5005 [crossbar], and Arnold Weinstock said to John Clark, 'Look John, there is only one real solution to this, we ought to put these two telecommunications businesses together.' That was the first time I ever heard that suggestion made. John Clark was not enthusiastic about it at all – it was nil response from him. We [GEC] did decide to take 5005 and from that emerged the whole Group Switching Centre (GSC) story.[5] The tragedy was that while Plessey had done a competent local system they had not done any work on 5005 in a GSC environment.

I remember one meeting when Arnold said to Bill Ryland that really his job was to run the PO and not to play politics. He was probably pretty good at running the PO but awful at politics. Let him purchase in the way that he thought was in the PO best interest.

In the next chapter we shall look at how it all turned out in the 1970s.

Notes

1. The distinctive characteristic of Strowger is that the switches which connect calls operate under the direct control of the impulses dialled by the subscriber. In very complex networks like that in London 'directors' are interposed between the customer and the connecting switch which translate the pulse trains dialled by customers into different pulse trains to steer the call through the network. But the principle remains the same. In common control systems like crossbar the pulse trains dialled by the customer pass into control equipment used in common by all callers which controls the behaviour of the switches directly by electrical means and not by pulse trains. All electronic systems operate on the common control principle.

2. Switching theory recognizes three different techniques on which the cross-connection process itself may be based.

   In Space Division systems it is accomplished by the making and unmaking of physical connections, for example by Strowger switches or by reed relays.

   There are two Time Division techniques, Pulse Amplitude Modulation (PAM) and Pulse Code modulation (PCM). In PAM, the technique used in the earliest trials like Highgate Wood and Goring, the population of customer lines is sampled in sequence at high speed. The instantaneous amplitude of the voice waveform (speech) on the originating line is passed forward into a 'highway' to which all lines are connected, in a particular time slot. The cross-connection process is accomplished by arranging that for the duration of the call both originating and destination lines access the highway in the same time slot. The pulses from the originating line therefore pass through the highway to the destination line. Given appropriate filter circuits and provided sampling occurs at a high enough rate, the complete envelope of the original voice waveform (that is the speech) on the originating line will then be reproduced on the destination line.

   The principle of PCM is the same, except that the instantaneous amplitude of the voice waveform on the originating line is converted into a value in binary (digital) code; and it is this value which is passed forward through the highway time slot to the destination line. Given a high enough sampling rate and appropriate circuitry on the destination line, the sequence of such coded values can then be converted back into the original waveform.

The key property of PCM is that the coded signals used to pass forward the information about instantaneous amplitudes are substantially unaffected by the transmission properties of the highway. This proved to give it a decisive advantage over PAM systems, where degradation of the amplitude-modulated signals in the highway transmission path proved an insuperable problem.

PCM digital technique forms the basis of all modern switching and transmission systems.

3. First Report of the Select Committee on Nationalized Industries – The Post Office, HC Paper 340 – I (HMSO, London, 1967), p. 268.

4. The long-distance transmission systems of the day operated on a 'four-wire' basis in which separate paths are provided for calls in the two directions so as to ease transmission problems and reduce costs. The switching systems of the day provided only two-wire paths. If trunk calls were to be switched automatically it was necessary to provide cumbersome and expensive equipment to convert from four- to two-wire and back again at the points of entry into and departure from the exchange. The purpose of four-wire trunk switches was to make this unnecessary.

   GEC eventually supplied a number of large Sector Switching Centre exchanges which used four-wire crossbar with SPC electronic control for installation in London.

5. In the original British STD system STD charging and routing was controlled at some six hundred large focal exchanges called Group Switching Centres (GSCs). Outside the five largest cities the units concerned also functioned as local exchanges for their immediate areas. Delays to GSCs therefore represented a significant part of the waiting list problem.

11 Technology, Modernization and Cuts

By now, in the early 1970s, the core of the supplying industry comprised three firms – GEC Telecommunications Ltd (GEC), a management company of the GEC group; Plessey Telecommunications Ltd (PTL), a subsidiary of The Plessey Company; and Standard Telephones and Cables Ltd (STC). There were two other significant equipment suppliers, Pye/TMC, a partly owned subsidiary of Philips; and Marconi, which was now a subsidiary of the GEC group operating in competition with GEC Telecommunications and supplying digital transmission equipment. Other firms such as Ferranti were making serious efforts to gain entry to the PO market.

There were four cable suppliers – British Insulated Callenders Cables Ltd; Pirelli Cables Limited, a subsidiary of the Italian Pirelli group; Standard Telephone Cables Ltd, a subsidiary of STC; and Telephone Cables Ltd, a joint subsidiary of GEC and of Delta Metals Ltd (now Delta Group).

By now Bill Ryland and Cadbury had reorganized the GPO procurement machinery, and the bulk supplies agreements were well on the way out. So far as purchasing policy was concerned, competition was now the overriding objective. With its own house put in better order, the GPO set out to bring some order also into the situation in the industry.

Roy Harris in the PO and his colleagues in industry were beginning to get seriously into the difficult problem of actually getting development going on a fully digital system. Mel Price:

> This design competition business finally had the rug pulled from under its feet and the Advisory Group on Systems Definition [AGSD – parented at this stage on the bulk supplies agreement and chaired by Roy Harris of the PO] was set up. Miraculously or otherwise the PO and the five companies did agree to that being set up. That was the first time ever that the whole lot of us sat down and said, 'What is it we are really trying to do?' Who uttered the first word I would not like to say but the lead in that came from the PO. I think that it had become recognized then that the idea of five switching systems and a design competition was just not on, because there just was not the resource to do it. I do not believe that GEC would have gone very enthusiastically in spending all their development resources [on a proprietary system] when they would have come out of it without any guarantee of any business.

But things had not yet gone the whole way to collaboration. David Leakey:

> For understandable reasons of inter-company rivalry, we could not achieve the close collaboration we knew was needed to develop a successful all-electronic exchange system. Initially we had to be content with a co-ordinating group called the Advisory

Group on Systems Definition where basic principles could be discussed and agreed, but detailed design work was left largely unco-ordinated.

Things began to happen also in the procurement of the current technologies. Price again:

Arnold [Weinstock] was saying after our experience with going competitive on transmission that there was not enough groundwork done; there were going to be problems with ending the [exchange bulk supplies] agreement. The outcome of that was extending the agreement for a year and a half. Then was set up the Bill Humphries [GPO Director of Telecommunications Development] working party on which the problem was certainly talked out. Whether people liked the answers must be open to debate; but it certainly was talked out. In the end it saw off the agreement, which was the obstacle to any real reform of the industry.

Things were deteriorating on the production side of the industry. Growing pains following the structural changes among the firms were having inevitable effects. There had been changes in attitude to mundane but important matters like the money allowed to be tied up in piece parts held on inventory in the factory awaiting incorporation in finished goods, which affected lead times for production.

The original decision of the Plessey management, which had taken over AT&E and Ericsson in the early 1960s, to go into crossbar had been a bold one. John Flint says:

John Clark [recently appointed Chairman of Plessey] knew nothing about the telecommunications industry at all. He had got two very large companies with masses of employees and overseas connections – agreements with India, Australian, Brazilian and Portuguese companies all making equipment. It must have been a terrible miasma for him to see everything through.

Suffice it to say that the 5005 crossbar did go in to the factories in Brazil and into Portugal. The local companies sold it successfully. But you had to re-engineer the thing for that local network. And the network had already got common [control] signalling. It was not step-by-step in the usual sense. The PO sat back on Strowger step-by-step.

By now in 1969 it was becoming clear that the undertaking given by Plessey back in 1964 that they could meet the shortfall in Strowger by production of 5005 crossbar was not being fulfilled. Flint again:

I think it was probably over-ambitious build-up, particularly of a new electro-mechanical system. Plessey came up to [the old AT&E factories in the north] and saw these enormous areas of machine shop – dark satanic mills going on and on. Being in the advanced south [Plessey itself] did not bother about that. They called in machine parts from outside firms – screws and so on. A lot of firms had grown up round Plessey Ilford who were feeding them in all the time. There was a sudden rush to get the old [northern] machine shops clear. But there weren't any firms around. In fact the firms that grew up eventually were run by inspectors and foremen off the [AT&E] floor who were wise enough to take those machines and put them in their garages.

There were other problems. The crossbar local exchanges used the original electro-mechanical common control. Plessey had passed the 5005 design to GEC, who had taken over numerous orders for crossbar Group Switching Centres (see Chapter 10, note 4, p. 102). Plessey were dependent on GEC for design information on the GEC processor, which it had been agreed that they would use as the control on their own GSC orders. They were therefore as affected as GEC was by delays to this development.

Crossbar deliveries were in crisis: 450 detailed design changes to 5005 were identified as required *after* the product left the development laboratories. The factories were expected to make these changes to equipment already on the production line or being installed. This was a recipe for chaos. A great number of contracts were affected, dating back to the mid–1960s. STC crossbar was in similar delay. Contract deferments continued to accumulate. As a result the PO eventually found itself with a waiting list of 450,000 would-be customers.

The PO faced a dilemma between a hands-off approach, which could form the basis for punitive action for damages but which would do nothing to help reduce the immediate delays, and involving its own staff in trying to help sort the contracts out, which would prejudice any later legal action. It really had no choice. Immediate service to the public had to take priority and the PO had to get involved. There was a limit to the contribution which the PO could make to the firms' technical problems, because of its lack of familiarity with crossbar. But it formed a specialized contract control group, with the task of winning the firms' confidence and doing all it could to monitor and promote their ability to meet dates. At the same time PO staff on the ground were allowed to become involved in actually trying to make the exchanges work.

The situation was an unwelcome mess. The GPO had started the trouble with inadequate forecasting. But a primary cause of the difficulties was the failure of the industry with the development and introduction of proprietary systems. The PO remained determined to secure competition in supply. But so far as development was concerned, the traditional PO approach of a standardized design developed with PO involvement still looked the best bet. The creation of AGSD, bringing together as it did the best development engineers of the PO and all three firms, offered a real chance of unifying future British development effort to this end. There was an obvious problem in reconciling this with competition in supply. But even firms making a standardized design would have plenty of room to compete on working efficiency, overheads and profits.

The most worrying thing remained the overall state of the industry. Despite the mergers of the 1960s and the efforts of the IRC it was still seriously fragmented. The combination of the abrupt rise in requirements and the proliferation of new technology had presented it with a challenge which most managements would have been proud to meet; but it had signally failed to rise to the occasion. The new telecommunications business had a home supply industry on which it could not rely.

During his brief term of office as Chairman, Lord Hall made his own attempt to address the structural problem of the industry. He was a Labour peer and Bryan Stanley was in his confidence. Stanley – in an account coloured by concern with union interest – says:

[Lord Hall] had a direct clash with [Christopher] Chataway [the new Minister of Posts and Telecommunications]. [Hall] was very friendly with Geneen, who was running ITT, who at the time owned STC. Geneen had said to [Hall], 'Look, I am fed up with this lot in STC. Are you interested in taking them over?' Hall told me that he was very interested in taking them over; and that he felt it was the way to break the power of the contractors who from his point of view had got the PO in a straitjacket. And that unless he found a way of having direct control of part of the manufacturing process he was not going to be able to break that stranglehold any more than his predecessors. Therefore what he wanted was a significant piece of the manufacturing capacity under PO control.

He wanted to talk to me about our existing factories, what they did, whether it was possible to combine the factories that we had with a manufacturing unit. I had to tell him it was going to be very difficult to do but obviously not impossible to do. It might mean some changes, depending on whether they saw the people working in the [STC] factories as being on a par with the people working in the existing [PO] factories. From our point of view we would want that and we would want them recognized by the union and there would be a clash because they were represented by other people. So he said, 'Well, we can probably bring in the General Secretaries of the other [industry] unions and do some kind of deal with them then.'

So he wanted very much to do a private deal with Geneen. But of course although it was the PO corporation there was still a Minister. Shortly after Lord Hall was appointed there had been a change of government and the Heath government had taken over. Chataway had been appointed Minister of Posts and Telecommunications. Hall had to put this idea up to Chataway to tell him that this was what he was going to do. And after a bit Chataway came down and said, 'There is no way we are going to allow you to go out into the private field and get involved in manufacture.'

So Hall told me he said to Chataway, 'Look, I am Chairman of the Corporation and you and your predecessors have been blathering about the greater independence that this is going to bring, and how it is necessary for the Corporation to develop in this modern age the potential of the PO and of telecommunications and I am going to do it.' Chataway said, 'Well we are going to stop you doing this.' Hall said he told Chataway, 'Over my dead body.' So he said [to me, Stanley], I realize that I am in some danger because he may take me literally. But I don't think [Hall] believed that it would happen, because he went on with many things that we found of great hope.

Lord Hall did of course leave, as we saw in Chapter 4. The aspirations of the POEU and its members to widen the role of the PO in manufacturing were to rumble on and to have to be contained by THQ right up to the time of privatization of BT.

The politics and economics of the industry were dominated by exchange switching. To recap, after all the complications of the late 1960s the PO was now purchasing no fewer than five different switching systems (official PO designations are shown in parentheses):

- PO 2000 type Strowger (TXS)

- Strowger-based Motor Uniselector Switching for the mechanized trunk network

- Plessey/GEC 5005 Crossbar, in its local and Group Switching Centre applications (TXK1)

- STC (ITT) BXB 1100 Crossbar, in both local and trunk (four-wire) applications (TXK3 and TXK4)

- the new British small reed system (TXE2)

The PO now undertook studies which showed that the maintenance, training, stores stocking and other costs arising from this variety were excessive. The studies were seen as underlining the need in the long run to move back towards standardization and rationalization of technology.

Despite its diversity, however, the existing catalogue of systems still had one important gap. The question of whether a satisfactory British reed system could be developed for the modernization of large local exchanges remained unresolved. Reed systems developed by companies overseas were beginning to appear on the world market. The ITT 10C system was available from Bell Antwerp, and people in the PO including Bill Ryland began to wonder about it as a candidate.

In taking over Ericsson, Plessey had inherited the TXE2 small reed exchange development. By now this system was in volume production for the PO and Plessey were strongly and successfully identified with it. In the large exchange area, however, they were equally strongly identified with 5005 crossbar, which they had taken over from AT&E. GEC had been involved in the large reed development ever since it took over AEI; but as we have seen with PO encouragement they had joined in on 5005 crossbar in the late 1960s. They had made a commitment to 5005 production. They now decided to drop out of the large reed development and to join Plessey in concentrating on crossbar. STC stepped in where they bowed out and took over development responsibility for what was to become TXE4. Ken Frost, responsible for the PO interface and for STC switching marketing strategy at the time, said:

> We took a chance on going into TXE4. In the first place without any firm commitment from the PO. And then we got into the great modernization programme, in which we argued for modernization with TXE4 while Plessey and GEC made their case for crossbar with some electronic control in it.[1]

The question of large exchange modernization had been hanging over the PO for a decade. Many of the existing population of large Strowger local exchanges dated from the 1930s and had gone through the Blitz. They were over thirty years old and ageing rapidly. The problem was at its most acute in London and the other big cities. By 1969 it had become urgent; service was visibly beginning to deteriorate. There were three linked questions to consider – first the decision to modernize in principle, second how rapidly to carry the programme out, and third which system to employ.

At the end of 1971 the PO telecommunications business made a proposal to the PO Board for a replacement programme using TXE4. The Board was not satisfied and turned the matter back for further study. Seizing their opportunity, GEC and Plessey began to lobby intensively on behalf of crossbar with electronic control instead. Whyte had been appointed Director Operational Programming in THQ. He now mounted a major investment appraisal operation using the Discounted Cash Flow (DCF) technique and an elaborate and comprehensive computer model to establish the case for modernization in principle and the correct choice of system as between TXE4 and crossbar.

The inputs to the model were thoroughly validated, with GEC, Plessey and STC fully involved. The discount rate used was set by the Treasury. Special forecasts were made of the growth of lines and traffic on the network and of PO financial parameters. The PO went to great lengths to ensure that the suppliers endorsed the inputs for their respective systems. Prospective prices, including the details of pricing structure with normalised profits, were agreed with them. The profile of deliveries assumed for the rival systems was agreed with them and then validated by the PO contract control group. The model showed that, of all the options, modernization completed in 1992 using TXE4 had the best positive Net Present Value (NPV). Modernization with crossbar showed a negative NPV.

Work was already in hand between the PO and STC in developing a version of TXE4 with electronic (SPC) control, to be known as TXE4A. It was an explicit assumption at this time that TXE4 would be superseded by the SPC version TXE4A when that became available and was demonstrably to be preferred on economic grounds. Also that TXE4A would be superseded in its turn by the AGSD product, now referred to by the intentionally anonymous title of System X, once it was developed and to be preferred in the same way.

At this time the suppliers' factories were essentially concerned with manufacture and assembly of metal piece parts for electro-mechanical systems. The manufacture of electronic equipment involved very different processes, centring on the assembly of components on to printed circuit boards. One of the principal requirements for the future and especially for System X was to give the switching industry a base load on which it could develop electronic production skills. Even though it was intended to adopt electronic SPC control, the crossbar switch itself remained essentially an electro-mechanical device. It was very much in the interest of the PO to encourage its suppliers to convert to modern electronic production technique. With his experience on the manufacturing side of the industry before he joined the

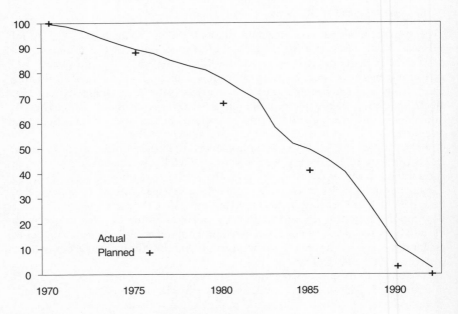

Figure 11.1   Percentage of lines on Strowger 1972–92

PO, Fennessy judged that TXE4 and especially the TXE4A SPC version would be a better vehicle for this than crossbar.

On the basis of the result of the appraisal and of considerations such as these early in 1973 the PO Board decided to go ahead with modernization to a target date of 1992 using TXE4 and TXE4A. In order to go some way to meet the wishes of GEC and Plessey and to help their export efforts, and because TXE4 was not yet available in volume, substantial amounts of crossbar were to be used as well in the early years of the modernization programme. STC subsequently agreed to transfer the TXE4 design information to GEC and Plessey and in due course they became major TXE4 and TXE4A suppliers on a competitive basis.

Figure 11.1 shows what actually happened. The programme for replacement of Strowger went ahead throughout the next twenty years as the PO had planned in 1973. There were hiccups from time to time; and for most of the period achievement lagged about two years behind plan, owing primarily to supplier delays. The programme was, however, completed almost dead on time, eight years after privatization.

The inter-exchange transmission side of the business was more than keeping pace with switching. It was already going digital. The first PCM digital systems were installed on short-distance inter-exchange junctions before the end of the 1960s. They were highly successful, and in the early 1970s the PO proceeded to a series of funded development contracts for long-distance digital transmission systems. Waveguide was considered as a transmission medium but discarded in favour of optical fibre. The early digital transmission systems were developed to North American standards, for example using the 24 channel (1.5 mbit/s or T1) standard for the first-order system used on junctions. The PO, however, subsequently decided to adopt the CCITT family of standards, based on 30 channels (2 mbit/s) for the first-order system. All its systems were re-engineered on this basis. The switching modernization programme was accompanied by a similar programme of modernization of transmission plant based on these developments.

As we saw in Figure 5.2, the service given by the network improved strikingly over the twenty-year period of the modernization programme. The whole operation was one of the biggest and least recognized modernization programmes in British utility history.

The PO was now discovering weaknesses in the contract arrangements put in place after the ending of the bulk supplies agreements. The new terms governing progress payments allowed the companies considerable cash flow on a given contract well before it was completed. In a situation of markedly expanding production requirements this helped the companies with funding of work in progress; and in theory the financial benefit it gave them would be cancelled out by competitive pressures on future contracts. But in the case of Strowger these pressures were muffled, because the companies had also succeeded in persuading the PO to negotiate a cumbersome agreement designed to protect them from too abrupt changes in market share following the ending of the BSAs. The PO became uneasily aware that by legitimate means its contractors were amassing a substantial cash flow on individual contracts well ahead of completion. This reduced the incentive on them to finish the contracts off and so to reduce the waiting list. (It also undoubtedly contributed to the extraordinary bulge in spending in the early 1970s, shown in Figure 5.1.)

The PO was determined to make as sure as it could that nothing like the delays of the late 1960s ever happened again. It now commissioned a major study by McKinsey of the whole exchange provision process, from its own demand forecasting right through manufacture and installation to opening. The suppliers co-operated, and the consultants went through the firms' procedures as well as those of the PO. They identified a very large number of improvements. The PO set up an implementation team of its own and carried though its share of the changes. It was up to the firms to make theirs.

Bill Ryland and the PO remained deeply committed to promoting competition between the three established suppliers. But there was more to it than that. The three firms' poor performance on deliveries, the unease about contract terms and the way the post-BSA situation was developing generally all pointed to competition being needed from outside.

There were two main candidates. At this time Philips were mounting a serious drive to enter telecommunications internationally. The Philips thrust in Britain was built round the British firm Pye/TMC, which had occupied a position as a niche supplier to the PO for some years and which Philips now acquired. Ryland had become seized of the possibility that a group·with the weight of Philips might be an effective challenger in Britain. At his behest THQ manoeuvred throughout the next few years to create an opening for Philips, first in Strowger and later as we shall see in System X.

Fennessy believed that L. M. Ericsson, the principal Swedish manufacturer, also had the potential to become a powerful competitor for PO business. By 1971 the international service was becoming a really serious problem. The level of congestion had passed the point of acceptability. Telecommunications were already important to the City and to exports and becoming more so almost daily. Plessey had been given an order for a crossbar switching unit for the international service early on in the crossbar story. By now this was turning out to be one of the all-time disasters of PO procurement. It never performed properly. It was to be twelve years from the date of the order to the time when the commercial negotiations about the contract were finally wound up. With this experience fresh in his mind Fennessy decided to make a bid to purchase a major international crossbar exchange from L. M. Ericsson. After prolonged arguments with Plessey and GEC, and with DoI to whom they appealed, he finally succeeded. The order was placed in early 1972. As a kind of consolation prize Plessey were awarded a similar order for a second international crossbar unit at the same time.

The international service situation was critical and there was no time to buy a site and construct a purpose-made building in the usual way. The PO found a large disused factory at Stag Lane in north-west London and the two exchanges were installed side-by-side. PO people and others from DoI and elsewhere went out there in large numbers to compare the extremely well organized Ericsson installation operation with its Plessey equivalent. Even the most detached observer could hardly avoid the conclusion that Ericsson was efficient and Plessey was not.

Returning to the general situation, the delays to exchange contracts were just about coming under control when the country hit the oil price shock of December 1973. In his statement on 18 December the Conservative Chancellor, Anthony Barber, announced an abrupt 20 per cent cut in funds available for nationalized industry investment in the following financial year. The Post Office had no option but to make very extensive deferments in spending on contracts already placed. The operational consequences were less serious than they might have been because subsequent events, including the three-day week, themselves retarded growth in the economy and therefore reduced demand for service. But the consequences for the industry almost defied description. From an atmosphere of urgent pressure to accelerate, companies found themselves overnight facing equally urgent demands to decelerate. Even the most perfect production control systems would have been hard put to it to cope.

The outfall of expenditure on any given contract was spread over anything up to three years. In the case of the delayed contracts it was considerably more. This meant that, to find the sums which it was required to save, a large part of the various factory throughputs had to be deferred. It was impossible to make a sophisticated selection of contracts by reference to operational priorities. The PO contract control group, with myself as Director, found itself facing a series of heroic decisions on slipping complete blocks of contracts, which simply had to be accepted if the required cuts were to be made. Damage to service was inevitable.

The problems were far from being confined to switching. They extended over the whole purchasing field. Merriman and I had a joint bad moment over the future of the only silicon tetrachloride plant in Britain. It too would have disappeared but for Post Office support at the critical moment; and Britain would have lost all chance of an indigenous supply of processed silicon for its infant semi-conductor industry. I had another bad moment when I had to decide whether to sustain a PO contract which was all that was keeping alive Footprint Tools, one of the most distinguished hand-tool suppliers in the country. I decided in their favour.

The country went through the three-day week, the problems of secondary picketing and the fall of the Heath government. Towards the end of 1974 the country, the PO and its suppliers were beginning to lick their wounds. But 1975 had a new set of difficulties in store.

One afternoon early in the year the Chairman of the Telephone Cable Makers' Association confessed, in Cadbury's words 'black with shame', that the members had been operating an illegal price ring ever since the ending of the cable bulk supplies agreement. The disclosure had been forced by one of the member companies whose top management were unwilling any longer to be involved in such irregularities.

The issue itself was serious enough. After protracted negotiation it was settled out of court by a compensation payment of £9m by the suppliers, in respect of improper profits. But the effect on confidence between the Post Office and the industry was more serious still. Two of the companies, TCL and STC Cables, were subsidiaries respectively of the GEC and STC groups. It was impossible to avoid doubt being cast on the probity of the parent companies. Equally seriously, the Board also felt a grave loss of confidence in PO Contracts Division and its Controller, who had had personal responsibility for approving cable contract awards.

The Board reaction was vehement. Procurement practices were to be sharply tightened up at once. The Director Central Audit was commissioned to make an internal efficiency audit of the affairs of Contracts Division. It is a tribute to the Director, Tim Ball, that the audit itself was regarded by all concerned as fair and moderate. Ball issued reports on seven different issues of whose handling he was critical. The Controller of Contracts retired and was succeeded by Air-Vice-Marshal Howard Cadwallader.

In March 1975 I had become Senior Director Planning and Purchasing. In June I had to call in the representatives of GEC, Plessey and STC and tell them that the Board now insisted on the unprecedented requirement of cost investigation on *competitive* contracts – in effect requiring the companies completely to open their books to the PO; and on the PO owning all patents on development contracts it was funding. The reaction of the suppliers was, perhaps not surprisingly, negative. A freeze descended on Post Office industry relations which lasted until the spring of 1976. It was a particular piece of bad luck that the episode coincided with the critical stage in the commercial negotiations for System X, which are discussed in the next chapter. PO people could not but feel sympathy for Plessey, who had no involvement in the cable scandal but were paying the same price as the others nevertheless.

The damage done by the episode to Contracts Division morale could have been very serious. Contracting work had to go on, cable dispute or no cable dispute. It was asking a lot of the staff of a Division under such a cloud to expect them to continue to show the firmness in negotiation which their work demanded. But to their lasting credit they did it. In early 1976 the Board released a pile of frozen contracts and Contracts Division could begin to breathe again. But even then a long hard slog lay ahead before relations would get back on a sensible keel.

Faced with all the evidence of problems with the industry, the PO reviewed in depth the possibilities for using its procurement power to bring about change in structure beyond the changes made at the end of the 1960s. It was a received view among many people in the PO that the success of Western Electric products and the resulting quality of the service to Bell customers in the USA sprang to a great extent from the intimate dialogue possible between AT&T and Western Electric as operating and manufacturing arms of a single vertical monopoly. The IRC had at one stage suggested that the PO itself should acquire STC, which could have been run as a model company to stimulate the other two. The PO now considered similar arrangements for in-house manufacture and many possible permutations of regrouping among the firms themselves, but reached no agreement on a course of action.

Other people were thinking along parallel lines. At one stage L. M. Ericsson considered acquiring Plessey. They were discouraged by the prospect of defence complications which would have been hard for them to handle.

The problems of the industry as it stood were far from over. The effects of the recession in the national economy began to make themselves felt on the growth of telecommunications lines and traffic. At the same time the new asset utilization system began to produce its first estimates of the surpluses of Strowger in the network, which were serious. The industry had to be told that Strowger ordering was to be cut substantially below previously forecast levels.

This was particularly difficult for Plessey. John Flint says:

The mood in Plessey Telecoms was twofold. We all knew that Strowger was a cash cow and Sir John Clark and the people at [Plessey headquarters at] Millbank looked at Liverpool as the cash cow for Plessey, because there was no development effort involved. Then the Barber cuts came and the whole existence of Plessey was threatened. There was another angle as well. The background of Willetts [Managing Director of PTL] was in the north-east – the 1930s Jarrow march and all that. He was very considerate of the workforce. Other people might have said, 'We have had a major cut in our orders – we will get rid of 5,000 out of Liverpool's 25,000 people.'

The manufacturing industry unions became involved. Labour was in power and the unions used their influence up the line to Ministers. There was a serious row, which ended up at Number 10 Downing Street. The Government backed the Post Office but it gave an uncovenanted hostage to fortune. Without the knowledge of Gresham Street the Prime Minister assured Plessey that there would be no further cuts. His words were read with misgiving in THQ. They knew what was out there in the field and they knew that the asset utilization system had growing pains yet to come.

In the middle of all this the PO successfully negotiated with STC for transfer of the TXE4 design information to GEC and Plessey, who now began vigorously to develop production capacity for this system. It was an encouraging demonstration of how design information could be passed around among competitors in supply on a sensible basis. The System X arrangements were being hammered out at this time; and the experience with TXE4 increased PO confidence that the same companies would collaborate in development and compete in supply for that system.

During the summer of 1976 it became clear that there would have to be further substantial reductions in Strowger ordering. The reality was that the Post Office was close to having all the Strowger it was ever going to need. As the industry and especially Plessey saw it, the situation had become intolerable. It was PO requirements which had caused them to retain such a large Strowger capacity and Strowger-trained workforce; the PO had suddenly cut away the ground it had built up under their feet; and it should not be allowed just to get away with it. They decided to commission an independent enquiry by the distinguished Cambridge economists Cripps and Godley. When the report appeared it was highly critical of the PO and especially of its forecasting procedures and of the lack of warning of the extent of the reductions. The PO and the government agreed that a second inquiry should be commissioned from Professor Michael Posner, another distinguished Cambridge economist. Professor Posner made a thorough investigation of the events and of Post Office forecasting procedures. His finding was that five professors of economics could not have done better than the Post Office on demand forecasting but that the Post Office had given the industry insufficient warning of the programme changes. The reduced programme stood.

A second big international order (Keybridge) was placed in the mid-1970s, and a third (Mondial House) in 1978. The Mondial contract included a substantial quantity of digital (AXE) equipment. The pattern was the same each time – a competition won by L. M. Ericsson on lead time and dependability with a second palliative order to Plessey after appeal to Ministers. As a result of Keybridge LME decided to build their switching factory at Scunthorpe, which provided the essential launch pad for their eventual entry into inland switching. Taken together the three exchanges were worth some £70m at 1970s prices, or well over £100m at present-day prices. They represented a major L. M. Ericsson inroad into PO requirements.

Whyte, now Director Purchasing and Supply, now made an important visit to the USA, as a result of which he drew attention to another force of growing importance to the industry besides the ups and downs of operating requirements. A 10,000-line crossbar exchange needed four hundred 4 ft 6 in by 10 ft 6 in racks full of small metal piece parts which had to be punched, assembled, adjusted and maintained. The equivalent System X unit was to consist of about fifteen 3 ft by 7 ft racks containing cards which the manufacturer assembled using bought-in components and printed circuit boards. The effect was going to be to reduce sharply the unit cost, price and absolute profit per line to the final equipment manufacturer and also to reduce the proportion of finished product value it could add. The cash flow base available to the manufacturer from production of a given number of lines was going to reduce greatly.

By 1996 all this is a matter of history. The effects on the industry have been dramatic. In 1973 the companies had a total work force on telecommunications plant manufacture of some forty thousand. In order to make electronic switching and transmission systems efficiently and competitively, this work force has had to be reduced by a factor of something like ten. At the same time R&D costs have inexorably risen. Co-operation and mergers between final equipment companies have become inevitable if they are to survive.

The writing about the character of electronic production and its implications was already beginning to be plain on the wall in the mid-1970s. But the UK industry was seriously slow to react and to carry through the necessary change and rationalization. From this point of view, painful though they were, the PO Strowger cuts were a matter of being cruel to be kind, because they forced the industry to begin the conversion process.

Altogether the 1970s were a difficult decade for British telecommunications manufacture. The switching suppliers took a series of knocks which taken together were perhaps harder than anyone should be asked to bear. The cable scandal did disproportionate damage to the industry as a whole. The PO missed an important opportunity to end the fragmentation of the industry when it was weakened in 1975. But, at least as the PO saw it, a start was made on hauling the manufacturers into the era of electronic production. And, by fighting and winning the setpiece battles on the three big international exchanges and establishing L. M. Ericsson on British soil, Gresham Street had presented UK industry with a major competitive threat on its doorstep. This was particularly admired in Germany, where the Bundespost was struggling to get free of Siemens. We shall see in the next chapter, dealing with System X, how the British firms responded to this threat.

Note

1. Quoted in John Young, *Power of Speech* (Allen & Unwin, London, 1983), p. 169.

12 System X

The work of AGSD had laid the foundations for a completely new concept in switching. It was to have stored programme control and a digital pulse code modulation switching matrix. Roy Harris and the AGSD team also conceived the important idea that it should be modular, so that each element – processor, switch proper, interface elements with the rest of the network, maintenance and administration unit and so on – would be a distinct entity, interacting with the other elements through prescribed interfaces. In this way design changes could be made within any given element of the system without affecting the others, so that the system could evolve and new capabilities could be added with maximum ease. The capacities of the various elements in the exchange could also be tailored to traffic requirements independently of one another. The idea was later adopted for the circuit digital systems of other suppliers.

There was no precedent in Britain for a design undertaking of the scale and complexity which now had to be addressed. There were however some very definite starting points so far as the PO was concerned. As a result of the studies of cost of variance and its experiences with competing proprietary designs in the late 1960s the PO was firmly wedded to the idea of a standard design, and to itself being involved in the design process. It was taken for granted that this meant that the development would be funded with PO money. At the same time the PO was equally firmly wedded to competition in supply of the developed product between the three British firms. Discussions began between the PO and the firms on how to address the problem in the autumn of 1973.

The Australian Post Office had a good reputation for procurement practice at that time. Plessey made an imaginative contribution by co-opting Roger Banks, a senior Australian official, to advise them on the question. He worked closely with the PO for some months. At that time the suggestion was for a 'dumb-bell' organization – a unified industry development structure interacting on equal terms with the PO. There was a great deal to be said for this but it never came off, primarily because the firms could not bring themselves to co-operate in the depth needed.

The PO was visited by a delegation from France. They said that General de Gaulle had lost patience with the state of the telephone service. A national plan had been formed to create a manufacturing industry with the capacity to renew the French network over a short period of years. The French government was well aware that this industry would before long have surplus capacity and would need to export on a large scale to stay in business. They wished to know whether the UK, in effect, would be prepared to become a second market for French switching. In the climate of 1973, with all eyes focused on System X, the suggestion was not surprisingly rejected. But the episode illuminates an important underlying issue.

The British firms were accustomed to a situation in which they were given regular forecasts of PO needs up to five years ahead – far in advance of the placing of actual orders. They had taught the PO that they needed planned build-up profiles for new products, followed by plateaux of ordering at a steady level, and this was what they got. The firms were also getting a considerable concealed subsidy through the payment terms on current production contracts. The PO had good reason to support the industry in this way because it knew from the crossbar experience just how unreliable their delivery could be, especially on new systems. It had a telephone system to run and it had to order its priorities accordingly. The French industry on the other hand was creating a sharp peak of capacity to meet short-term domestic requirements which was bound to be underloaded by domestic business within a few years. The effect was to create an 'export or die' climate in the French manufacturing sector which the British conspicuously lacked.

Intensive discussions continued about possible permutations of development arrangements for System X but the standpoints of the senior managements in the three companies differed so much that no solution emerged or seemed likely to. The situation was becoming really worrying because serious development could obviously not start without a proper framework. By mid-1974 it seemed to Roy Harris and me that if progress was to be made at all the only thing to do was to take an initiative at our level and devise a formula for the PO to act as *primus inter pares* co-ordinator of collaborative development between all four parties, building on the AGSD foundations and looking forward explicitly to competition in supply. Harris took the lead in working this up on the engineering side. I and my commercial opposite numbers played our part. The four Managing Directors gave their support. In March 1975 they met to ratify a commercial memorandum of understanding which had been hammered out on the essentials of the arrangements.

Unfortunately in that very month it became publicly known that the four cable suppliers, including GEC and STC subsidiaries, were conducting the illegal price ring referred to in the previous chapter. Not surprisingly Bill Ryland and the PO Board reacted violently. One most serious effect was to cast serious doubts on the integrity of the GEC and STC parent groups. GEC Telecommunications and STC were of course participants in the System X discussions. The System X arrangements therefore came under very close and critical scrutiny indeed. Ryland now insisted that the development contracts must include explicit provision for the entry of a fourth supplier; they must include extremely rigorous cost investigation and pricing clauses; and the PO must own the patents. These were going to be very difficult requirements to impose. GEC in particular but also STC were in no mood to make such sweeping concessions in the switching area because of irregularities involving their cable subsidiaries. Plessey were an innocent party with no reason to give in to moral pressure.

If the country and the industry were to have System X at all there was nothing for it but to buckle down again at working level and try to hammer out solutions which the PO Board and the companies' managements would go along with. There were other problems besides those resulting from the cable situation. The problem of control of big development programmes is notoriously difficult, and in the System X case hundreds of millions of pounds were going to be involved. In the climate of

1975–6, with the cable scandal fresh in everyone's mind, it was obviously essential to get as bomb-proof a control as possible on the spending of PO money by the firms on development.

An acceptable contractual framework was finally hammered out. A clause satisfactory to the PO which provided a mechanism for the entry of a fourth supplier (assumed to be Pye/TMC) was negotiated; the industrial property problems were resolved by a formula under which the companies owned the patents but the PO had complete free use; and a fully organized system of expenditure control was devised. All this took time. The first development contracts – the so-called feasibility contracts – were placed in the summer of 1976 and formal development work could begin. The main development contracts were negotiated in the spring of 1977 and signed in July.

It was obvious at the time that the fragmented foundations on which the development machinery had had to be built represented just about the worst starting point one could think of for ground-breaking development of a large high-tech system. The odds against three sovereign firms, each facing outward to its own shareholders and each with its own priorities, achieving the cohesion needed to produce a system as complex as System X with the speed needed were just too great, however hard the PO might try. So much effort was going to be needed to make things happen at all. The final textual negotiations on the main contracts required thirty-three all-day meetings between the four parties in six weeks. This was a vivid portent for the future of the sheer effort which the people working in the technical development programme itself were going to have to bring to bear to get results. But given the circumstances there was no other practical way forward.

The Carter Committee, which reported in 1977, perceived this and other problems:

> The situation as we have found it causes us the gravest misgivings. The three manufacturers are not a natural team; in particular, the British-owned firms (General Electric Company (GEC) and Plessey) are suspicious of cooperation with the American-owned Standard Telephone Cables (STC), lest their position in the export markets should be weakened. The manufacturers face serious problems in moving from electromechanical to microelectronic technology, including large-scale redundancies and the obsolescence of much of their equipment. Their immediate interest would be better served by a rapid expansion of the telephone system using older types of equipment, such as Crossbar, which have some years of life in the export markets still before them. They are being asked to cooperate in a development project which so far has no firm orders at the end of it, and which may yield a product with no export market at all. This project is falling behind schedule, retarded by a complex apparatus of committees and discussions. Minor details, we are told, pass upwards for consideration at high level in the Post Office. Crisp and final decisions on specifications are difficult to obtain. The management of the project, a particularly difficult task where jealously independent manufacturers have to be coordinated, appears to be receiving neither the measure of authority nor the status in the Post Office which it requires. Unless specifications and management can be effective, in the context of a realistic timetable leading to firm orders, serious waste and grave harm to the national economy could result.[1]

The criticism of the PO reflected the viewpoint of the senior managements in the firms. The picture as it presented itself to the PO was somewhat different. It was the day-to-day work of co-ordinating development and simply causing things to happen on the ground which mattered; and the task at this level was enough to deter any but the most dedicated spirits. John Martin, the PO project controller under Harris, says:

> The real burden fell to my engineering team which had the task of harmonizing the design and manufacturing processes of the different sovereign partners who expected to compete on supply. Remember each company had its own entrenched investment in everything from the style and skill base of its employees and their training methods through software practices, component coding, documentation systems, production testing and installation methodology. It was the evolution of effective harmonised working practices between the four that had to be solved, plus the forcing of our meetings' structure on the engineering organization. This was the real achievement and the key to our ultimate success in creating a system that could be made and tested and which is our legacy to the industry. The need for this work has never been recognized and indeed our methodology has been held up as evidence of *poor* organization and the cause of delay.[2]

Roy Harris, John Martin, Bill Jones and the others on the PO side of the fence were to have to work ceaselessly throughout the next few years just to keep the project on track and collaboration flowing at all. The fact that they succeeded with such obstacles to face and that the programme resulted in what as we shall see was an outstanding product in the technical sense was a signal achievement, with few if any precedents in British public procurement history.

The divided structure of the project was to create problems in other respects. It was natural for the PO as the operator to take the lead in specifying the detailed performance required of the system. It was equally natural for the PO engineers who found themselves writing the specification for the first wholly new development in British switching history to set out to get the most perfect system they could. In a properly ordered world it would have been the natural role of the development engineers in the companies to challenge these PO aspirations in detail as work proceeded, so as to end up with a product saleable to other customers. In the case of TXE2, for example, the facilities had been pared right back with GPO co-operation. But the way the System X project was divided among the four parties made the necessary intimacy of dialogue impossible. The inevitable result was over-specification and delay.

The Carter Committee heard other eloquent criticism by the firms of the PO. The evidence of the ASTMS union said:

> However, there appears to be some uncertainty over the timetable for System X, which is not now expected in service until the mid-1980s. We understand that the Post Office has a clear idea about the functions that it wants System X to perform, and how these requirements should be satisfied. But we are concerned that in its search for the ideal system, the Post Office may be placing too much emphasis on being involved in the early stages of development of the new system, and may therefore be favouring potential systems that are at an early stage of development rather than systems whose development is further advanced.

It seems to us that the Post Office is reacting to the possibilities of the new technology rather slowly; indeed, the Post Office sometimes gives the impression that it does not regard the development of System X with any great urgency. The main supplying companies, however, seem keen to proceed with System X as fast as possible. For example, recently, Plessey proposed to the Post Office a project called Félicité in order to get ahead more quickly. Félicité involved the combination of a French digital switching system called E.10 and a Plessey processor, PP 250. However, The Post Office did not seem interested at the time, and Plessey have now virtually dissolved their previously close link with CIT-Alcatel.

The Post Office's attitude to the development of System X has far reaching and potentially serious implications for the supplying industry. The Post Office is not alone in developing electronic systems. Most of the industrialised countries are working on similar projects, and in many countries they are further advanced than we are. Most notably, the Swedish company, L. M. Ericsson and the American multinational, International Telephone & Telegraph have both developed electronic digital switching systems, known as AXE and Metaconta respectively. France is likely to modernise its telecommunications service by re-equipping it with a combination of the [Ericsson] AXE and the Metaconta systems. This will not be France's first electronic digital system: the CIT-Alcatel E.10 system is already in use in Brittany. Apart from L. M. Ericsson and ITT ATT-Western Electric have developed the ESS4 system (Western Electric have recently announced that they intend to re-enter the export market for the first time for nearly half a century) and Japanese companies are also carrying out field trials for their electronic digital switching system. Yet the British Post Office, in an attempt to develop what it believes will turn out to be a near perfect electronic system, seems to be proceeding rather slowly.[3]

Bill Ryland retired in the late summer of 1977. During his last few months he made a personal study of System X and became seized of its central importance to the future of the business. He made a number of recommendations on project organization, including the immediate placing of substantial advance orders for System X trunk exchanges to provide a base load on which industry could create production capacity. These orders were duly placed in 1978.

Clive Foxell, eventually BT Board Member for Technology and at this time in PO procurement, says:

> There was a feeling [at this time] of a very turgid, slow-moving situation in which there was a heavy contractual element. As time went on I saw that this foreplay was very much the companies trying to establish their rights and positions in something very much larger, in which time was not of the essence.

All over the world the telecommunications manufacturing industry was now re-orienting itself to electronics and the digital era. John Flint:

> There were other things happening – there was SPC telex and packet switching, there was Frank Thomas's programme on PCM, there was Plessey buying a company out on the west coast [of the US] to do electronic switching and Arnold [Weinstock] setting up Marconi Canada. Everybody was looking in all sorts of directions. The global village was in sight. Europe was there. L. M. Ericsson was stomping around successfully in all our markets, particularly in Australia.

The moral for the System X programme was obvious. It needed to be got on with fast. Development work was going ahead within the various constraints but it became obvious that progress was too slow. William Barlow, who had joined the PO in late 1977, says:

> I was very impressed with the quality of engineering in the PO. It was quality in depth. There was a terrific tradition in the old research place at Dollis Hill. They had moved into Martlesham. There were people all around the Regions and the engineering organization that had been very well trained. Courses were good. I was very satisfied indeed with the quality of engineering. Some of the people who had come through to the top were quite outstanding internationally.

> The biggest subject they had on their plate was the development of System X. The concepts were good. The execution was very slow. The costs were high. I found that I had a very difficult situation. The PO was footing the bill. The need for a digital system was very clear. The more I looked at it the more I felt that we were in a very serious situation to the extent that either we were going to have to decide to stop and turn to an overseas company and bring in the technology; or we were going to have to decide to go and reorganize the way the it was handled. I took the view that British engineers ought to be capable of designing their system; and that if they were quick enough about it it should have the same chance as others to be a world system. It was true at the time the French had what they claimed to be a digital system but it wasn't. The Americans were working on this theme but had not got very far. The Germans and Philips were in it. But the only people who had made real progress at that time were Ericssons, the Swedes.

> So I decided that we would go on with System X. What I did was I got the three executives [the Managing Directors of the firms] together. I said, 'Look, if I decide to go on with this you are the ones that are going to benefit, you in your companies. You have got to give me solemn undertakings that from here on you will put in proper resources and proper management effort; and you will take a personal interest in doing it.'

> I was not satisfied with the management of the project in the PO. I thought the PO was far too lenient with themselves and their collaborators in terms of project milestones and time and cost. In parallel I arranged to bring in the US civil construction company called Bechtel to project manage the system until such time as they had trained our people in project management techniques well enough to be allowed out again. Bechtel were very surprised to be invited. But they did come in, they did give a lot of help on the organization and project management. I myself had regular progressing meetings with the Managing Directors of the firms and we got some impetus and momentum behind it.

> One of the complaints was that the firms did not have any orders on which they could count and thus make their capital investments. We gave them some initial pipe-filling orders quite early on before designs were complete so at least they knew they had got them. We took years out of the programme as it was when we started addressing it in the beginning of 1978. In fact the first System X exchange [the Baynard House pilot] went on stream in September 1980, which was in line with the new programme that we worked out with Bechtel in 1978.

> I was convinced there were too many cooks. I decided STC could conveniently be dropped. I tried to get them out of the quartet. I ended up with a terrific row in

Peter Carey's office [Permanent Secretary of DTI] at which Lord Caccia, himself a former Civil Servant and head of the Foreign Office, and Kenneth Corfield [respectively Chairman and Managing Director of STC] fought vehemently against being dropped. At the end Caccia turned to me and said, 'What are you going to do, Sir William, if you can't get the government to back you in dropping us?' I said, 'You will wither on the vine.' In fact up to the time I left they were still there.

Before 1969 the GPO had been the sponsoring government department for the manufacturing sector, with responsibility for export promotion. Whatever its earlier reservations about crossbar, the PO had embraced it in good faith in 1964. If difficulties in the home market had weakened the crossbar export sales drive in later years, they were due to the industry's own poor delivery performance rather than to lack of support from the PO. After 1969 the Corporation continued to be acutely aware of its influence on exports. It was regular practice for the PO to provide test and demonstration sites for industry export products and to support industry when they had export visitors. Fennessy himself had come from Plessey and was deeply aware of the need to support the companies' export efforts. The companies were allowed to own the patents on the System X designs not least because this helped them so much on the world market.

At PO suggestion a special committee had been set up within the System X structure to consider and cater for export requirements in design. A company owned jointly by the three firms called British Telecommunications Systems Ltd was formed with PO support to co-ordinate the export marketing effort. The PO played an important role in assembling the UK stand at the Geneva exhibition, which was the world launch event for the first generation of digital exchanges. The PO regularly participated in sales visits to other countries. The PO formed its own overseas consulting arm, Telconsult, with a brief to give all the help it could to UK exports consistently with the need to present a balanced view to its customers; and so on. The PO pushed its luck in using its home customers' money to support export effort as much as it did.

But it did not work. Barlow again:

System X was an opportunity missed. It was obvious to me that to be effective in the international market and for the PO to know that it was getting international prices you would have to sell the system all over the world. We set up a company of which the PO and the three firms were shareholders. We appointed a chairman, Christopher Chataway. Plessey provided John Sharpley to be Chief Executive. This company was there to promote System X overseas. But the three companies could never agree amongst themselves about anything. They made life impossible for the Chief Executive and after some years it petered out.

The PO had earlier persuaded STC to pass the TXE4 and 4A design information to Plessey and GEC without undue difficulty or delay. It was fundamental to both the spirit and the letter of the System X contractual arrangements that design information would pass freely between companies in the same way. Nevertheless the firms now began somewhat belatedly to jockey for the commercial advantage of being the developers of the high-volume sub-systems. Foxell:

A lot of the infighting between the companies was due to the recognition that, although on day one the cake had been divided up [on the basis of] 'how many sub-systems have I got to develop and have I got as many as the other companies?', some sub-systems were more significant in production than other sub-systems. For example for the network synchronizer you only needed a very small number of units, where obviously the line card was a crucial sub-system in terms of volume.

The line card turned out to be the most difficult sub-system. When I came on board STC were developing it on the basis of a North Electric line card which had been developed by that ITT subsidiary in the States. They made poor progress with it and there was a continual battle over something that was going to run to millions of units in production. There had been a similar battle much earlier over the choice of processor. In a collaborative development there was this undercurrent of 'what is the commercial implication for me – this company – rather than for System X as a whole?' We moved at the speed of the lowest common denominator. So the programme slipped and slipped and slipped.

The broader issues now surfaced again. The government involved itself, and Jeffery (now Lord) Sterling became involved as a mediator. Foxell again:

> We [in the PO] were aware of the inefficiency of dealing not only with such a large number of companies but with such a large number of sites. Plessey subdivided the development to Roke Manor, Poole, Taplow, Caswell and Liverpool. All of them had this net of development activity – multi-site, everything. I analysed the effect purely of that number of sites in terms of procurement. Everyone was saying that this was blatantly inefficient – we should reduce the number of sites – the number of companies.
>
> I feel that John Smith [STC] had probably decided that he did not necessarily want to be in System X. He believed that the System X market was not big enough for three; and saw an opportunity to maximize TXE4A and use the ITT switch to compete with System X. Reynolds of GEC was playing it long. Clark of Plessey believed they should do it all; they were forward-looking and I had great respect for him in that sense. You almost needed Clark and Weinstock to be put in a blender to produce the right mix of enthusiasm and prudence.
>
> In view of the ongoing slippage in System X development, BT tried again to bring in an alternative switch in order to ginger up the UK suppliers. Again this failed due to DTI reservations, but this pressure plus acrimony over the funding of export models opened the door to streamlining the System X production arrangements. The agreement that was worked out was that Plessey would become the prime contractor from the development point of view. Production would be shared between GEC and Plessey for a certain period and then it would become competitive. STC would pass all the System X information over and be entitled to all the remaining TXE4A orders for a certain period.

The long-distance application was the simplest to perfect – for example it involved no customer line cards and no customer administration or billing – and this part of the programme proceeded according to plan. The first long-distance System X exchange was brought into service at Coventry in 1983. The entire network of fifty-four long distance digital main network switching units was installed and working by 1985–6. Looking forward to Part VI, it is important to remember that all but the very last stages of the work which lay behind this were carried out by the public sector monopoly. It was a final public sector achievement in the network area.

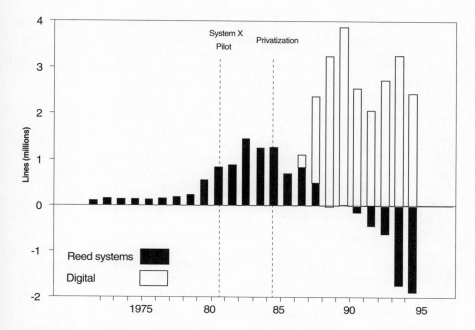

Figure 12.1   Electronic lines added to or removed from network in year 1972–95

So far as the local application of System X was concerned, on the other hand, it took five years from the signing of the first formal development contracts to the opening of the first local exchange to carry traffic, at Woodbridge in Suffolk in 1981. Figure 12.1 shows that no less than nine years then elapsed before the peak of the profile of introduction of the local application into the home network. (The peak in 1983 was of TXE4 and TXE4A.)

The operating units inside the PO had been awaiting digital switching with growing impatience for several years. The Regions were well seized of its prospective advantages over reed systems like TXE4 and TXE4A in terms of improved performance and facilities, lower maintenance costs and space savings. With the pressures they were under from THQ on operating efficiency, they wanted the best technology they could get. With the local pilot in service the Regional managers responsible for local exchange ordering decided that the time had come to run down orders for reed systems in anticipation of System X. As can be seen in Figure 12.1, the pace of modernization of the network checked accordingly. The expectation at the time was that the peak of local digitalization would be reached in the mid-1980s. It was not actually reached until 1989; and, as Figure 12.1 shows, reed systems did not begin to be replaced by digital and taken out of service until 1990.

The defects of the development arrangements were not without very real virtues of their own. David Leakey:

> System X ended up as probably one of the best modularized designs in the world, spurred by the need to split up the design between quasi-independent design teams.

This in turn has eased considerably the evolution of the System X design as more modern technology has become available, to the point where the System X of today is the result of several major detailed design upgrades. This has enabled the design to meet the ever-increasing requirements of size, power and special facility support required as the demands on the overall telephone network have increased well beyond that originally envisaged.

System X is respected today as among the best of its generation. Its concepts, in particular its modular structure and the power it gives for forward evolution, have influenced designers around the world. They are set to survive into the next generation. The system has been bought in volume by BT and in lesser quantities by its competitors in Britain; and some sales have been made in other countries. System X exchanges are performing very well in service. But, as the first real opportunity for Britain to break into export markets with its own technology, it missed its chance. William Barlow:

> I am sorry to say that after I left the momentum seemed to slow down and it was many years before System X was supplied in quantity. Although in the event it has turned out to be a first-class system, fulfilling all the wishes of those who were instrumental in the initial design, it came on the international scene too late to gain its share of the digital market which was going on round the world.

The early difficulties with development organization contributed at least a year's delay. The cable scandal and the reaction of Bill Ryland and the PO Board contributed a second year's delay for which the cable industry, which included two companies whose parent groups were also parents of two of the System X participants, must take a share of responsibility. The difficulties arising from the fragmentation of the industry spun the development process itself out over many years. The collective decision to award the line card development to STC was to lead to disproportionate stresses and delays, not appreciated at the time it was taken. But the most important single reason why System X failed in the export market was the time it took to get the local version into volume production once the pilot exchange had opened. It would be difficult to find a more graphic demonstration of the weakness of British industry in getting newly developed products into volume production.

The way companies organize themselves, the way they co-operate with partners, the resources they devote to development and industrial and production engineering, and the manufacturing capacity they create, are matters for the managements concerned and they must bear a corresponding share of responsibility for the System X story. But the PO and the IRC have responsibility also. They had an opportunity to catalyse the concentration of the industry on to one firm in 1968. The PO had a second opportunity to do so when the industry was weakened by the three-day week and the cuts in Strowger in 1975 and when two of the three firms were discredited by the cable scandal. There is a very good chance that had either opportunity been taken the development of System X and its manufacture could have been organized from the outset as it should have been, through a single sovereign firm. Had it been, what the engineers finally developed was such a good product technically that all the odds are that it would have succeeded on the world market.

Both in 1968 and in 1975 there were good pragmatic reasons for not seizing these opportunities. The PO was into the period of roller-coaster demand for connections described in Chapter 6, and modernization of the switching in the network was urgent. The delays that were actually to develop were bad enough. Measures severe enough to force change in the industry would have created violent dislocation of supply at the worst possible time. But the real reason these opportunities were not seized was much more basic. There would have been a major confrontation between the PO and one or more of the GEC, Plessey and STC parent groups, which would certainly have ended up on the desk of the Secretary of State. In the last few days of Ryland's term of office in 1977 I was present at a meeting with Eric Varley, then the Labour Secretary of State, who asked him why the PO did not use its procurement power to bring about the restructuring of the industry. Ryland replied, 'Because we could not be sure that you would back us.' Varley did not reply. Barlow's experience when he tried to detach STC told the same story. The real problem was the lack of political will for restructuring of the industry.

The long battle fought by the PO in the 1970s to establish Ericsson as a serious competitor on British soil finally paid off under George Jefferson after privatization; although even then BT's freedom to run its own procurement was constrained. The OFTEL report for 1985 summarizes what happened:

> Following BT's announcement that it intended to purchase a second range of digital exchanges – System Y – from Thorn Ericsson Telecommunications Limited instead of solely relying on System X produced by Plessey and GEC, the Director General received a number of representations and responded by making a thorough examination of the issues involved. The outcome was the document 'British Telecom's Procurement of Digital Exchanges' published by OFTEL in July 1985. After considering the broader implications for UK employment, exports and competitiveness, the Director General concluded that BT's decision to second source was acceptable and reflected normal commercial prudence. However, as set out in paragraph 1.53, he did put forward the view that, unless supply of System X suffered a major failure, BT should restrict purchases of System Y for the next three years to allow Plessey and GEC time to adapt to the new situation. BT expressed some reservations about this advice, but has since announced an acceleration of its programme of digitalization which may produce broadly the same effect.[4]

The cumulative effects of home telecommunications industry delays in the 1960s, 1970s and 1980s on service to the public and on the competitiveness of their colleagues in British industry generally can never be calculated. To anticipate the argument in Part V, the *threat* of operator competition from Mercury and cable TV certainly played a part in the BT decision to introduce Ericsson as a supplier of inland exchanges. But even with this powerful stimulus on their doorstep the British companies still took a disproportionately long time to get System X on the market in real volume. Operator competition and privatization were actually followed by a *delay* in digitalization and modernization compared with operating aspirations and expectations in the closing days of the PO management.

In Part IV we pick up again the story of the operating side of the industry.

Notes

1. Report of the Post Office Review Committee, Cmnd 6859 (HMSO, London, 1977), para. 12.17.
2. From a letter written for publication in the author's possession.
3. Appendix to Carter Report, Cmnd 6954 (HMSO), London, 1977), ASTMS Evidence, p. 446.
4. OFTEL Report 1985, para. 3.20.

Part IV
The Birth of BT

13 Collision of Cultures

At the time William Barlow left in the spring of 1980, senior management morale in Gresham Street was high. Whatever the immediate image of the service, the business had a remarkable ten years behind it. The wind was blowing more and more clearly in the direction of separation from posts; and that was what its managers wanted. Barlow had completed the necessary groundwork before he left, and Gresham Street was impatient to get on with it. At long last telecommunications would have its own board sitting in its own headquarters. The way should at last be open to introduce staff and finance structures which would help rather than hinder. There were other reasons for optimism. The change of government was clearly going to alter the industrial relations environment. Competition was going to bring its own excitements. The mood was one of expectation.

In the summer the government appointed Sir George Jefferson as Deputy Chairman of the PO. He took over as *de facto* Chief Executive of telecommunications and began to prepare to take over as Chairman of BT when it separated out.

Jefferson had had a distinguished career in high technology manufacturing industry. He had grown up in British Aerospace and had led its guided weapons division. Aged fifty-nine, he had a very clear personal vision of the way a successful company was organized and managed.

The world in which he had formed this vision had certain important similarities with that of PO telecommunications. He was himself a professional engineer. Electronic technology had an important role in both BT and British Aerospace. His former company had gone through its own series of constitutional changes, from private company to nationalized company and back again. The government – more precisely the Ministry of Defence – had been its principal customer and Jefferson had long experience of the defence interface between industry and Whitehall, as well as of selling in the exceptionally loaded environment of the world arms market. But there was nevertheless a big difference between Jefferson's world and that of PO telecommunications. British Aerospace was a big company. But PO telecommunications was bigger still and quite different in character. Jefferson, accustomed to manufacturing and to large groups of staff concentrated at a limited number of sites, now found himself in charge of a service industry with a quarter of a million people scattered across the whole face of Britain.

The conglomerate structure of the Corporation and the physical separation between Howland Street and the business headquarters had reinforced the idiosyncrasies of telecommunications. Sheer size, rate of growth and the all-absorbing character of the work had had an important influence also. The telecommunications business had become a world on its own. Jefferson had a certain amount in common with Howland Street, which had a strong admixture of people from outside, looked into the wider establishment and thought largely in its terms; but very little with Gresham Street or the Regions. Yet it was from the latter that he had to forge a new organization and a new way of doing things.

The insulation of Gresham Street from the world outside telecommunications had created an environment in which the business could continue to function – certain *mutatis mutandis* – as an enclave of Civil Service ways of doing things; and it was happy to do so. Apart from Fennessy and Benton at its head and Kember and Swallow in charge respectively of finance and procurement it had been and was still staffed almost entirely by people bred in the Civil Service; or at more junior levels by the generation recruited in the 1970s whom they had trained.

In the next few years Jefferson was to oversee a remarkable collision between business and Civil Service cultures which to this day has few if any parallels in scale or impact.

Fennessy had been dealing with the GPO for many years when he took over as Managing Director in 1969. He understood it. His approach was to accept the virtual impossibility of changing the system overnight in the circumstances of 1969, and to turn it largely as it stood to the running of telecommunications as much like a business operation as he could get it. When Fennessy first arrived he was speaking to Baldry, then Director Purchasing and Supply. Baldry said how much Fennessy was expected to change the organization. Fennessy, ever the realist, replied, 'I won't change you; you will change me.'

Many of the people in PO telecommunications had the instincts of outside business far more than the system had ever allowed them to realize or display; and Fennessy was able to bring out their qualities. As we have seen, under his leadership and that of Peter Benton PO telecommunications was remarkably successful in tackling the daunting operating problems it faced in the early 1970s. But the machine itself remained a square peg in a round hole, straining to do something for which it was not really built.

Jefferson's approach to this situation was the reverse of that of Fennessy and Benton. He had his vision of the way a company should be run. He did not take up time trying to understand the organization he had inherited or the mixture of disillusion and idealism which drove many of its most senior people. The THQ structure as it had stood just before his arrival had been based on close analysis of the special needs of a telecommunications operator, coupled with some of the best consultancy advice available in the world. Tom Peters, later to write *In Search of Excellence*, had been involved. But it still reflected the functional characteristics of the Civil Service system. Procurement, R&D, network matters, marketing, field operations and business planning were all functionally organized at headquarters level; and in some ways the relationship between the Senior Directors in charge of the main functions, the Managing Director and his two Deputies still resembled the top structure of a government department. There was good reason for these arrangements and all the indications were that they were working. Jefferson however now introduced an organization based much more clearly on division into line units, with each unit head responsible for his own command.

His overriding priority was change. He had a way of doing things which he was determined to make stick; and he was a determined man. The experiences of

Gresham Street once he arrived provide a rare opportunity to compare business and Civil Service cultures alongside one another in a very large organization. Thrown into relief in this way, the differences were profound.

The requirements of higher Civil Service work are unique and as different from those of business as chalk from cheese. Over the years a lot of very intelligent people had put a great deal of thought into the way in which the British Civil Service operated. It was one of the best in the world for reacting to Ministers' requirements. It could assess events, develop recommendations, secure Ministerial reaction and approval and initiate action at extraordinary speed. It was also good at follow-up. Its proven way of working at all levels was a piece of paper circulated to interested units, usually followed by a meeting whose outcome was meticulously recorded and then by equally meticulous follow-up by lower levels in the machine. Ministers and top officials lived in a world in which they had to be ready to move from one policy topic or event to a radically different one and then on to another almost at a second's notice month after month and year after year. The pressure was intense and unremitting. There was a premium on dissemination of information. With very good reason one of the worst crimes a department could commit was to land its Minister in a situation in Cabinet where a colleague complained that his department was not consulted on an important issue affecting it. There was a similar premium on co-ordination before action. Such practices are what we call bureaucracy when they get out of hand. But correctly channelled and driven against time they make for a very effective way of working.

Senior Civil Servants carry high personal responsibility but it is of quite a different kind from that of their opposite numbers in business and industry. The political positions of Ministers and even of governments can be rocked by failures in Civil Service work. Intellect, discretion and adroitness secure approval. Egos are the prerogative of Ministers and are at a discount for Civil Servants. Policy is by definition the personal responsibility of Ministers. Once decided, policy is executed by serried ranks of Civil Servants, but it is still Ministerial. Implementation may involve thousands, millions or tens of millions of individual cases and hundreds or thousands of junior Civil Servants to handle them. The system is designed to ensure that all of them have a clear picture of the principles Ministers wish to have applied. Internal communication is of the essence.

In an executive department like the old GPO some of these characteristics of course became blurred. If the primary business of the department is the collection of revenue and the spending of money on providing services, in practice officials have to carry heavy executive responsibilities personally. Ministers cannot determine detailed budgetary allocations, select and recruit staff, make technical judgements, disentangle service failures or answer for the handling of billions of pounds. But because the GPO was part of government the more important technical and operating issues were politically sensitive and had to be put to Ministers. One of the most delicate responsibilities of officials was to make sure that the terms in which this was done were balanced and correct. They had both to reflect the merits of the case and to be intelligible to busy Ministers preoccupied with Parliamentary and political business, reading them perhaps in the small hours of the morning after a gruelling day in the House. A single turn of phrase could swing a decision. It was not surprising that many hours were spent agonizing over the exact wording of submissions.

Senior GPO Civil Servants were well aware of the mismatch between the mix of responsibilities they carried and their pay and status. They often discussed it among themselves. But they knew there was nothing they could do about it.

The nationalized industry environment of the Corporation after 1969 imposed a new set of priorities. More and more of what had to be done resembled the tasks in business, with only limited openings for display of policy skills. Officials found themselves with personal responsibilities for spending or for technical decisions barely distinguishable from those of their colleagues in industry; except that the sums of money and the responsibilities involved were often enough to daunt the most self-reliant private business executive. The mismatch with private sector pay and other rewards was becoming more and more obvious. But the way the people thought about their responsibilities and the way the machine went about discharging them was still fundamentally that of the Civil Service. Chairmen and Board Members were seen as a kind of equivalent of Ministers. Policy decisions and the formal responsibility for them rested with the Board. If a policy was seen as wrong down in the machine it would still be meticulously carried out. (The Senior Salary Structure story was a peculiarly significant example.) Practically everyone had been a career Civil Servant and thought about their jobs in career terms. Knowledge was there to be shared. Group loyalty was immensely strong.

Nationalized status fitted the atavistic instincts of many PO people much better than Whitehall and in some ways better than full-blown private business would have done. As individuals many of them absorbed the nationalized environment and throve on it. Their job was to provide a specified service to the public at an acceptable level of quality; and steadily to improve the economic efficency with which they did it. They had to stay in the black and there was trouble if they did not; but they were not there basically to make profits.

The special demands of public monopoly could not be denied. If PO officials failed to do something, no one else was going to do it for them. As telecommunications expanded and ramified, the personal pressures this created were rising all the time.

The world of British business for which the organization suddenly found itself heading in the early 1980s was much more different from Gresham Street than either side really appreciated. Companies exist for making profits. The character and quality of services or products is called forth by the marketplace. Top management has considerable choice in how hard and in which directions it drives itself and its business. Excess demand or unpromising openings can be left to competitors. A new subject or a new product is worth pursuing only if it can make a contribution to the bottom line. Products and approaches may change but the budgetary, production and marketing processes and the priorities remain basically the same year in year out. Genuine policy issues do arise from time to time, especially in big companies, but by the standards of Whitehall they are few and far between. Their handling is the preserve of Chairmen and of Boards. Management rarely has much to do with it. Managerial prestige goes with the winning of business and the making of profits. Responsibilities are personal and advancement is gained by personal success. Egos are at a premium and diffidence is at a discount. Knowledge is power and should be kept to oneself. Group loyalty takes second place to self-interest. Paper is just a nuisance and bits of paper are often ignored. Managers are expected to be motivated by pay and perks. People often change employers several times in the course of a working life and think nothing of it. Things could not be more different from the Civil Service.

There are hundreds of thousands of businesses in Britain, of every conceivable kind. But because at bottom their objectives are common, business people share a common basic way of doing things and a sort of *lingua franca* of thinking and talking. There is only one Civil Service. Knowledge of its way of doing things is confined to those who work within it and is not shared with business people. Civil Servants have a very special language of their own. They do not generally speak the language of business, though some may learn it in the course of their work. This in itself creates a barrier between the two cultures.

The organization was accustomed to leaders who communicated. In the old days it had been used to Ministers, most of whom were long on speeches and grand designs even if they were short on action. As Chairman, Bill Ryland had dealt with Gresham Street on the perfectly justified basis that since most of the top people other than Fennessy had worked with him for years before 1969 they could be expected to know before they started what he wanted done; whether they did it was of course another matter. Fennessy had been pragmatic and downbeat but he had always made sure his objectives were thoroughly understood down the line. He had intervened in the design of a new management appraisal form to ask for emphasis to be given to results – a key lead. Peter Benton had an exceptional gift for communicating his vision.

The organization liked Jefferson and it earnestly wanted to learn his way of doing things. But his style was quite different from anything that had gone before. He had grown up in the secrecy-shrouded world of high-tech weapons. If there was to be any master planning it would be done and kept in his head. He expected the people immediately below him to know without being told that they had to work out their own salvation and what it would look like; and to compete with one another to achieve it. He judged them on their success in line with his own undisclosed criteria. The boundaries of the formal jobs he had appointed them to counted for a lot less than personal enterprise. It was a good mechanism for natural selection of entrepreneurs, and many individuals were to thrive on it. Anything more different from the Gresham Street way of doing things could hardly have been devised. But it was at least debatable whether breeding internal entrepreneurs should be the first priority. The organization was after all still a huge monopoly doing one essential job which needed a high degree of co-ordination.

Some important things were on Jefferson's side. BT staff were nothing if not members of the general population, caught up in the currents of national thinking. Many of them shared the growing public impatience with big 'corporatist' structures. They were conscious of their talents and wanted to exercise them and enjoy the fruits of their efforts as individuals. Jefferson went without hesitation for the jugular of the old system – the hierarchy. He went out of his way to flatten the sides of the pyramid. If a subject came to his attention he would deal directly with the middle-ranking specialists responsible, with little or no regard for the layers in between. The people concerned found themselves suddenly in direct touch with the very top authority of the company. They were encouraged to express themselves and to go away and act on their own judgement. They had never known anything like this before and many of them loved it. They responded accordingly.

But this approach had its downside as well. The old structure was repressive and intimidating. But it had important logic behind it. The PO hierarchy was a hierarchy not just of rank but of knowledge, experience and co-ordination. Bosses usually knew more about the work and had more experience of it than their subordinates. If they had come in higher up the system without having had to work their way up, they were expected to learn and learn fast and to contribute their own talents to the collective process. Bosses who did not understand what they controlled were not unknown but they were rare and they did not last. Jefferson's approach discarded the good as well as the bad of this. Important babies began to go out with the bathwater in what was after all the management of an essential public service with a daily job to do.

PO THQ had been a very busy place, with much less time for bureaucracy than its critics asserted. In the core of the headquarters, corner-cutting and bypassing of levels were essential if the work was to be got through. They were the rule rather than the exception. But, mavericks apart, the conventions were always observed, with good reason. Co-ordination was still at a premium, as it had to be in a business where everything interacted so much with everything else. A mistake in a detail of an engineering design installed in Land's End could cause accounting confusion in John o'Groats. Superiors and subordinates in direct touch across two or three levels always made sure that the intervening levels knew what was happening. Directors had an acknowledged right to intervene when they were bypassed in dialogue between their Heads of Division and Senior Directors. They were expected to use it to prevent things going off the rails.

The headquarters was expert at reading the wishes of top brass from small signs. Jefferson's style was read as meaning that he wanted no such conventions in the new set-up. People who were bypassed or left out had to fend for themselves. The 1979 headquarters reorganization had been meticulously administered and promulgated to everyone affected. The 1981 reorganization was not. People realized that they now had to find out the hard way where they fitted and what they were expected to do.

As usual personnel practices were central to what was happening. Under Jefferson's direction two key changes began to make themselves felt. The new BT was not to be a career organization. People at every level had suddenly to get used to the idea that they were quite likely to leave the company well before the end of their careers; and that people from outside would replace them, not promotees. They had to think in terms of finding other jobs in the world outside – something they had thought they had left behind for ever when they got into the PO. Many of the people who were to leave were good and relatively young. The chance to stand on their own feet and to recalibrate themselves by outside standards was to be something many of them would appreciate in retrospect. But it was still a sharp shock.

At the same time management was changing to personal contracts with confidential salaries and normal business perks like cars and health insurance. The significance of this change to people brought up in the old system is difficult to overstate. From pay being something which came up with the rations – with personal pay levels known for all to see which individuals could do only little to increase by their own efforts except by working for promotion – management pay suddenly became a personal thing. It was now dependent to an unsettling extent on personal performance. High pay levels were suddenly there to be attained by effort. Share options for managers and even golden handshakes for people who could get to the very top were on the distant horizon. Money abruptly talked. The value system by which the individuals lived was being changed for them. Some loved it. Some had reservations.

Jefferson was fanning an irresistible wind of change, and people had to go with it. The bottom line was adapt or leave. Jefferson knew that the new omelette was not going to be made without breaking eggs. He made clear that he knew that mistakes were going to be made and that he would tolerate them. But that did not make the growing pains comfortable. For some of those involved, before long they were to be very uncomfortable indeed. The whole thing was an excellent way of administering a shock to the people as individuals; and it was probably the only way the old mould could have been properly broken. But all sorts of stresses and inefficiencies developed as a result.

In retrospect Jefferson's achievement was extraordinary. For generations people had discussed the problem of Post Office reform. Benn and Ryland had grasped the stem of the nettle but they had not really succeeded in getting to its roots. In the seven years from his arrival in 1980 to his departure in 1987 Jefferson finally did the job for telecommunications; and he broke the back of it while BT was still a nationalized industry. At the same time so many other things which had created problems in the 1970s had also been changing for the better. The businesses had been properly separated and telecommunications was at last fully independent of posts. The extraordinary industrial relations environment within which telecommunications had had to work had been transformed. The way was clear at last for sensible personnel practices. In short the old set-up with its encrusted legacies from the past was gone, never to return. Jefferson and his colleagues had a clean sheet on which to write. They could look forward to a very different environment from that which their predecessors on the board of the PO Corporation had faced in 1969. The question now was what they were going to make of it.

The collision which Jefferson presided over between Civil Service and business cultures was the precursor of many which were to follow and which are still following as functions continue to be moved out of Whitehall proper to executive agencies or the private sector. Many people will read many different lessons into these experiences. The most important is perhaps that the central policy machine of a Civil Service department is designed for a totally different job from the managerial machine of an outside business. The sensible relationship between the two is one of mutual respect and of keeping off one another's patches. There are distinguished exceptions but generally speaking trouble comes when people from either try to do the other's job. The cards are just as much stacked against business people trying to pick up the work of central policy formation as against Civil Servants running business operations. Neither Civil Service nor business experience is a universal qualification for any walk of life.

The actual introduction of competition and the birth of BT as an organization in its own right took place in 1981. This is the subject of the next chapter.

14 Competition and the Birth of BT

As far back as the passage of the 1969 Act a young Conservative backbencher called Kenneth Baker had supported the separation of posts and telecommunications and had been one of those pressing for competition in customer apparatus. Baker was now appointed Minister for Information Technology in DTI. In *The Turbulent Years* he says:

> The [Telecommunications Act 1981] was essentially a paving measure which gave us powers to liberalize the telecommunications industry and to end its eighty year monopoly. To achieve this, first BT's monopoly of equipment had to be ended. When it came to telephones it was a case of Ford's famous dictum 'any colour you want so long as it's black' and there was a waiting list of 250,000 fed up customers. We wanted to see shops in the high street selling telephones and businesses being allowed to own their own private networks, using them as they wanted rather than how BT determined.[1]

The case as he states it here is somewhat off target. The first non-black telephones had actually been introduced in the 1930s. The first PO telephone of truly modern design had been the Trimphone, dating in conception from 1958. We saw earlier that the business had been responding to the prospect of competition in customer apparatus for twelve months before the Conservatives gained power. The 250,000 waiting list had had nothing to do with telephone instruments as such; and by 1981 it was a thing of the past. Legally, businesses had always been free to own and run their own networks. But however imprecisely Baker reflects the mounting pressure for customer apparatus competition at this time.

Pressure was also beginning seriously to stir for carrier competition. This undoubtedly owed much to the example of MCI in the USA. But it also owed a good bit to the distinctly unsatisfactory PO service record in the City, especially in relation to the local ends of private circuits for the financial community. They had an understandable desire to have another company to turn to for a resource of such importance to their operations. As we have seen, the rapidly growing demand for private circuits had become something of an embarrassment to the PO, not least because the clumsy arrangements needed to provide them cut across the pressing priorities of the public service. Private circuits were underpriced and unpopular in the field and as Peter Benton had found earlier it was not easy for top management to get them the attention they deserved.

The case for competition in provision of private network facilities had in fact been recognized in Britain since Victorian times. It is important to understand that neither the PO nor the GPO ever had a legal monopoly of in-house communications ('A-

A' in the jargon of the industry). As I myself can testify from my work on the 1969 Act, both the 1869 monopoly and the 1969 monopoly were carefully framed to exclude companies' internal networks. The crucial handicap which held companies back from constructing their own facilities or having them constructed in the old days was not our monopoly but the lack of wayleave powers for anyone but the PO, which would equip them to take the right to lay plant on other people's land; and corresponding powers in highways. All that would really have been needed to meet the aspirations of the City for private service competition was to make such wayleave powers available to other carriers providing private communications facilities for businesses. Had this been done in 1980 the way would have been clear legally for the private facility operations of the modern companies like Mercury and MFS without further ado. (In the event provisions in the Telecommunications Act 1984 had this effect as part of the wider changes made at that time.) In fact where physical paths independent of the PO already existed, as in the vacuum tube network under the streets of the City or alongside railway tracks, there was no reason why competing facilities to carry companies' internal traffic should not have been installed at any time.

Any lawyer could have told the companies that from this point of view the private circuit situation did not of itself either require or justify the ending of the monopoly of public carrier communications. It is difficult to believe that the motives of the City in pressing for the ending of this public service monopoly were unmixed. On published figures international public services were visibly highly profitable and inland long-distance public service only slightly less so. It was natural for City and Stock Exchange to want a piece of the action.

On 21 July 1980 the Secretary of State for Industry, Sir Keith Joseph, made a statement to Parliament about the relaxation of the monopoly generally. In the course of the statement he said that he had decided to commission an independent economic assessment of the implications of allowing complete liberalization for what are commonly referred to as value-added network services. In September 1980 Professor Michael Beesley of the London Business School was commissioned to undertake a study of the implications of allowing complete freedom to offer services to third parties over PO (BT) circuits.

The Beesley study also extended to the question of competition by operators constructing their own facilities. Since it was inevitable that companies who did this would want access to the profits available from long-distance public telecommunications, this automatically gave rise to questions to do with the public carrier monopoly.

The PO knew all about MCI and about the case for long-haul competition in the public service in the special case of transcontinental communications in the USA, fuelled as it was by the artificially high profit margins built up by AT&T Long Lines on long-haul calls (see Chapter 9). But the idea of a systematic policy of competing public infrastructures throughout a country as small as Britain was another matter altogether. As Part II showed, the PO could be proud of its achievements in public network matters in the 1970s and there was no justification in the record for ending the public service monopoly at all in this respect.

Peter Benton and the marketing function in THQ therefore mounted a spirited action in defence of the public carrier monopoly. But it was obvious to me from the start that it was going to be difficult to construct a completely watertight theoretical defence against policy-makers determined to introduce infrastructure competition on grounds of political or economic doctrine. There was no doubt that there would be considerable losses in efficency due to duplication in most of the network. But the principles of telecommunications engineering economics said that public service routes where the number of circuits was above a certain level, including many of the heavier long-distance routes in Britain, could be subdivided between two operators with no theoretical loss of efficiency. In one way or another this was going to be seized on by the proponents of competition.

In his Report published in January 1981 Professor Beesley proposed to allow what was termed resale of circuits in the home market – that is the selling-on of circuits rented in the first place from the PO; and his Report was favourably disposed to resale of international circuits.

So far as the public carrier monopoly was concerned, his Report said:

> Possible entry [of competitors] into transmission and switching is important as bearing on the options open to lessees of BT's circuits and on the basic direction of policy towards the regulation of BT's monopoly. *Economic evidence is poor* [italics added], but we see no merit in resisting such entry on the score of possibilities of increased costs; and a context of increasing competition in this sphere makes more tractable the task of regulation.[2]

On this lukewarm foundation were to rest a sequence of changes and approaches to policy in Britain which were to culminate in the investment by competitors of many billion pounds in competing public infrastructures.

The British Telecommunications Act became law on 27 July 1981. It duly established British Telecommunications (BT) as a nationalized Corporation standing on its own feet. After over a hundred years together, posts and telecommunications were finally separated. Section 15 of the new Act conferred licensing powers under the carrier monopoly on the Secretary of State, while leaving the Corporation in possession of the monopoly itself, which remained cast in the wording of the 1969 Act. Section 16 of the Act adapted the situation in respect of customer apparatus to give the Secretary of State or a person appointed by him the power to approve apparatus for connection to the BT network. The monopoly was ended.

The significance of these developments, and of the way the British government was to use its new licensing powers not just for Britain but for Europe and indeed round the world, cannot be overstated. The legacy of policy problems to which they have led is discussed in Parts V and VI.

With the monopoly brought to an end, the British customer apparatus industry began to square up to the new world it had so long sought. Its problems were yet to come. In the carrier area the Secretary of State used his new power to license Mercury Communications Limited. It had three owners, Cable and Wireless, itself recently privatized, BP and Barclays Bank (the two latter were later to drop out).

Sir George Jefferson had been recruited to chair BT as a nationalized Corporation, and that was the responsibility he now formally assumed. In the summer of 1981, rolling back the frontiers of the state was known to be on the government's agenda as a general matter. But there was no specific plan to privatize BT (see the next chapter).

Jefferson had gone out of his way to evaluate and recognize the qualities of the people he found at the top when he arrived. He had chosen all four of the line heads on his new Board from within the business. The allocation of responsibilities among the new executive Board Members and the resulting organization reflected his personal picture of how to run a company.

He was party to the general perception at the time that the future lay with service industries rather than with manufacturing. Translated into BT terms this meant an expectation that future growth in income and profit would come primarily from development of new services and applications, rather than simply from multiplication of the revenue of the existing services led by the telephone. So far as the network was concerned it was a necessary means to the end of development of new services rather than an end in itself.

The Marketing Executive (ME), created under the 1979 reorganization for just this job of developing new products and services, was beginning to get into its stride. It was deeply involved in the launch of the products of the Benton years of ferment, like Monarch, Herald and Prestel. With such an agenda on their desks the senior staff of ME were more than a little surprised to be lectured by Jefferson on 'thirteen wasted years' in the marketing area.

Jefferson now transformed ME into BT Enterprises, with the flagship role of developing the new activities on which the future would rest. Peter Benton was appointed to lead it as Deputy Chairman. I was appointed Managing Director Inland Division, with responsibility for the network and the Regions. Jim Hodgson was Managing Director International. Whyte was appointed Managing Director Research and Procurement. To the great pleasure of a lot of people Jefferson revived the title 'Engineer-in-Chief' for Whyte in his second role as overseer of engineering matters throughout the organization. Mike Bett was Board Member for Personnel; Doug Perryman Board Member for Finance; and Iain Vallance Board Member for Organization and Business Systems. The non-executive Board Members were Sir George Macfarlane, a distinguished engineer who had served on the Carter Committee and had been associated with the PO ever since; David Cormie, a distinguished accountant who was later to die prematurely; and John Lyons of the Engineering Managers Association. Apart from the Chairman and Benton the executive members were still a public sector group of people. Relative pay levels made that almost inevitable. Even Bett and Perryman came respectively from the BBC and the Coal Board.

Jefferson was under pressure both from government and from his friends in private business and the City to show results and show them fast. Telecommunications was becoming daily more important to business and to the finance sector in particular. They were not the people to accept less than the best in their supporting services and they were not hesitant to say so. He already knew from hearsay about the failings of PO telecommunications. He was determined to end them once for all by root-and-branch change; and he was impatient to get on with it.

In fact, as Chapter 9 showed, the operating situation Jefferson had inherited was better than it seemed or than he was disposed to take on board. It was a whole order better than that which Lord Hall, Bill Ryland and Fennessy had faced in 1969. Outside central London the machine was running reasonably smoothly. The job to be done now was to get London and private circuits right and then to lift operations generally from a plateau more or less of acceptability up a slope towards genuine excellence calibrated by North American standards.

Customer relations were a key part of the remaining problem. We senior people in Gresham Street felt thoroughly uncomfortable with the 'take-it-or-leave-it' and 'passed from pillar to post' approach over which we presided in the field. Theoretically it should have been easy to change to a system where the public could have a single point of contact for all their needs except actual service functions like operators; and to staff that point of contact with understanding and helpful people. In practice it was extremely difficult, not least because of the deeply rooted hierarchical psychology and the interest of the unions in preserving separation of functions. Such difficulties were typical of the reasons why the business was not getting the credit it deserved for the advances of the 1970s. There could not be a more a vivid example of what BT had to gain from the coming changes in the national industrial relations climate.

Internally Jefferson had spent the year since he arrived in 1980 building the bridgehead of his attack on the old set-up. Now he was his own master he was ready for the break-out. He began the real campaign.

Over the years since the Bridgeman Report the PO had evolved a complicated balance between devolution to the field and centralization on headquarters, which bred its own tensions. Jefferson's first year had made him particularly aware of the field side of this coin. With his experience running a British Aerospace division he could empathize with the Regional Directors and General Managers in their critical view of headquarters. He now placed great emphasis on the principle of devolution. He wanted to see the field units develop as independent profit centres, with maximum freedom from centralized domination. Soon after his arrival Jefferson had asked to see the documentation which embodied the Regional budgetary process. It did not fit his conception at all. He re-examined the McKinsey 'Red Book' and made clear that he thought it should have been implemented. He announced the intention to appoint a properly qualified accountant in each Area so that proper accounts could be taken out as a basis for treating Areas as profit centres. He seemed to have taken the measure of the field management and to have decided that as a group they could handle the freedom of fully devolved authority. These were ideas the field could understand, and it seized on them. The folk-consciousness of Areas and Regions had hankered after true devolution for fifty years. It seemed now really to be in sight.

The GPO way of managing the organization and its services had been strongly hierarchical. After the Corporation was created in 1969 things had gone on in the same way. Orders had continued to flow down and reports and information up through official channels just as they had done for four hundred years. The old structure had devolved a great deal of authority as far down as the Managing Directors of the businesses and their Managing Directors' Committees, which is where the real action was.

In the early days before the separation out of BT, Jefferson had set up a Chairman's Policy Committee which concentrated on personnel and similar issues. Those present at the meeting when Jefferson reported the discovery that there were now *eighteen* shelf feet of headquarters instructions would never forget the look in his eye. It resembled the look in William Barlow's when McKinsey told him there were four hundred committees; but it was steelier.

After the formal creation of BT, Jefferson did not institute a Management Board or any organization-wide equivalent of the old Managing Director's Committee. The headquarters had a huge amount of day-to-day business for which it had been required under the old hierarchical organization to seek high level sanction. It had been trained to go to the Managing Director's Committee for most significant operating decisions. It now found itself without any similar organ to go to or any laid-down channels through which to operate upwards. With the old authorization mechanisms gone the headquarters staff had to find a new way to operate and to handle issues, taking more responsibility themselves. The experience and the challenges it posed were an important element in the transition from the Civil Service environment to that of business. But there was more to it than that. Telecommunications as a discipline breeds intricate and loaded situations, in which technical, operating, personnel and finance issues are inextricably intertwined. Progress can often only be made by systematic discussion at high enough levels for all the issues to be brought into a single focus. People now had to hammer out their own ways around such problems.

The two new Executives created by the 1979 reorganization of THQ had just had time to build up their momentum when Jefferson began his programme of change. It was now interrupted as the business absorbed its second reorganization in two years and while Jefferson worked through his learning curve. It was to be further held back while government felt its way through the problems of privatization and the creation of the new regime. To people like Benton and me, seized since 1978 with the sheer urgency of change and impatient to exploit the spur of competition, the frustration and delay was not easy to bear.

The principle behind the new structure was devolution of operating responsibility to the Managing Directors of the line divisions. There was no difficulty in Whyte's command. Procurement and R&D had clear compact briefs which everyone understood. Things in BTI did not need to change much to fit Jefferson's perception. The unit had stood on its own feet for many years. Even with its limitations the PO accounting system had been able to separate out the financial performance of the international services. They were traditionally the most profit-intensive sector of the business. Now he was a Board Member Hodgson was able to forge ahead into the future on his own responsibility.

BT Enterprises on the other hand had a problem. The difficulty of the overlap with Inland and the 'thick slice/thin slice' issue discussed in Chapter 9 remained unresolved under the new organization. With McKinsey help it was re-examined in depth during 1982. But it was to persist in one form or another until the organization of the whole company was changed in the late 1980s.

The place which presented the real difficulties was Inland Division. The Division employed four-fifths of the staff of the business and represented corresponding proportions of revenue and expenditure. For these reasons alone the most challenging managerial problems had to be in Inland. The question was how best they could be tackled: there were various possible weapons in the armoury.

The first was to find a way to devolve authority and responsibility to the field units as they stood in a way which would really stick. For 40 years since Bridgeman the PO had been striving to find an effective formula. The experience with the implementation of the McCarthy settlement for the Shorter Working Week dispute had shown the limitations of devolution on the basis of the exisiting systems of the business. On such a basic matter as the hours worked by engineering staff, the exisiting pattern of controls and the efforts we had made to make answerability under them stick down the line had not been enough to prevent some Areas from making unduly generous settlements on the proportion of nine-day fortnights.

Would Jefferson's more thoroughgoing approach accomplish what the PO had never been able to do and provide an effective formula?

The second weapon was internal reorganization. Over the years there had been much discussion of possible ways of restructuring field operations. The problems had a lot in common with those of local authority organization. The 1969 reorganization had preserved the three-layer structure, with an intermediate regional level for planning and various specialized engineering and other functions. But as far back as the 1950s there had been talk of eliminating Regions and concentrating all field functions on larger 'super-Areas'. Such an arrangement would go a long way to expose Area management more directly to the real imperatives of the business at headquarters level.

The third was competition. Competition was now a fact. Could we find a way to use it to stimulate the great monolith of field operations?

I was impatient to give effect to Jefferson's lead on devolution. My time as Regional Director in Leeds had convinced me beyond peradventure that full devolution was the right way to run the field. If people were given the real responsibility they would respond. Headquarters could stop spoon-feeding the weaker field units and my own life should get easier.

One of the most important keys to improvement and to making devolution work lay in attitudes among first- and second-line supervision. The first priority was to reverse the damage done by the decision to exclude second-line supervision from the Senior Salary Structure, which was still a very definite factor in the situation. I had learnt from Tom Peters about the nuances of business organization. I knew the people and the value they placed on first-hand contact. I wanted to mark the start of my office as Managing Director by a clear sign that I regarded second-line supervision as management; and to couple this with a personal exposition of devolution to them and their superiors.

The obvious way to do this was to call together all Area management down to and including the second-line and talk to them in groups. In a normal organization this would have been easy. But in the existing BT organization the logistics were daunting. There were fifty Area offices and no one had ever contemplated a systematic tour of all of them in one go. In the autumn of 1981 I tried. But the experiment had to be ended with one visit left to make. My stamina gave out and I had to seek medical help. The old format was not going to be reformed simply by strenuous personal effort on the ground.

Iain Vallance and Mike Bett now began a radical programme of restructuring of the field operations of Inland Division and a programme to reduce overheads and headcount in face of the expected pressures from competition. The old three-layer structure of headquarters, Regions and Areas was replaced by a new two-layer structure with Districts formed roughly out of pairs of old Areas reporting direct to BTHQ.

Before Jefferson came we MDCT members in THQ had looked forward with real expectation to a Board which would steep itself in the problems of telecommunications and of the business itself. But priorities at the level of the main Board itself were now developing quite differently from that. There was only a minimum of discussion of the performance of the services and their problems; or of personnel or managerial issues. Uneasily the staff became aware that the fact that the Board now sat in Gresham Street did not guarantee the longed-for change in the Board's understanding of the business and its priorities.

The background to the decision to privatize is discussed in the next chapter. It was conveyed privately to the Chairman and by him to Board members. Derek van der Weyer, then Deputy Chairman of Barclays Bank and later to be Deputy Chairman of BT plc, was appointed to the Board to handle the BT end of the act of privatization itself. From then on, preparation for privatization became the overriding concern of the Board.

I had not been involved in the debates with Beesley. Now that carrier competition was visibly coming I had high hopes for it. I had spent the best years of my life trying to counter the slow-moving and reactive climate of monopoly. No one who had not experienced it could ever quite understand what it was like. It looked at last as though the time had come really to break out. If, as we were told, I and my colleagues had grown arrogant with the pride of monopoly, at least we could embrace its fall with alacrity. The prospect of competition had been engendering anticipation and apprehension among management and staff for several years. These attitudes were there to be built on. The performance of the inland operation had reached a sort of Camp Two on its upward climb. The next stage was going to be the hard slog of lifting the tolerable towards the best. I saw the impact of competition on the attitudes of management and staff as the most important single force to help with this. Led on by what I and my ex-PO colleagues were told about competitive business in the world outside, we had a vision of a regenerated organization operating in a completely new environment, with its remaining failings rooted out by the pressures of the market.

The PO Network Planning Department (NPD) and its predecessors, responsible for the development and operation of the long-distance exchange and transmission network, had a remarkable track record. Each generation of transmission technology since the 1930s had been taken up and exploited with real vigour. Long-distance transmission unit costs had been dropping for decades. Digitalization of the long-distance transmission network had been under way since the early 1970s. The PO was actually ahead of AT&T in this respect. NPD had a fierce and independent commercial tradition. Its people had long had aspirations to form a separate managerial unit to run the long-distance service as a whole, on the analogy of AT&T Long Lines.

With the help of McKinsey an organizational boundary was defined between the central main network including the new Digital Main Network Switching Centres and the rest. In the spring of 1982 a new unit was formed within Inland Division to run this central long distance core, to be called National Networks (NN). Inland Division was now divided internally into two – NN under Back and Local Communications Services under Iain Vallance. The idea behind NN was to create a unit symmetrical in responsibilities with the new long-distance carrier competitor. NN would have to compete because it would have nowhere else to turn. My hope was that competitive psychology would spread out from such a unit to the rest of Inland Division. I remained as Managing Director of the complete Division. The Commercial Secretary to Inland Division, G. J. Jones, reported direct to me on inland tariffs and relations with competitors, but otherwise all the work of the Division was devolved to Back and Vallance.

As I saw it, long-distance competition would give indispensable experience of how to react when local competition developed. The business knew its long-distance operations were efficient. Its inefficiencies centred in local operations. It was competition to these that would really matter and on which managerial hopes for the future were built. NN had ten thousand staff and it would form a real bridgehead for competitive psychology within Inland Division as a whole.

Back and his staff embraced their role with enthusiasm. NN began to separate out and run its field operations. The Specialized Services unit under Sidney O'Hara took the first serious steps into the new world of advanced business communications. John Boag measured up to the well-understood problems of long-haul network planning and began to face the quite new world of competitive tariffing. War games were held to try to understand how competition with Mercury would develop. Morale began to rise in a way never possible under monopoly.

I could see that a fair deal for Mercury on interconnection was absolutely essential if it was to develop the weight to match NN. I felt that it would be wrong for Back and NN to have to negotiate directly with Mercury, as their competitor. I took on the job myself, supported by G. J. Jones, the Commercial Secretary. We negotiated an agreement with Derek Evans, the first Managing Director of Mercury. (Both my 'Chinese wall' between the competing unit and the people concerned with negotiation with the competitors and this first interconnection agreement itself were swept aside when OFTEL was set up in 1984.)

The idea of organizational separation between long-distance and local brought up difficult problems of internal accounting. At first sight it should have been possible fully to separate the finances and to arrange a system of transfer pricing. Camilla Crump studied the question in depth. It turned out that the problem was as close to insuperable as made no difference. The intrinsic nature of telecommunications networks makes them very hard to subdivide for accounting purposes while they remain in the same organization. The only truly valid separation is that between sovereign units, of the kind which operates for example between operators in the international service. (In another form this problem continues to bedevil the present system of regulation, in a way discussed in Chapter 17.)

The creation of Mercury was bitterly opposed by many people in the unions. In the spring of 1983 the POEU began a programme of limited industrial action in protest. It was called off when the 1983 election was announced.

The government's plans for carrier competition at local level were progressively being unveiled. The basic idea was that competition would be mounted by companies offering a combination of telecommunications service and cable TV. Jefferson regarded it as of great strategic importance for BT to have a presence in this new world. In the spring of 1983 I established a new unit (which was later to become BT Vision) in Inland Division to organize and run this operation, under the direction of Donald Wray. BT bid for cable TV franchises in the first competition in the autumn of that year and secured five.

The most urgent questions arising from carrier competition were in the procurement area. As George Jefferson saw it, coming from the fiercely competitive world of aerospace manufacturing, competition in carrier operations coupled with the inexorable pressures of the stock market was going to make it imperative to bring about competition in procurement for real. As we saw in Chapter 13, he pushed the presence of L. M. Ericsson to its logical conclusion and introduced them into provision of exchanges for the inland service. The emphasis of general R&D policy was also changed. The long tradition of development funded by the PO and carried out jointly with the British suppliers and the idea of competitive purchase of a single standard product, which had reached their apotheosis in the System X arrangements, was abandoned. In future BT intended to rely more and more on proprietary products developed by the manufacturers on their own and selected by competitive processes.

Peter Benton resigned as Deputy Chairman at the end of March 1983; policy differences with Jefferson, particularly on regional devolution in customer equipment and systems, had become intractable. Whyte reached sixty and retired in the summer of that year. I myself had been struggling against ill-health ever since my tour of Areas in 1981. I resigned from the Board and left BT in the autumn of 1983. After a bare two years only Hodgson now remained of the original four line heads who had been found from within the business.

Jefferson now formed the Board which would lead the plc in its first years of life, with himself as Chairman, Derek van der Weyer as Deputy Chairman and Hodgson as Vice-Chairman. Inland Division disappeared. Its place was taken by Local Communications Services with Iain Vallance as Managing Director, and National Networks with Back as Managing Director.

Privatization is dealt with in the next chapter. Its effects and those of competition are taken up in Part V.

Notes

1. Kenneth Baker, *The Turbulent Years* (Faber & Faber, London, 1993), p. 75.
2. Liberalization of the Use of the British Telecommunications Network (The Beesley Report) (HMSO, London, 1981), para. 140 (j) (p. 36).

15 The Act of Privatization

[Lady Thatcher's] most celebrated achievements, the taming of the trade unions and the invention of privatization, emerged as much from events as from pre-meditation.

Joe Rogaly, *Financial Times*, 7 July 1995

PO telecommunications people had always been impressed by the performance of AT&T in the USA and the advantages it gained from being in the private sector. The bolder among them had canvassed the idea of transfer of their own organization to the private sector as far back as the 1960s. The idea had been seriously discussed under Labour in the 1970s.[1] As the decade wore on, discussion at the lunch tables in Gresham Street turned to the attractions of the BP fifty-fifty state/private ownership arrangement and the public dividend capital formula.

In *The Downing Street Years* Lady Thatcher made the economic case for privatization as her government saw it as forcefully as it has ever been put:

> But of course the narrower economic arguments for privatization were also overwhelming. The state should not be in business. State ownership effectively removes – or at least radically reduces – the threat of bankruptcy which is a discipline on privately owned firms. Investment in state-owned industries is regarded as just another call on the Exchequer, competing for money with schools or roads. As a result decisions about investment are made according to criteria quite different from those which would apply to a business in the private sector. Nor, in spite of valiant attempts to do so (not least under Conservative governments) can one find an even moderately satisfactory framework for making decisions about the future of state-owned industries. Targets can be set; warnings given; performance monitored; new chairmen appointed. These things help. But state-owned businesses can never function as proper businesses. The very fact that the State is ultimately accountable for them to Parliament rather than management to shareholders means that they cannot be. The spur is just not there.[2]

The echoes of her experiences with the problem state industries she inherited are unmistakable; and one can feel with her. British Leyland, coal and steel were becoming bottomless pits for subsidies, and the government was understandably losing patience with them. But her eloquent analysis did not fit BT.

In *A Conflict of Loyalty* Lord Howe gives an account of how the idea of privatization gained political impetus under the Conservatives:

> 'Privatization' was always a more conscious objective than reform of public sector pay, but for years it was never quite on the agenda. For most of my political lifetime

the much more negative label of 'denationalization' had been in use. So I am glad to accept the tribute paid by Christopher Johnson that 'it was a master-stroke of public relations on the part of the Thatcher Government to coin and put in world-wide circulation the word as well as the concept'. David Howell is credited with the invention of the word. But even with the more trendy name the idea's momentum was destined to increase only with the passage of time. This was also true of the extent to which the policy was able to command increasing political and public support. Our long-term aim was spelt out specifically in 'The Right Approach to the Economy' in 1977: 'to reduce the preponderance of state ownership in our community'. The key members of my Economic Reconstruction Group – Keith Joseph, David Howell, Nigel Lawson, John Nott and I – took that seriously. But our 1979 manifesto was light on specifics: we were committed to privatize only the National Freight Corporation and the 'nationalized shipbuilding and aerospace concerns'. Margaret had been fearful that a more extensive catalogue might frighten the floating voter . . .

But British Leyland was far from being the only public sector corporation that was to test my commonsense close to breaking point. Much the least predictable component in the whole of public finance during my years at the Treasury was the huge but erratic demand of the nationalized industries for cash: the Coal Board's annual subsidy in the 1980s exceeded £0.5 billion, and British Steel's worst single year cost almost twice as much.

And so it threatened to go on. This was probably the main reason why I spoke so strongly in a speech on privatization which I delivered to the Conservative free-enterprise body, the Selsdon Group, on 1 July 1981:

> It is only since the Election that the issue of privatization has moved to the very forefront of politics. Our experience since we have been in Government has convinced us . . . that the need for privatization, competition or, at least, private sector financial disciplines in the nationalized industries is even greater than we imagined in Opposition.

It was on the strength of that kind of diagnosis that we had launched early in 1981 two initiatives: first, a search for new ways of financing some nationalized industry borrowing for investment by means of private capital, thus enabling us to exclude it from the PSBR; and second, a fundamental shift in the relationship between sponsoring ministers and the boards and chairmen of industries, such as might transform their performance beyond recognition.

The Central Policy Review Staff, then under Robin Ibbs' energetic guidance, produced within a very few months an elaborate response of objectives, performance targets, reviews, reporting structures and the like, all under the oversight of a new Cabinet sub-committee (E(NI)) under the Prime Minister's chairmanship. And I began to put this into effect in face of a less than enthusiastic response from the Nationalized Industry Chairmen's Group. The limited practical results served only to fortify the case for a more radical approach.

The other proposal (for private sector capital) ran more or less similarly into the sand. Bill Ryrie, then one of my second permanent secretaries, conducted a study of the scope for this, as did Parliament's Treasury and Civil Service Select Committee. To the dismay of the industrial lobby, they came to much the same conclusion. In the words of the Select Committee: 'The arguments put to us for greater freedom for nationalized industries to borrow more on the private market do not seem to us to be convincing.' This conclusion, from which the Treasury certainly did not dissent, put a stop to the seemingly hopeful idea of privatizing the financing rather than the ownership (the debt rather than the equity) of the nationalized industries.

The Select Committee's report was published in the same month as my privatization speech. Taken together they were seen, in Christopher Johnson's words, as 'a very clear signal to many, in Whitehall as well as Westminster, that it was time to break the mould of the nationalized industries'. This all happened at a time when the key ministerial positions were held by enthusiasts for further privatization: Nigel Lawson at Energy, Nicholas Ridley alongside me as Financial Secretary to the Treasury, Patrick Jenkin at Industry and David Howell at Transport. Privatization was thus an idea whose time had come. The way was open for the extensive privatization agenda that was to find its place in our 1983 manifesto.

The privatization of British Telecom took place in 1984, as well as that of Jaguar and Enterprise Oil. Between 1986 and 1989 there followed British Gas, British Steel, British Airports and, finally, between 1989 and 1991, the water and electricity industries. One of the most successful privatizations, British Airways, was one of the longest to put into effect. The enabling legislation had been produced in 1979 but it was only after protracted litigation had been settled that the sale could go ahead in 1987. I have explained that one of the main arguments driving forward this whole process, from my earliest days in the Treasury had been the basic search for efficiency in the management of resources. The other main dynamic had been, in the words of my 1979 Budget speech, 'participation by people in the ownership of industry'. During the 1980s both these objectives were fulfilled.[3]

Telecommunications became caught up in the unsuccessful attempts to find financing sources for public industries independent of the PSBR to which Lord Howe refers. There was prolonged discussion of the possibility of issuing a 'Buzby Bond' to raise £100m. But the amount of money involved was marginal so far as the main finances of the business were concerned; and it had no real significance for the investment programme, which continued to rise steadily, funded essentially from internal sources.

July 1981 was to prove a fateful month so far as BT was concerned. In the first place it was the month in which the British Telecommunications Act gained Royal Assent. The businesses were legally separate and the new BT Board was formally taking up office. But there was a lot more going on than that. In *The Turbulent Years* Kenneth Baker, who by now was Minister for Information Technology in DTI, says:

> On Sunday 5 July 1981 [Lord] David Young and I had supper with Keith [Joseph] at his house in Chelsea in order to persuade him to push ahead with the privatization of BT itself. I had prepared a paper setting out a timetable; a Bill by the spring of 1983; a regulatory authority which would police the market and promote competition; Mercury licensed in 1983 to provide the first tranche of competition; other service providers licensed for private networks; sale to the public in 1983/84; more competition to be provided from local cable companies by 1990/91. This was the strategy that was agreed at that meeting.

BT would benefit enormously from being privatized. As a Minister responsible for a nationalized industry, in this case BT, I had to approve its tariffs, its wage settlements, its investment programme and its board appointments. Ministers are not best suited to do this. We were blamed for every little service failure; blamed if tariffs went up; blamed for any shortfall in investment and blamed for any strike. I could not see any upside at all. A business like BT should be run by businessmen and businesswomen, not second-guessed by Ministers who are birds of passage.[4]

The timetable was genuinely prophetic. There is perhaps a certain confusion of logic between the exasperation of Baker's colleagues with nationalized industry managers as a breed and his own sense that responsibility still rested with him as a Minister. But everyone in Gresham Street at the time would have cheered the last sentence to the echo.

Issues about the structure of the operating industry now surfaced, but they were pushed aside in the interests of progress. Baker again in *The Turbulent Years*:

> [In April 1982 Lady Thatcher] launched a spirited attack on BT and its monopolistic practices and overmanning – 'I want more liberalization before privatization'. As always there was a grain of truth in what she was saying, and she had been very well briefed by goodness knows who. She wanted new money to go into new telecommunications systems and not BT. She fought everyone like a tigress for an hour, landing broadsides on Patrick Jenkin, Nigel Lawson, Lord Cockfield and myself . . . I explained to her patiently that the strategy behind our policy was to give Cable and Wireless a licence to establish the alternative network, Mercury. If we tried to set up small networks or to break BT up into regional companies then the privatization would have to be postponed for five or ten years.[5]

Under Baker's urging the proposal to privatize BT in short order gained momentum rapidly. On 19 July 1982 Patrick Jenkin, the Secretary of State for Trade, made a statement to the House of Commons announcing the government's intention to go ahead (Appendix 1). In the course of this statement he made the following observations on finance:

> As a nationalised industry BT does not have direct access to financial markets. Its borrowing is controlled by Government and counts against the PSBR. To bring inflation under control these borrowings have inevitably to be subject to strict limits. But external finance is only part of the picture. In the past monopoly power has enabled BT to raise prices to finance investment without doing all that could be done to increase efficiency. Around 90 per cent of BT's investment programme, about £2,200 million this year, has been self-financed. By 'self-financed' I mean of course 'customer financed', BT's charges to customers not only cover current running costs, but are also paying for 90 per cent of new investment. As a result, charges have risen steeply while investment is still not enough. Unless something is done radically to change the capital structure and ownership of BT and to provide a direct spur to efficiency, higher investment would mean still higher charges for the customer. The Government, BT and the general public would find that unacceptable. We need to free BT from traditional forms of Government control.

The logic underlying telecommunications finances at this time and the government attitude to them deserve consideration in a little detail. The financial performance of the telecommunications business in the ten years up to 1982 is summarized in Table 15.1, taken from the BT Report and Accounts 1981-82.

What Patrick Jenkin said about BT finances may appear less than ingenuous. As Figure A2.2 shows, the business had actually been *reducing* prices in real terms for four

Table 15.1 PO telecommunications finances 1973–82

	1973	1974	1975	1976	1977	1978	1979	1980	1981	1982
Profit/loss for year (£m)	−9.7	−61.4	−194.5	154.7	365.4	326.6	336.4	129.1	123.9	457.8
Fixed assets net expenditure (£m)	625.5	696.4	787.2	915.9	834.6	844.6	996.5	1240.8	1304.8	1456.1
Changes in working capital (£m)	−1.7	111.3	139.8	−220.9	−63.4	67.7	49.3	111.3	−319.8	381.5
Capital requirements (£m)	623.8	807.7	927	695	771.2	912.3	1045.8	1352.1	1985	1837.6
Movement in net liquid funds (£m)	−7.5	−216.3	−22.4	216.9	278.9	79.1	−108.7	−460.2	41.8	−79.1
Net requirements (£m)	616.3	591.4	904.6	911.9	1050.1	991.4	937.1	891.9	1026.8	1758.5
Financed: internal resources (£m)	240.8	298	368.7	641.9	841.9	1039.5	1110	1070.3	1102.2	1630.9
external borrowing (£m)	375.5	293.4	535.9	270	208.2	−48.1	−172.9	−178.4	−75.4	127.6
Self-financing ratio (%)	38.6	36.9	39.8	92.4	109.2	113.9	106.1	79.2	111.9	88.8
Return as % of capital employed at replacement cost Target	–	–	–	–	6.0	6.0	6.0	5.0	5.0	5.0
Achievement	–	–	–	–	7.6	6.1	6.9	4.6	4.4	6.5

Note: 1973–80 PO Accounts Basis. 1981–82 BT Accounts Basis.

of the preceding five years. So far as efficiency was concerned, as Appendix 3 shows, the PO had been containing its costs at least as well as BT plc was to succeed in doing.

The factor which was really driving the increase in internally generated funds was not price increases but the growth of business and revenue, due to the inexorable growth of customer demand, as predicted by the Carter Committee. The volume of business at constant BT prices had been growing at the truly remarkable rate of 7.5 per cent a year, equivalent to doubling every ten years, ever since 1970 and was to continue doing so throughout the 1980s (Figure A2.1). The factor which was holding back investment in the network was not shortage of funds but industry performance and the delays to System X.

The truth was that the cash flow and the profitability of the business had grown to the point where over time it was now self-supporting in terms of capital for investment in its plant. Even in a completely abnormal year like 1980, with costs going through the roof owing to outside inflation and a return on assets artificially suppressed below normal target requirements, it could still finance 86 per cent of its requirement for investment from internal sources. Right up to 1996 BT plc has never needed to go to the market for money for investment in fixed assets.

It was straining belief just too far to imply as Margaret Thatcher does that a private management operating a business with a cash flow as assured and growing at such a rate as that of telecommunications would have been motivated in the real world by fear of bankruptcy. An objective observer might have seen the situation in 1982 in very different terms from the Ministers of the time. PO telecommunications, as a public sector authority, had had its financial target reduced by the Conservatives. But partly as a consequence of private sector shortcomings it was still generating more cash than it could invest. This situation was being exploited by government for political purposes to reduce the Public Sector Borrowing Requirement.

The profitability figures in Table 15.1 and Figure 15.1, which plots cash profits over the whole twenty-five-year period, provide a similarly different perspective on the decision to privatize; and they also suggest an explanation for the replacement of the target system after privatization by the price cap mechanism (see Chapter 17). The information in Table 15.1 was published in the 1981–2 report and accounts, just at the time of Patrick Jenkin's statement. It was obvious to anyone who cared to look at the figures that, given a system of regulation which did not directly constrain profits, BT could rapidly become a profit-generating machine of a remarkable kind, with all that that meant for the stock market and for the price the government would get if it was sold. Once the programme of privatization was decided on in principle for ideological reasons, BT was an obvious candidate to put near the top of the list.

With the government committed in principle to privatization, attention now shifted to devising the regime within which BT was to operate. It was a job which had to be done virtually from scratch.

One issue was absolutely central. It was essential to convince public opinion that the new company would operate in a regime which would guarantee restraint of prices and profits. Given the picture of overstaffing and so on which Ministers had chosen to paint, it was also necessary to be able to point to a new mechanism for encouraging improvement in efficiency. US experience with the Bell system had vividly demonstrated the limitations of regulation of large private sector telecommunications companies. Logic, as well as the government's own political

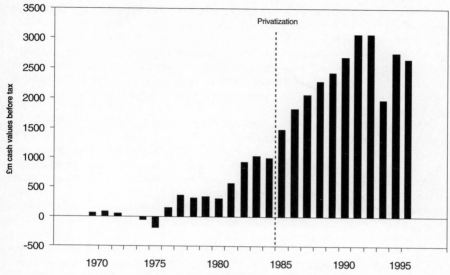

Figure 15.1   PO and BT declared profit 1970–95 (£m cash values before tax)

doctrine, pointed to maximizing competition and minimizing dependence on regulation. It was obvious that BT was going to have to work within a framework of regulation at the start. The question was how to frame a regime which would enable Ministers to predict convincingly the development of competition across a sufficient range of activities within a sensible time-scale.

(The basic framework for competition had been set by the 1981 Act.)Work had been going on for some time on the arrangements for competition in customer apparatus. Mercury was up and running and long-distance competition could fairly be said to be in prospect. But it was BT's local carrier activities which constituted the bulk of the operation and the core of the problem. Local telecommunications were a notoriously unpromising area for the making of profits. How could a regime be created which would promote competition in this area?

The government faced something of a dilemma in undertaking work on such issues. The great weight of UK expertise and experience in telecommunications matters was concentrated in BT itself. But the whole point of the new arrangements was to create counter forces which would contain BT and put pressure on it. The poacher could hardly be invited to participate in drawing up the tactics of the gamekeepers. BT must be given the right to comment and to argue its own case; but the government turned elsewhere for help with its formative thinking. BT people like me and Gordon Pocock had been used to dealing with DTI in bilateral discussions conducted in private, at which we had the standing of experts from a major public sector authority dealing with their sponsoring Department. Suddenly we found ourselves attending meetings called by DTI to discuss policy which were also attended by an intentionally wide range of outside interests, from professional trade associations to consumerists. Not only had BT lost its privileged status almost overnight, it was now in the dock.

The trade associations were as expert as BT itself in their respective fields. But through no fault of their own the other participants in the discussions were a long way back down the learning curve. The government turned to the academic community. Professor Stephen Littlechild of Birmingham University contributed the idea of 'price cap' as distinct from return on asset regulation of prices (see Chapter 17). But advice was needed from people with hands-on experience and knowledge of running telecommunications who were independent of BT. The government turned to the USA.

Developments there had already proved a very important source of inspiration for competition in customer apparatus and long-distance carrier operations. The US cable TV industry was very well established. Cable was big business in the States, and the industry was profitable and assured. It was beginning to eye telecommunications as a related field which it might set out to conquer. The cable TV and telecommunications customer distribution networks had a good bit in common, even though they were dissimilar in the details of their functioning. In Britain the Carter Committee had devoted a section of its Report to cable TV.[6] It had foreseen that the wideband cable TV systems of the future would in principle be able to carry telephone service as well as TV programmes. The government and its advisers realized that such a coupling of local telecommunications with cable TV might hold the answer to the problem of fostering viable competition to BT at local level.

The cable TV industry had a chequered history in Britain. There had been private operations in certain areas which were notoriously hard to reach from the main off-air transmitters, like parts of the south coast. Under Labour the PO itself had mounted limited operations to make aerials unnecessary in new towns. But cable TV remained a niche operation. The British private interests were well aware of the money that was being made out of cable TV in the USA. They saw a golden opportunity in the developing thinking of the government. A natural alliance rapidly formed between them and the DTI. The idea of a unified 'grid' to deliver all kinds of electrical communication – telecommunications proper, TV and computer communications – had been around for a long time. James Martin had just written *The Wired Society*, whose closing chapter had overtones of encouragement of enterprise by smaller business which appealed to Thatcher thinking. Now it seemed it was all coming together. Enthusiasm abounded. The government set up a high-level Information Technology Advisory Panel parented on the Cabinet Office to map out the new world of combined cable TV and telecommunications and begin to build the Conservative Information Society. BT was invited to give evidence to the Panel. But it was now firmly in the position of defendant in a court presided over by government itself.

In April 1983 the government issued a White Paper, The Development of Cable Systems and Services. The paragraphs summarizing the position in telecommunications said:

> Cable's relationship to the national telecommunications structure has to be considered against the government's wish to increase competition in the provision of telecommunication services and apparatus so that industry and the consumer can benefit from resulting improvements in efficency.
>
> The existing national telecommunications operators, BT and Mercury will not be given the exclusive right to run cable systems nor will their participation in every

cable consortium be mandatory. *They will however be free to compete with other cable providers* [italics added]. In addition:

> (1) BT and Mercury will retain the exclusive right both to link local cable systems and to provide voice telephony services on local systems . . .[7]

With the dies of privatization and competition now fully cast in principle, Baker and his colleagues were impatient to gain political mileage. As 1983 wore on, things began to move rapidly. (For a detailed account of events in this period see Baker, *The Turbulent Years*).[8] A Telecommunications Bill was drafted to convert BT into a public limited company owned wholly by government, to embody the new statutory framework and to establish regulation. A parallel Bill was drafted to give effect to the cable White Paper and to establish a regulatory authority. Bryan (later Sir Bryan) Carsberg was appointed as the first regulator (see Chapter 17). Both Bills were introduced into Parliament and became law in the summer of 1984. The government offered just over fifty per cent of its shares in BT for sale on the market in late 1984. The issue was over-subscribed several times over. (A second tranche was sold in 1991 and the remainder in 1994.)

BT had been privatized; and in political and City terms government had a major success on its hands. All the stages of the process, from the first knockings of work on competition to the act of privatization, had been carried through in something over three years, interrupted by the 1983 election. The changes which culminated in the PO Act 1969 had been substantial but considerably less radical and far-reaching. They had taken nearly five years, interrupted by the 1968 election. Baker and the government had accomplished a full-scale revolution in UK telecommunications. But it had been carried through too fast for proper thought and proper attention to basic issues like structure; and with the principal focus of know-how – BT – largely excluded from the formation of policy.

The first of the dynamics driving forward Lord Howe's personal belief in denationalization and privatization was the basic search for efficiency in the management of resources. Whatever Ministers thought, Gresham Street had shared this dynamic for a decade or more and it had the results to prove it. We former PO people also echoed from our hearts Lord Howe's conclusion that a fundamental shift was needed in the relationship between Ministers and Boards and Chairmen. Against such a background we accepted without hesitation the prospect of privatization and pressures from the stock market.

In Part V we shall see how it has all worked out.

Notes

1. See T. O. Lloyd, *Empire to Welfare State* (OUP, London, third edition, 1986), p. 483.
2. Margaret Thatcher, *The Downing Street Years* (Harper Collins, London, 1993), pp. 677–8.
3. Geoffrey Howe, *Conflict of Loyalty* (Macmillan, London, 1994), p. 253. There is a footnote on p. 255 of *Conflict of Loyalty* which says: 'There was in fact only one possible – and perverse – advantage in having any of these industries in the public sector at such a time of economic turbulence: the government's almost open-ended ability (if such it was) to fund short-term losses in face of strike action, until the strike was defeated. It was this consequence of nationalized status which led to management "victories" in steel and coal in 1981 and 1984.' This note was correct in its application

to telecommunications. The ability of the business to borrow from the Bank of England on state security had enabled it to sustain without difficulty the effects of the CPSA action holding up billing – see Chapter 8.

4. Kenneth Baker, *The Turbulent Years* (Faber & Faber, London, 1993), p. 78.
5. *Ibid.*, p. 80.
6. Report of the Post Office Review Committee, Cmnd 6859 (HMSO, London, 1977), p. 108.
7. The Development of Cable Systems and Services, Cmnd 8866 (HMSO, London, 1983), paras 243–4.
8. Baker, *The Turbulent Years*, p. 80.

Part V
The 1980s Regime

16 Privatization at Work

British Telecom was forced yesterday to admit that its services had deteriorated this year as a highly critical report by a Government watchdog showed the number of complaints had risen by 130 per cent in 12 months.

The Times, 27 October 1987

Once competition had been introduced and BT had actually been privatized, the political imperative was to try to make the new arrangements work and to present the effects of privatization and the working of the regime in the best possible light. No prizes were going to be given for dispassionate scrutiny of how things were working out in reality. Competition had by 1996 been running for fifteen years and privatization for twelve. The regime is well past the running-in stage. The time has come to look critically at its performance with a mind to the future.

In *The Downing Street Years* Margaret Thatcher summarized the effect of privatization on BT as follows:

The consequences of privatization for BT were seen in a doubling of its level of investment, now no longer constrained by the Treasury rules applying in the public sector. The consequences for customers were just as good. Prices fell sharply in real terms. The waiting list for telephones shrank and the number of telephone boxes in operation at any particular time increased. It was a convincing demonstration that utilities were better run in the private sector.[1]

This confident statement provides an agenda for examination of the effects of privatization in practice.

It is true that in cash terms investment doubled between 1983 and 1990; but it is also true that in the same terms it had doubled between 1978 and 1982. In both cases the expansion was in line with five-year plans for both investment and its funding agreed between the Corporation, DTI and Treasury well before privatization. As we have seen, the rise in expenditure due to digitalization was actually delayed compared with the last public sector five-year plan. Also as we have seen, apart from the special circumstances of 1973–4, after 1970 investment in the main operations of the business was never constrained by the Treasury under either Conservatives or Labour. The only real constraints on the ability of the PO to invest in the 1970s had been the performance of the private sector suppliers and the delays to System X. So far privatization has had no significance for the funding of investment in plant; BT plc has not raised any money in the market for this purpose.

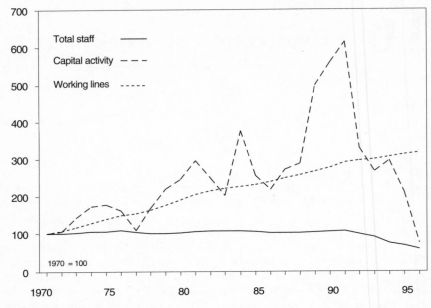

Figure 16.1   Staff and activity (capital activity-lines added or modernized) 1970–95

The clear implication of what Lady Thatcher says about prices is that the improvement in management and cost control following privatization led to an unprecedented drop in real prices. Appendix 2 examines in detail the pricing record in terms of real changes in overall PO and BT prices over the whole period 1970 to 1995. The cost control and service record is examined in Appendix 3.

Many people regard staffing levels as a measure of efficiency. PO staffing was and BT staffing is dominated by field requirements. As we have seen, field staff productivity had steadily improved throughout the 1970s. By 1982 field staff had been three thousand fewer than they had been in 1970, where the network and the annual growth of the network had both more than doubled in size, and investment activity had risen by even more.

PO planning around 1980 assumed that the huge field machine which had had to be built up to handle growth and modernization and its labour force were going to have to be kept in being up to the mid-1980s. Strowger maintenance procedures were so labour-intensive that this in itself was going to continue to add to requirements until Strowger was eliminated. The problem, and it was a testing one, was to hold numbers constant in face of this ever-increasing workload. But from the mid-1980s onwards we expected that requirements and especially engineering staff requirements would begin markedly to contract. There would be a substantial reduction in workload, arising from the reduced rate of growth of lines, the reduction of capital activity due to completion of modernization and digitalization and the effect of these on maintenance and other costs. The back would also finally have been broken of computerization of office processes. The effect was bound to be a major reduction in field staff requirements.

The contraction in workforce we were expecting as a result towards the end of the 1980s was very considerable. In 1980 the combined staff in all the categories affected by the expected contractions in workload in the later 1980s numbered a hundred thousand. The effect due to the contraction of capital activity alone was going to be considerable whatever happened; staff on capital works accounted for 29 per cent of the engineering workforce in 1980, or about thirty thousand people.

Figure 16.1 shows what actually happened. After privatization numbers remained constant up to 1990. Capital workload then dropped dramatically; and growth in lines, which had peaked at 1.29 million in 1979, dropped to 0.5 million a year (see Figure 6.1). New technology finally bit into maintenance and office workload. Overall the task of the company's labour force reduced by a whole order. Just as numbers had had to be held up to face the ever-growing workload of the late 1970s, so the right thing now was to shed labour. Outsourcing was also saving heads if not costs (see Appendix 3). Staff dropped by 40 per cent.

There is only one correct way to manage staff numbers: to adjust staff continuously as workload fluctuates, maintaining sensible levels of pressure on individuals and sensible levels of overtime, and seizing every opportunity offered by advances in technology or changes in working practice to reduce workload and increase productivity. That is what the PO had done since the 1960s and what it was planning to continue to do before privatization; and it is apparent from Figure 16.1 that this is what BT plc continues to do. That is good management.

To sum up the staffing story of the whole twenty-five years:

- The field productivity record before privatization was highly creditable. Between 1969 and 1982 field staff declined by three thousand, where the network and the annual growth of the network both more than doubled in size and investment activity rose by even more.

- By the end of the 1970s headquarters staff in the broad sense accounted for 16 per cent of total staff, owing in part to the absorption of a share of the old CHQ at the time of separation of posts and telecommunications.

- Within this group the headquarters proper undoubtedly became overstaffed in the year or two immediately before privatization.

- Following privatization and competition, total staff numbers remained remarkably constant up to 1990.

- Since 1990 total staff have dropped by a hundred thousand or 40 per cent.

- Total current account expenditure at constant prices has, however, dropped only by 9 per cent (see Appendix 3).

The PO managed its main mass of manpower well and BT continues to do so. The stringent price caps imposed since 1990 (see Chapter 17 and Appendix 2) may well have reinforced management's determination in tailoring staff to load. But *no* reduction in head count is traceable to privatization or competition as such.

The findings on economic performance overall from earlier chapters and from Appendices 2 and 3 may be summarized as follows:

- As we saw in Chapter 5, there was a violent price increase in 1975. It arose partly because increases which should have been made earlier had been suppressed for political reasons and partly because up to that time the PO had had no effective budgetary or money cost control mechanisms.

● In the years following 1975 the PO instituted such mechanisms and they visibly worked.

● Prices were consciously held down between 1978 and 1980 (see Chapter 8) but were forced briefly to spring back up again in 1981, following exceptional general inflation in the preceding period.

● Apart from this there have been real price reductions in every year since 1976; and those in the years 1978-80 were actually greater than those in the years which followed privatization.

● The principal factors driving these reductions both before and after privatization have been technology and the continuous rise in volume of business and revenue, foreseen by the Carter Committee as long ago as 1977 (see Chapter 5).

● Cost control has made a contribution to the reductions, but there is an unmistakable pattern of *relaxation* of cost control in the years following the formation of BT compared with the closing years of the PO, coupled with a marked decline in service in 1987 (see Appendix 3).

● The PO pace of improvement in economic efficiency was restored only after the regulator intervened with stringent price caps in 1991 (see Chapter 17).

Contrary to what Lady Thatcher asserted and to the received view there is therefore *no* evidence so far that significant gains in efficiency or real reductions in the overall price envelope have arisen as a result of privatization or of competition as such. It is true that certain prices have dropped under the influence of long-distance competition. But the overall price envelope within which these reductions have occurred has been dropping and continues to drop anyway in real terms, basically because of the effects of growth of business and advance in technology on unit costs. It appears that within this dropping envelope all that competition has done is to push in the price 'balloon' in one place and cause it to go out in another, as BT has rebalanced prices between long-distance and local calls.[2]

Privatization as such has therefore produced very much less improvement in BT's economic performance than Lady Thatcher was led to believe or than is usually claimed for it. The same is true of competition, a point to which we shall return in the next chapter.

If we turn to the other features of Lady Thatcher's summary, we find that, as Chapter 6 showed, the 1980 waiting list was due more than anything to the extraordinary and unforeseeable behaviour of the national economy in the mid- and later 1970s. In contrast to earlier waiting lists it was fully mastered within a year or two. On the other hand she was more right to refer to coin-boxes than perhaps she knew. The PO had never learnt properly the lesson from the USA that coin-boxes are so visible that the service is judged by them almost to an unfair extent. The original 1950s pay-on-answer STD coin-box had turned out to be a serious liability. The design of kiosks had not changed since the 1930s. While still state-owned, BT had set in hand a programme of re-equipment with the 'blue' boxes familiar today and with cardphones; and redesign of the kiosks. It was left to the plc to shake off the ungenerous provision policies of the past and actively to increase the numbers on street corners, correctly treating kiosks as an integral part of the main service.

Lady Thatcher made no reference to service in a general sense. So far as the quality of the telephone service itself is concerned, the most striking feature of Figure 5.2 is the steady improvement which began following the PO decision to modernize the network in 1973. The only obvious effect of privatization or competition on this is the temporary setback in 1987. There was a significant setback to other features of service at the same time (see the quotation at the head of this chapter). Since 1987 however there has been a substantial improvement in public perception of the service and of the way it is offered.

In stock market terms the original flotation of just over fifty per cent of BT in 1984 was the first and perhaps the greatest success of the early programme of privatization of state industries. The shares were over-subscribed to record levels. Also, it may have been more luck than judgement but it turned out that the timing of this first tranche of sale of equity could hardly have been bettered. The national economy and with it the company were about to enter the longest single period of sustained growth in recent history. The back had been broken of the problems of growth and service. Digital and cellular radio technology were becoming available. The long-drawn travail of the development of System X and the associated wrestlings with procurement arrangements were nearly over. Telecommunications had just been separated from posts, and government was embarked on the reform of industrial relations. As a general matter, and in very marked contrast to the years of the Corporation, the mid- and later 1980s were to be remarkably free of serious external problems. Overall, the strain on the organization and its management was greatly reduced.

Against this background it is not at all surprising that the act of privatization emerged as it did as a success and that the share price rose abruptly just after privatization and continued to rise steadily throughout the first decade of privatized operation. The resulting euphoria has pervaded attitudes ever since. But this is not an adequate basis for consideration of future policy, either in Britain or in the many countries who are looking to Britain as a model. We need to look more closely and dispassionately if we are to arrive at the real story, which is much more complicated and much more of a continuum with the past.

In the first place many important changes other than privatization and competition occurred in the early 1980s, many of them instituted by the Thatcher government itself. The separation of posts from telecommunications ended the awkward relationship between the telecommunications business and its directing Board which had so bedevilled the 1970s; and made possible for the first time personnel and industrial relations approaches geared to the characteristics of the businesses. The persistent failure to recast the personnel structures of the basic staff was one of the biggest single handicaps which the business faced under the combined PO Corporation. The separation out of regulation and the creation of OFTEL were important advances in their own right. Finally there were the growth of consumerism, the rise in public expectations for public services and the industrial relations reforms.

Internally both service and field workforce productivity had been improving steadily for many years by 1984. Even George Jefferson's appointment dated from 1980, before any serious mooting of the privatization of BT. The internal revolution for which he was responsible was already well under way by 1984.

The fundamental changes in technology and especially in network technology had already been going on for well over a decade by then. The first digital transmission systems were introduced into the PO network as far back as 1967, and the first trials of stored-programme-controlled exchanges were carried out at much the same time. By the early 1980s the changes in PO procurement policy made in 1969 and the early 1970s were finally beginning to bear fruit. Ericsson had been established as an alternative UK-based supplier. The convergence of computing and telecommunications in customer apparatus and services had been under way and the PO and its successor had been responding for several years. The computerization of telecommunications office processes which was at last gaining speed had been in gestation for over a decade.

In such a complicated situation it is not possible to pick out effects attributable to privatization or competition as unique agents; and it is artificial to try. We need to look at the story in a different way.

As we have seen, the PO Act 1969 which applied to the PO the formula devised by Herbert Morrison for the main Labour nationalization programme in the 1940s was regarded at the time as a major advance. On paper it gave the PO considerable freedom to manage its own affairs. But in reality there was a long way still to go. The most important single reason why the Morrisonian formula did not succeed more than it did in the PO case can be expressed in one word – governments.

A struggle runs through the earlier pages of this book – the struggle by those who ran and run telecommunications in Britain to try to do the job as they perceive it, as they want to do it and as the public deserves. The story of the 1960s is about the struggle to shed the ill-fitting straitjacket of the Whitehall Civil Service, which achieved only partial success in 1969 and *mutatis mutandis* continued throughout the 1970s. The other feature of the 1970s was the struggle for freedom against union influence on Labour governments in telecommunications matters. William Barlow's experiences recounted at the end of Chapter 8 are a telling case in point of the difficulties of the relationship with the Conservative governments. The inability of the PO Corporation to achieve decisive freedom in this respect was the most important single handicap on its performance during its twelve years of life.

In these terms privatization seemed at the time to be something heartily to be welcomed as a final step on the road of freedom, which would be decisive in a way which none of the earlier steps had been. But things were not to prove to be as simple as that. Privatization has substituted the stock market for the unions and regulation for the direct oversight of the DTI; and the constraints which these new forces have turned out to impose are just as significant in their own way as their predecessors. But on top of that the involvement with government proper and national politics has not gone away. Telecommunications and the other main utilities are so big and so integral to the fabric of modern society that whatever the nominal freedom they enjoy in the private sector they will always be subject to political attention; and their boards will always have to take account of the pressures which it sets up.

This is important in considering basic policy. In theory privatization coupled with competition should operate to drive out inefficiencies in pricing, like the permanent disposition to over-price long-distance calls and to under-price local calls and rentals. But such matters have such great political significance that it is most unlikely that real market forces will ever be left free to operate in respect of them. Certainly they have not been in the UK case, where rentals in particular were constrained for several years in the recent past by their own price cap.

Judged in terms of telecommunications experience the most important single advantage of privatization is not that it confers anything like total freedom from government; but that it forces into the open relations between the industry, government and government agencies like regulators. Given that governments and their policies will always affect and be affected by the big utilities in important ways, the chairman of a plc is free publicly to criticize them and their regulators in a way in which a chairman of a nationalized industry could never do.

Privatization has had certain obvious and predictable consequences. Freed from the constraints of the public sector, Board and other salaries have considerably risen. The fact that salaries and wages under the Corporation were determined by public sector policies did not prevent very considerable advances for the mass of telecommunications staff in the 1970s; but it did severely reduce the incentives available at top levels and therefore the attractiveness of the posts to outside talent. By setting the company free to pay going rates for the people it needs, privatization has eliminated this problem. Privatization also offered a badly needed opportunity at last to reverse the damage done by the Senior Salary Structure decision back in 1971 and to raise the morale of first- and second-line supervision.

The financial target system held PO profits to a defined level, which was not supposed to be either fallen below or exceeded. Freed from this constraint, profits have markedly increased (see Figure 15.1).

But higher pay and higher profits are only part of the story. The managers of companies in general business face real nail-biting competition, and benefit from its stimulus. The acid test of the regime in which a privatized utility operates is how real the competition which is organized for it to face actually turns out to be. There is nothing more calculated to keep complacency alive than a threat which loses credibility as experience of it grows. This is one of the most important single issues for the future. We shall look closely at it in the next chapter.

In theory the stock market has brought a new and more powerful set of pressures to bear on BT's efficiency of operation and on extracting the maximum return from existing investment. The compulsion to face these pressures should give the management of BT plc the advantage of a major stimulus which the PO did not have. As a mechanism of pressure on the undertaking, the old system of financial targets and targets for reduction in real unit costs was a great deal better than nothing; but it was too easily diluted by Ministers in the interest of short-term political expediency. The stock market never wavers. But in fact, as we have seen so far, the pressures of the market have had much less effect in raising levels of efficiency than might have been expected. Profits may have gone up; but remarkably little ground has been gained in terms of the rate of improvement in efficiency. (This may of course have been partly because a 'golden share' owned by government protects BT from the hazard of take-over.)

In theory the freedom to raise money in the market for investment is one of the most important advantages of privatization. But, again as we have seen, in practice BT plc has not needed to raise funds for investment outside the business at all. As long as this situation continues the freedom to go to the market for capital has little practical significance.

If there was one area where the new regime was to be expected really to make an impact it was in product innovation. In the event telecommunications as a world industry has devised remarkably few new products of its own since 1984. So far as Britain is concerned there was considerably more innovation by the operator in the period between 1978 and 1984 than there has been since. In Britain digital PABXs, modern call connect systems, high-impedance telephones, cardphones, ISDN (2B+D) service, Prestel and cellular radio all date from this period. Since 1984 the industry has primarily trailed in the wake of the demands of the small specialized group of knowledgeable users; and indeed has relied on them to think up applications rather than doing so itself. All the real innovation in the industry in recent years has been driven by them. The growth of Value Added Network Services (VANS),[3] of electronic data interchange (EDI), of video-conferencing and of the use of telecommunications in computing, in CAD/CAM and so on has all been driven by users. The development of the Internet is perhaps the most striking case of all.

As a government-owned organization run by state employees and with a huge preponderance of power in its sector, the PO accepted a fundamental responsibility of service to and fair treatment for the citizens of Britain. It accepted a similar responsibility of fairness towards its staff and its suppliers, the latter even where, as in the customer apparatus area, they were would-be competitors.

At privatization all these relationships changed. The fundamental responsibility of the organization is now to its shareholders. The people of Britain are now customers to be wooed. The position of the staff is governed by the provisions of the contracts they accept for their employment. The relationship with the suppliers is now the normal one between companies doing business together. So far as the competitors are concerned, whatever doubts there may be about their performance so far (see Chapter 17), since privatization they have constituted a threat which is there to be seen off or at least bested so far as BT is concerned. Yet it still has the preponderance of power which the PO enjoyed. The consequence is inevitable. The more BT acts in its own business interest and that of its shareholders, the more its actions present themselves to competitors and regulator as unfair and 'predatory'. The result is growing and unproductive conflict. This circle can never be squared within the present structure.

There has been equally basic change in another respect. The *raison d'être* of the PO was service to users in Britain. It might become involved in ventures overseas, as in Intelsat or in joint ventures for laying submarine cables, but these were ancillary to the main objective. Once again things changed completely at privatization. The duty of BT plc to its shareholders means it must look for potentially profitable ventures anywhere in the world. As other countries progressively liberalize their telecommunications, the investment opportunities overseas grow and BT is responding accordingly. But in the present structure BT can never lose its inherited responsibility to users in Britain. As the potential of the new network technologies and the investment they would involve at home becomes clearer (see Chapter 19) the Board of the privatized company faces increasingly difficult problems in determining investment priorities.

The Board of BT plc must be guided in all such matters by its responsibility to its shareholders. The responsibility for balancing the interests of investors against the interests of the people of Britain now rests with regulation and with government. The extent to which they are succeeding or failing in this responsibility is an important test of their functioning. The regime continues to work the wrong way in this respect. As we shall see, price regulation since 1990 has operated to depress investment by BT at home. When the latest regulatory proposals are implemented, charges to the majority residential market will still be controlled by a price cap. The value chosen will continue to depress the incentives to invest in this market (see Chapter 17). What the regulator should actually be doing is taking positive steps to *increase* these incentives, but there is no evidence in the record that the regulator has ever done so. This situation of itself raises serious questions about the present regime and structure.

The political climate of the 1990s and the Citizen's Charter bred an exaggerated emphasis in Britain on detailed measures of day-to-day service. Such measures are an essential tool of internal management and they have their place in public presentation. But they have serious limitations as a way of getting at the really significant effects of changes like privatization. Detailed statistics for the service of any utility will always fluctuate under short-term pressures of demand and availability of resources and of things like industrial action. The deterioration in service which occurred in 1987 was the most striking since the 1960s; but we should not read too much into that experience. Periodic deteriorations are pretty well bound to occur in the future, whatever happens as regards ownership, competition or regulation. They are always retrieved by management, if only because it does not survive unless they are. The true test of utility service to the public should be its unobtrusiveness. In a really successful utility service would be so uniformly good and prices so unexceptionable that it would attract little or no public attention.

The changing national climate under the Thatcher government is vividly illustrated by the experiences of the POEU (later renamed the NCU) in the 1980s. In coming out to meet the staff and their apprehensions through the job security agreement and the audio-visual programme in 1978, Peter Benton and I had taken a calculated risk, justified by the potential benefits in the circumstances of the time. It did not come off. With Thatcherism and the acquisitive society encouraging a hard-nosed attitude, the union membership came firmly to believe that the militant line they had taken in overruling their officials at the January 1978 Special Conference on the Shorter Working Week had been vindicated. They had won a reduction which their officials had judged impossible. This gave them an ill-judged assurance which led the union to take industrial action against competition and privatization in 1983. This action was called off at the time of the 1983 election. The union mounted a second strike in 1986. In the changed industrial relations climate it had no hope of success. It was called off after only a fortnight. The power of the engineering union and of the Technical Officers within it was finally contained.

This story, and the perception earlier of the 1970s as years of struggle against undue union influence under Labour, should not carry the implication that unions in their proper role do not have an important contribution to make. Unions can and do bring an influence to bear on behalf of the staff which is essential to the proper running of big organizations. The story in Parts I and II brings this out well enough in our case. But it also brings out that union influence must be properly channelled. The 1970s illustrated vividly the damage which can be done by union power once it escapes from sensible bounds. As it turns out, much the same might be said of UK telecommunications' experience of the influence of the stock market under the Conservatives. It has a healthy contribution to make. But there is a permanent danger that the interests of investors may be put before those of the British public unless they are properly moderated by regulation.

To sum up:

- Privatization and competition have been followed by unquestionable improvements in the specific areas of public coin-boxes and private network facilities; and since 1987 in public perception of the service generally and of the way it is offered.

- Competition has resulted in a relative reduction in the prices for calls on certain long-distance relations.

- Internally, privatization has enabled higher salaries to be paid to managerial staff and so made it possible to attract good people more easily.

- Privatization has made it possible for BT plc and its chairman to speak out publicly in a way not open to their predecessors.

but

- Privatization has had no practical effect on BT's ability to invest and has not of itself led to increased investment in the network. If anything the regime is *discouraging* BT from investing in the home market.

- Contrary to the claims that are made, neither privatization nor competition has led to an acceleration of improvement in operating efficiency or to a reduction in head count in the big battalions in the field.

- Again contrary to the claims that are made, neither privatization nor competition has made any recognizable difference to the downward trend of BT's real prices overall.

- Their only obvious effect on the steady trend of improvement in the service given by the network inherited from the PO has been the minor setback in 1987. They have done nothing recognizable to accelerate it.

- Contrary to expectations there has been a *reduction* in the pace of innovation in products and services since privatization and competition.

- Such innovation as there has been has conspicuously been led by users.

The story of the PO and BT over the last twenty-five years is not that of a defective state monopoly suddenly and magically redeemed by the forces of privatization and competition. Merely because improvements follow a particular set of changes does not mean they have been caused by them. *Post hoc propter hoc* is not a sound logical principle. To the credit of both public and private sector managements BT performance has been on an improving trend ever since 1969. This trend continues up to the present time.

As we saw in Parts I and II, by the early 1980s the organization had been waiting with growing impatience for almost two decades for a sensible separation from government, for separation from posts, and for industrial relations reform. It and its customers embraced the new set-up in hope and trust that the right formula had at last been found. The question is whether these expectations have been borne out. Some of the answer to this question is in the conclusions above. But to make this answer complete we need also to consider the working of the regime within which BT now operates. This is the subject of the next chapter.

Notes

1. Margaret Thatcher, *The Downing Street Years* (Harper Collins, London, 1993), p. 681.

2. As matters stand about two-thirds of BT's revenue arises from regulated activities. In the case of these activities the external constraint on prices has been the price cap system, which can operate only at a global level.

    It is true that there has been pressure on certain charges within the regulated envelope due to competition. But it is impossible to trace this through to any practical pressure on costs. Calls dominate both the revenue stream and the cost base of an operator like BT and in the case of call charges the pressure from competition has arisen on a selective basis, route by route and destination by destination. However only an extremely limited element of an operator's direct costs, let alone overheads, can be accurately attributed to calls on such a basis and in practice such detailed allocation of costs is never made. It may be possible to trace a rather more direct relationship between price pressure and BT costs recouped by rentals; but even in this case the situation is so complicated by the highly disputatious subject of overhead allocation that it has doubtful real significance.

    The truth is that in the case of a telecommunications operator structured on conventional lines costs and performance in their control can meaningfully be assessed only on a global basis for the complete public service operation of the company. It follows that deductions about the effect of network competition on costs can also be made only on a similar global basis. Certainly nothing useful can be deduced about the effect of competition on BT's costs from the fact that competition has led to reduction in BT's prices on certain individual long-distance relations.

    For not dissimilar reasons what matters in assessing the effect of the regime on prices is their behaviour overall, regulated and unregulated, as plotted in Figure A2.2 (see also Note 2, Chapter 17).

3. Value Added Network Services (VANS) are services provided either from computers located in or attatched to the network or by human operators which provide services that add value to the basic network function of conveyance. Computer VANS have developed into a very important family of services, which include modern business services and the Internet.

17 The British Regime in Action

Section 1 of the Telecommunications Act 1984 provides for the Secretary of State to appoint the Director General of Telecommunications as the regulator. The Director General and staff form the unit known as the Office of Telecommunications (OFTEL). Section 55 requires the Director General to make annual reports to the Secretary of State and requires the Secretary of State to lay these reports before Parliament. In other respects OFTEL is an independent non–Ministerial unit of government, with no day–to–day answerability to anyone.

Sections 3 (1) and 3 (2) of the Act specify identical duties for the Secretary of State in respect of telecommunications and for the Director General. Both have an express duty to maintain and promote effective competition.

Telecommunications competition in Britain has gone through a series of phases.

The first was the era of anticipation in the late 1970s, when people believed competition was coming but no one knew the form it would take. As we have seen, in this period the prospect of competition strongly influenced the PO in the area of product and service innovation and marketing and in what it was saying to its staff and unions.

The second phase was the period 1981 to 1984, when statutory changes to introduce competition were actually made. Competition began successfully to be arranged in customer apparatus and in private value-added network services. Mercury came into being. A policy of 'duopoly' was established, which confined the right to provide inter-area fixed links to BT and Mercury. In the interest of the promotion of local carrier competition the BT licence was framed to exclude BT parent group from entertainment TV services; it had to operate through a subsidiary. As we have seen, the threat of carrier competition had an important influence on BT's internal structure at this time. It also lent weight to the case for the changes of policy in procurement.

The third phase of competition was the period between 1985 and 1988. Mercury was now investing what was in the end to be a total of over £2bn in constructing an extensive competing long-haul network and providing direct connections to it for a limited number of big business customers. Mercury reached and reaches the great majority of its customers indirectly over interconnections with BT plant.

A number of native British companies had secured combined franchises for local telecommunications and cable TV following the passing of the Telecommunications and Cable Acts in 1984 and they began to construct plant in this period. BT itself, acting through a subsidiary, had secured five franchises and began cable TV plant construction itself. Over the next three years it became apparent that the native cable TV operations were not going to succeed. They were not helped by general fiscal changes affecting investment which worked against them. By the end of 1988 it appeared that the policy of promoting local wired service competition to BT was close to failure. The role of prime agent of competition in local service for the general public passed to mobile and hand-held radio. We have seen that such competition as existed at this time failed to prevent BT service deteriorating markedly in 1987. The regulator made various changes to regulatory practice itself to prevent a repetition of such a deterioration.

The fourth phase began in 1989, when the threat of local wired service competition seriously revived. A number of overseas interests headed by certain Regional Bell Operating Companies (RBOCs) from the USA took stakes in UK cable TV operations. The RBOCs had their own reasons for setting up in Britain. They felt hampered and frustrated in the US regulatory environment. The UK offered a promise of much greater freedom. They hoped also to gain experience to use later in their home market when, as has now happened, they were authorized to enter cable TV there. The UK government had good reason to welcome them, both for saving its policies for local competition from collapse and because they held out the prospect, which has been realized, that they would be substantial inward investors into the UK economy.

The fifth and latest phase began with the publication of the White Paper *Competition and Choice in Telecommunications* in 1991. The BT/Mercury fixed link duopoly was ended and all parts of telecommunications were thrown open to all comers. It became possible for local competitors to install their own exchanges and linking transmission systems. There was one important exception to the opening of the market. The constraints on BT group entering the entertainment market were restated. Significantly, the new applications for licences since 1991 have been for long-distance or radio-based operations.

The effects of all this have varied markedly between the various sectors. Competition and genuine market forces, with all their implications for inefficient companies, now dominate the customer apparatus sector. Competition has worked satisfactorily for specialized value-added services for business. Building on the great suppressed demand which existed before cellular technology became available, mobile and hand-held radio has developed with considerable success under competitive conditions. (The indications so far are that hand-held and mobile radio as such are complementary to, rather than a competitive substitute for, wired service. There may well, however, be a limited role for fixed link microwave systems to deliver service to customers in competition with wired services – see below.)

The record of competition between wired service carriers calls for examination in detail. As we have seen, the threat of such competition undoubtedly influenced BT in the period 1978 to 1984. But after fifteen years the actuality of the effect on BT is less impressive. As the preceding chapter demonstrated, on proper analysis there is no hard evidence that such competition has had any direct effect in improving BT performance.

Mercury has been operating for well over a decade. Its share of the market has never risen above 9 per cent. In the early months of 1995 it began seriously to falter. Large numbers of staff were shed and operations were cut back. At the time of writing it is too early to say what will happen to Mercury in the long run; or whether the new competitors whose entry was made possible by the ending of the duopoly

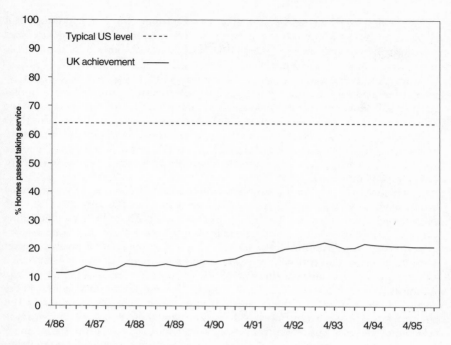

Figure 17.1 Take-up of cable TV in the UK 1986–95

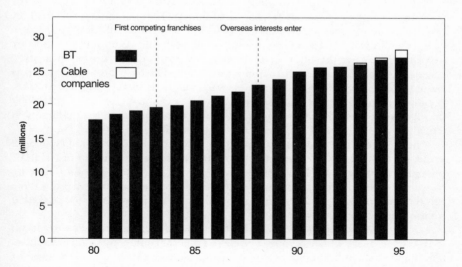

Figure 17.2 Progress of local competition 1980–95 (BT and competing exchange connections)

in 1990 will succeed where Mercury appears to be failing. But if they do succeed it is likely to be by following the example of what Mercury is doing now and concentrating on the busiest long-distance and international routes and the profitable specialized business services market.

It was predictable that long-haul competition would pull down tariffs on heavily used routes and eat into the high margins of profit traditional in this area. This has happened. Theory says that it should also have brought about an improvement in the efficiency of BT's long-haul operations and a reduction in their unit costs. But these operations were already efficient and set to become more so through the progressive introduction of digital technology long before carrier competition began. The track record of long-haul public service competition in Britain is unimpressive. No operator has emerged comparable to MCI.

In the local area some of the most powerful telecommunications companies in the world have now established themselves as competitors to BT wired service. The biggest single interests involved are the US RBOCs NYNEX and US West operating through jointly owned UK subsidiaries. French, Canadian and other interests are also involved. A third RBOC, Pacific Telesis, was also involved originally but later withdrew. These companies have made large investments and are committed to make more. In 1996 the take-up of cable TV, measured in terms of the percentage of homes 'passed' by cables who actually take service, remains obstinately low, in the area of 21 per cent, whereas the US figure is above 60 per cent (see Figure 17.1). But the operators have been more successful than they expected in winning telecommunications customers from BT. By 1996 telephony take-up was about 25 per cent of homes passed. Figure 17.2 plots existing market shares. Assuming take-up continues at the present level and with the build obligations the cable telephony share would rise to 15 per cent by 2005. (Figures 17.1 and 17.2 are taken from published BT and Cable Communications Association statistics.)

The great bulk of the customers whom the cable operators have won for telecommunications service are residential customers. They are traditionally the least profitable; and they have been won largely by low price offers, like low connection charges and rentals and such measures as free off-peak calls. Winning customers by price reductions at the unprofitable end of the market does not seem in itself calculated to lead on to long-run commercial success. The really profitable customers are those who make a lot of calls per line throughout the working day, like businesses, public sector organizations and so on. Rental charges make up a comparatively unimportant part of the bills of these customers and they are correspondingly less likely to be influenced by low rental and off-peak offers.

The stringent price caps currently imposed on BT are also of course telling evidence of the failure of competition to bring effective pressures to bear on BT prices and costs. Since the local competitors must match or beat BT prices if they are to gain and hold market share, their returns also are at risk. If matters go on like this there is a real danger that the overall profitability of this sector of the operating industry may be artificially depressed.

Local telecommunications service has traditionally been subsidized by profits on long-distance calls, which are not available to the local competitors as matters stand. The implicit assumption behind the policy of awarding combined franchises for cable TV was that profits from cable TV would subsidize the telecommunications operations. Given the undoubted profitability of cable TV in the USA this was perhaps a reasonable assumption at the time; but with cable TV take-up so low there is little sign of it in Britain so far.

In their home environment in the USA the telecommunications unit operating costs of the RBOC parents have always been lower than those of the PO and BT; and, as we have seen, BT has not so far succeeded in reducing its overall unit costs significantly below the levels it inherited. On this reasoning the competing companies should be able in theory to establish an enduring cost and price lead over BT in the UK and still maintain reasonable returns. But the UK is not the USA. At present the competing companies are a very long way from the scale of operations of the US parents, and have correspondingly less scope for economies of scale. In particular UK calling rates are much lower than those in the USA and US unit costs per call are correspondingly lower. On the managerial side the cable companies have yet to demonstrate that they can reach US levels of operating efficiency in the UK environment and with a UK labour force. They also have important handicaps specific to Britain. They have a requirement to lay all cables underground, unlike the USA where overhead distribution cabling is the norm in most areas outside big cities. The resulting civil engineering costs account for a large part of the companies' present investment. Most serious of all, at present levels of take-up the cable operators have a disproportionate and growing burden of infrastructure plant which is not earning its keep.

At present the telecommunications operations of the companies are confined to the operation of local distribution networks in franchises defined and selected by reference to the cable TV market, with a limited amount of switching and interfranchise links of their own. They are inescapably dependent on BT for the handling of the great bulk of their traffic. If the competitors are to pose a threat which will really impinge on BT they must gain real economies of scale and escape from dependence on the BT network and the drain which interconnection charges impose on their finances. The only way they could do either is by developing network operations which duplicate those of BT on a national scale; or by linking up with a partner to create such facilities. This would amount to duplicating the bulk of the existing BT network, both long-haul and local – that is, something not far short of a modern equivalent of the huge PO network programme of the 1970s. On the basis of the results achieved so far it would be very difficult if not impossible for them to justify or secure the very great investment this would involve. The parent company boards and the financiers from whom the money would have to come have many other calls on their resources; and present experience must be making them more and more hard-headed and cautious about involvement with infrastructure competition.

The companies are investing at a pace set not by their own judgement but by licence build obligations. True the political objective of choice is attained. But choice is one thing; getting competition really to bite is another. Figure A2.1 shows that, while the 1990 recession undoubtedly hit BT hard, its overall business volume has now resumed its long-term trend, competition or no competition.

The legislation which permits telecommunications companies to offer cable TV and vice versa in the USA has now passed into law. This must have important implications for the UK. It seems highly likely that the RBOCs will begin now to consider diverting future investment in this field back to the USA. Again, the original reason they gave for entering cable TV in the UK was to gain experience to help them in their home markets. This objective has been achieved. It would be logical for them also now to move the key directing staff who have gained experience and provided the momentum in the UK back to the USA.

The most effective argument for continuing optimism about the cable companies' prospects is that cable TV in particular is traditionally a long lead time business and that quick returns were never to be expected. But it was by 1996 eight years since overseas interests took over the cable operations in the UK. The patterns of Figure 17.1, in particular the very pronounced shortfall below US levels of take-up of cable TV proper and the doubtful economics on the telecommunications side, do not justify optimism that matters will improve, even in the longer run. The prospects must also be affected by digital broadcasting, which will enable satellite and off-air terrestrial broadcasters to offer a great number of channels.

Assessed in strict business terms, any prospect that the present cable operations will develop into competitors on the scale needed to pose a really decisive threat to BT seems highly debatable.

At the time of writing a new local competitor, Ionica, is entering the market. Ionica uses fixed radio links to customers' premises and intends to operate its own exchanges. It will offer both voice service and data at bit rates up to 28 kbit/s at acceptable quality. For obvious reasons, over a certain distance radio connections of this kind to customers cost less in new construction than cable connections. It is perfectly possible that in favourable circumstances Ionica will be able to offer service at a lower connection charge and rental than BT. But it faces much the same problems as the cable operators. There is an irreducible cost to establish radio service of this kind in a given area, made up of the cost of the base stations, of the links to them and of the exchange unit, which is independent of the number of customers and corresponds to the infrastructure cost for cable. Unless Ionica can secure a sufficient take-up it will find itself in the same position as the cable companies, with an expensive infrastructure which is not properly loaded. Again in the same way as the cable companies it will be dependent on call revenue to secure profitability; and dependent on BT for the disposal of the majority of its customers' traffic. It will face the same problem of BT's charges for interconnection, which will drain off a high proportion of its call revenue.

I have myself been a supporter of radio-based customer systems for over ten years;[1] and I am not to be seen as arguing against competition from radio in principle if it can be made to stick; or indeed against the use of radio loop systems as first comers for provision of telecommunications service in greenfield situations. I wish Ionica well. It has certain things going for it specific to radio. It is easy and fast to provide service to individual customers by radio once the base station infrastructure is established; and since if Ionica fails in one area it may move its radio installations, and even at a cost its exchanges, to other areas it has an advantage of flexibility which wired operators can never have. But it is very difficult to see it developing as more than a niche service.

The cable companies and Ionica will no doubt continue as the former have begun by offering low rentals and connection charges, free off-peak calls and other such inducements to customers to transfer. Number portability, when attained on the ground, could help them in this. They may win significant numbers of customers from BT in areas which are favourable to their various characteristics, especially low-user customers who are influenced by rental charge levels. An optimistic scenario might be that in combination they will bring some enduring pressure to bear on BT rental charges nationally in the long run. But it is call charges and revenue which matter. With their heavy and continuing dependence on interconnection with the BT network it is difficult to see how the competitors can ever really make money out of calls or bring serious pressure to bear on BT core costs, however successful they are in holding down their own operating costs. Even in combination it is unlikely that cable and Ionica-type services will emerge as a commanding challenge to the core of BT's local operations.

In short, after fifteen years and despite very considerable investments by competing operators and very considerable support from government and the regulator, notably through constraints imposed on BT, neither long-distance nor local carrier competition has really taken off or had any decisive effect on BT; nor do they offer any convincing prospect of doing so in the future.

Turning to regulation as such, its most important single element is concerned with prices. When the regime was designed it was decided not to regulate profits or individual price levels as such, but to apply a 'price cap', expressed as the difference for a specified period into the future between retail price inflation and permissible increases in a 'basket' of the BT prices concerned. The mechanism is usually called 'RPI-x'.

It had a number of theoretical attractions. It left prices and profits free to find their own level within the price ceiling set by the price cap. The theory was that this gave BT an incentive to increase operating efficiency which was not available from the financial target system or the return on asset system of price regulation used in the USA. The effect of telecommunications prices on inflation was constrained by the price cap, but subject to this BT was free to make whatever profits it could by gains in efficiency. The fact that as originally conceived the price cap operated only on a global basket of prices had the additional attraction that it gave the management of the privatized BT freedom as regards the details of pricing.

Unfortunately real events never conform to tidy models. For a long time the actual value of the increases in the prices controlled by the price cap turned out consistently to be significantly below the price cap value, so that it could hardly be said to be creating the stringent ceiling which theory said it would. The deterioration in service in 1987 made everyone realize abruptly that the regulatory system provided no guarantee of or protection for the quality of service provided. Public dissatisfaction was such that the regulator felt obliged to begin to take a close interest in quality matters, involving a much greater degree of monitoring of BT performance in this respect than government had ever applied to the PO. As the 1980s wore on, political and media attention also became directed to the very high profits on international calls, which had of course existed for many years. Concern also developed in government about the political effects of big increases in rentals, which always affect voters on small incomes. Subordinate price caps were introduced for international calls, even though this was becoming a highly competitive market, and for rentals.

As we have seen, the effect of recent price cap values has been to impose a very stringent requirement on BT indeed, equivalent to a 12 per cent real reduction in controlled prices in four years. It is the government which is embarrassed by utility profits and it is not difficult to deduce that it has been government which has insisted that increasingly severe price caps be imposed to limit those of BT. If these deductions are correct the price cap process as it has developed is nowhere near as different as one might have hoped or expected from the old PO price negotiations with government, influenced as they so often were by short-term political considerations.

Taken together these developments amount to a denial in practice of most of the theoretical attractions of the price cap system. The expectation that it would lead to freedom for management has not been realized at all. BT today is subject to more detailed control of prices and monitoring of quality of service by the regulator than the PO ever was by government.

The price cap system has one weakness of particular importance in a capital-intensive industry like telecommunications. Shareholder pressure on the stock market can tend to favour short-term returns, at the expense of long-run investment. The price cap system not only fails to balance out any bias of this kind in the market, it firmly reinforces it in the wrong direction. It restricts cash flow and therefore operating surpluses available for investment. As operated in recent years it has restricted profitability and therefore reduced the company's ability to raise money in the market. But it does more than that. A stringent price cap means that BT is not only short of money for investment but subject to pressure for the reverse since lower investment means lower capital charges on current account. The combined effect is to generate pressure actually to decrease the investment programme. The price cap system and in particular the severe price cap values imposed on BT since 1991 therefore have serious implications for investment in the regulated services for the home market. This is an important matter because BT is and is likely to remain the principal national operator for the foreseeable future.

The traditional basis of regulation of Bell companies in the USA and of targeting for PO telecommunications in the public sector was return on assets (RoA). This has the correct effect on investment. It puts a premium on new network investment, since this increases the asset base and therefore the profits available for a given return. (The traditional objection to RoA is that it amounts to cost plus. There is some truth in this; see Chapter 20 for a discussion of how this weakness of RoA might be eliminated in an improved regime.)

As already noted the stringent price caps currently imposed on BT are telling evidence of the failure of competition to bring effective pressures to bear on BT prices and costs. In themselves they amount to an admission of the ineffectiveness of competition in the period up to the present and of the political need for greater pressure on prices.

Perhaps the most obvious of all the weaknesses of the system is that the price cap does not tell you whether the actual level of prices is acceptable at all. In consequence it hamstrings government politically in answering criticism of the regime.

The Achilles' heel of RPI-x is the value of x. Whereas the rate of return used in RoA regulation can be checked against comparable performance by others, the value of x has no independent meaning and cannot be checked by outside reference. It may be right, wrong or wildly wrong. There is no way of knowing. There is no defensible way of settling it in advance other than the way used in practice – that is by negotiation between the parties starting from forecast values for a number of inputs – economic variables, volumes of business, investment, cost and productivity forecasts, price changes and so on – and taking in predictions of return on assets. Few if any of the forecasts of input variables ever turn out to be right. One or two of them – usually including the economic ones which are the foundation of the whole process – are almost always going to be found to be wrong, especially in the later years of a price cap period. Obviously if real inflation departs seriously from that assumed, the working of RPI-x itself is going to be wrong in favour of one party or the other.

To sum up, whatever the elegance of the price cap system in theory, in practice it has proved impossible to make it operate to affect costs unless it is used in a completely arbitrary way. It has operated seriously to depress returns in the industry and provides a disincentive to investment in the home market as distinct from overseas. It has played an important part in drawing the regulator into a spiral of more and more detailed prescription of what BT is to do or is not to do, which has gone a long way beyond any similar government involvement in the affairs of the PO. And it has failed to provide any yardstick to help government in answering politically damaging charges that BT is making excessive profits. The only thing it does about which there can be no dispute is to provide a theoretical justification for lack of constraint on profits, which if one stops to think is a strange basis for utility regulation. In short it is seriously unsatisfactory.

Interconnection of networks has proved to be a second area of difficulty. The record of the last ten years is marked by steadily increasing conflict between the operators over the charges made by BT for the use of its plant for competitors' traffic and increasing appeals to OFTEL, with no prospect that the tensions will ever be resolved.

The natural disposition of regulators is to look for solutions to these problems by finer and finer chopping of accounting logic. But this is fated not to work; it goes against the grain of telecommunications. One of the most basic issues in the interconnection debates revolves round the assumption that a valid accounting division can be made between what are now called the 'Access' business and the 'Network' business; and that when such a division is made it can be used fairly to determine the amount of compensation BT deserves from its competitors for their use of its access facilities to reach customers. An earlier form of the idea that such a division can and should be made underlay thinking as far back as the 1955 White Paper. But this division has never been accomplished on a watertight basis, not (as it may be tempting to assume) because of the inadequacies of past accounting practices but because of something much more fundamental.

A moment's reflection will show that the 'access' network exists only to permit people to make calls; its only function is as the outer end of the call network. It has no meaning separate from the rest of the network and no true accounting identity of its own. For these reasons it cannot be a 'business'. The existence of separate rentals may seem to argue the opposite but it proves nothing. It dates from 1929, long before the application of modern accounting thinking. In those days rentals and connection charges were no more than an arbitrary way of collecting some network revenue which looked understandable to the general public, was therefore politically convenient and increases in which could be got away with separately from those to call charges, on a sort of analogy to 'divide and rule'.

The commercial problems of interconnection really amount to an equivalent involving outside parties of the problem of transfer pricing between subsidiaries internally within groups, which always gives rise to difficulties of division of overheads and profit. Three separate attempts were made to arrive at transfer charging arrangements between elements of BT before privatization. The last was in 1982 when the separate long-distance unit National Networks was set up. Despite any amount of trying it proved impossible to get out a valid system of transfer pricing as between the long-haul operations of National Networks and the local operations of the rest of the division. The reasons were that profit could be allocated only by reference to return on assets, and that approach involved setting an arbitrary return 'target' for one or other element of those being divided (or both); and that there was no logically sound basis for allocation of overheads.[2]

The truth is that no logically watertight basis exists for allocating overheads and profit as between parts of the telecommunications network operations of a single company, and it never can. Forty years of financial wrestling since the 1955 White Paper, with Treasury and distinguished outside firms of accountants and consultants repeatedly involved, has never got round this simple fact. The only way satisfactorily to subdivide network costs and profits would be to divide the network itself and to apportion the parts to completely separate sovereign companies.

The engineering side of interconnection is also fraught with difficulty. Theory assumes that all the requirements for smooth interworking between competing networks can be met if each conforms to international standards at its interfaces to the other segments. Such an ideal picture is quite unreal. In the real world the catalogue of standards is never complete or up to date; and whether by accident or design they are invariably implemented in ways which differ in significant detail from operator to operator and supplier to supplier. These characteristics are accentuated in the modern environment of all-out operator and supplier competition. Moreover the technical requirements for proper interworking are becoming steadily more complex. Work undertaken by the DTI on standards for the Intelligent Network illustrated how conditions which may affect interworking on sophisticated facilities are buried several layers deep inside modern network structures and cannot be properly accommodated just at peripheral interfaces. These problems will get steadily more involved as technology advances (for an alternative approach to the problem see Chapter 21).

The regime has more deeply rooted problems involving technology than these. For as long as competitors continue to duplicate one another's plant there are obvious risks of them getting out of step on generations of technology. If the network of competitor A were to fall seriously behind in technology compared with those of B, C and D, the service available on the main mass of relations, A–B, A–C and so on would be determined by the capabilities of the least advanced segment – that is of A. The danger of serious disparities developing is real and will obviously increase as the number of competitors increases and as the years go by. If as a result of the entertainment bans, of the effect of the price cap on investment or for any other reason BT were to fall into the position of competitor A, this would create a really serious situation for UK telecommunications.

Finally there is a long history of complaint by BT's competitors about its 'uncompetitive' behaviour; and by BT about the unfairness of regulation. Friction between competing parties and between them and the regulator is inherent and natural in regimes of the present kind. By itself it would hardly be a matter for remark or concern. But when the friction is getting more and more obvious with no obvious way out in sight; and when it is coupled with a situation in which the business prospects of the competitors are so visibly uncertain, in which the impact of competition on BT's performance is so limited and in which the company's continuing dominance is a matter of such concern, the working of the regime has to be seen as basically unsatisfactory. If things continue as they are the industry is fated to a future of interminable and unconstructive wrangling between BT, its competitors and the regulator to little or no useful effect. The question that has to be faced is whether it is practical to arrange properly working regulation of competing modern high-tech telecommunications networks at all. The British experience says that it is not.

If things are to be improved, a good place to start is with a critical look at the nature of the regulatory task itself.

In its original form telecommunications regulation concentrated primarily on control of monopoly pricing. This is well suited to regulation and the disciplines which come naturally to regulators. It is concerned with financial and statistical facts and predictions, with only limited interplay with technology and managerial matters. It is when regulation is extended to administering and promoting competition between interdependent networks that the problems arise.

There are several reasons for this. In the first place network telecommunications is *par excellence* a forward-looking high-tech business which constantly aspires to change. Regulation on the other hand is like financial audit. It requires a tidy body of established fact which can be analysed and re-analysed for as long as it takes to get an answer. The advance of network technology will not wait while regulation catches up. The more influential the regulator becomes, the greater the danger that his or her activities will have the effect of slowing-up technical advance.

A second reason is that it is impossible to get to the bottom of commercial or regulatory issues in network telecommunications without a sufficient technical input, and it is asking for trouble to try. If they know what they are doing people with non-engineering responsibilities in telecommunications will always check their thinking on any important issue with sufficiently senior and authoritative engineers. Five times out of ten they find when they do so that they are pursuing the wrong question or acting on the wrong set of assumptions.

This problem gets steadily worse as the technology advances. In 1964 the GPO was running a Strowger network using first-generation carrier transmission equipment, with all-copper distribution and low-impedance calling telephones which were an integral part of the exchange circuitry from the electrical point of view. The only services available were basic telephone service and elementary call diversion and similar services provided the hard way by relay sets in exchanges. Data transmission between computers was in its infancy and was seen as a specialized problem for transmission engineers. Even under these conditions the mix was already such as to give rise to complicated and difficult commercial issues. It was just about possible for non-engineers to have a sufficient grasp of all facets including the technology to handle them; but the limit was rapidly being reached. In 1996 the network is dominated by first-generation electronic switching, digital transmission and software control; high-tech systems are penetrating distribution plant; and high-impedance telephones working off plugs and sockets are the norm. There is extensive interaction with computers and computing technology, and services have multiplied enormously. The second generation of electronic telecommunications technology, using extremely high-tech fast packet switches, gigabit capacity transmission and a whole new order of software complexity is already well above the horizon.

The situation even of the engineering profession is one in which the demands of the technology are creating a serious risk of over-specialization if it is to be handled at all. True engineering generalists are becoming a rare breed. On the other hand privatization and competition have created a completely new family of commercial problems in which the regulators must specialize if they are to succeed. It is essential for them to deploy the skills of accountancy and to be versed in telecommunications law and policy if they are to do their job at all. The person has not been born who can combine all this with a sufficient grasp of modern telecommunications technology. The regulators can only survive by treating what is in fact a technology which is constantly evolving in a kaleidoscopic way as a series of black boxes with fixed characteristics, to be moved around on a sort of chessboard to suit policy and commercial requirements. This cannot work. The companies under regulation hold the initiative and they have immensely greater resources and know-how. The issues at stake are so loaded that the companies will bring to bear the most sophisticated mix of engineering and commercial ingenuity of which they are capable, both in the marketplace and in their dealings with the regime.

The separation of regulation from operation and the creation of OFTEL was one of the most constructive and distinctive changes made between 1981 and 1984. Sir Bryan Carsberg's most important single achievement was to avoid the regime developing the cumbersome litigatory processes taken for granted in the USA. Compared with the US machinery British regulation is efficient and effort-economical. But as time has gone by, the British regulators have begun to get more and more out of their depth with the problems of promoting competition between networks and of administering interconnection between them. In the long run if not in the short run the arrangements will become unworkable. This is the exact reverse of a criticism of OFTEL. On the contrary it is a tribute. The regulators are making a basically unsatisfactory regime work as well as anyone could expect; but it needs to be changed.and the regulatory task badly needs redefining on a manageable basis.

As I was finalizing this chapter it was announced that OFTEL was proposing a radical change of approach to the regime for the next pricing period up to 2001. It is now proposed that price cap regulation should apply only to residential and smaller business users and that the price cap value for them should be reduced to RPI-4.5 per cent. Prices for larger users would be left to be determined by competition. At the same time the regulator is to take much wider powers to root out what he considers unfair competitive practices by BT.

To the extent that they reduce the area covered by the price cap these proposals are to be welcomed. But unfortunately they have important deficiencies.

In the first place they involve a truly remarkable act of faith by the regulator. They depend crucially on the assumption that competition alone will provide a sufficient check on BT pricing over a very considerable part of its revenues – revenues caught by the new price cap would account for only a quarter of the total. It is certainly true that competition for international and business services seems set to be fierce in the future. But for the rest of the services concerned such confidence is simply not warranted by the experience summarized in this book.

Second, the approach hinges on the regulator's new powers to enforce competition. Only time will tell if these powers can be used to bolster competition sufficiently to make it more effective in the future than it has been in the past; but the omens are not good. What is certain is that if the regulator sets out to use them to effect he will become embroiled in a degree of oversight of and dispute with BT which has no parallel hitherto either before or after privatization. The whole idea of increased freedom for BT due to privatization is being negated.

But the most serious weakness lies in the fact that, while revenue from the users affected by the new price cap may account for only a quarter of BT's total revenue, they represent some 80 per cent of its customers – the majority of the residential population. We shall see later that very important questions to do with the future of services for this majority remain unresolved. A primary aim of policy should be to encourage investment in new network facilities on their behalf. But because of changes in the make-up of the price cap basket the 4.5 per cent future level will be as stringent so far as they are concerned as 7.5 per cent overall has been in the past, with all that that means in discouraging invesment.

Once again the regulator is only doing the job as laid down by the Act. The real defect of the regime lies in the assumption implicit in Section 3 of the 1984 Act that competition is a holy grail which provides the answer to everything. This is just not true of telecommunications networks, for reasons we shall examine in Chapter 19.

To sum up:

- The regime introduced in Britain under the 1981 and 1984 Acts has been found to work well in customer apparatus and value-added services for business; but the key criterion for its success concerns its working in the network area.

- The policies in this area centre on infrastructure competition and price cap regulation.

- The challenge posed to BT by infrastructure competition has been found to be ineffective, with little indication that it can become more powerful in the future.

- The business prospects of the network competitors remain highly uncertain.

- The associated regulatory arrangements are getting into more and more serious difficulty.

- The price cap system has been shown to be thoroughly unsatisfactory.

- The latest proposals by the regulator do not offer a satisfactory solution.

In short the fundamentals of the carrier regime have been shown to be defective. Part VI considers an alternative approach.

Notes

1. See J. M. Harper, *Telecommunications and Computing – The Uncompleted Revolution* (Communications Educational Services, London, 1986), Chapter 9.
2. For a more detailed discussion of the problems of allocation of network costs see J. M. Harper, *A 21st Century Structure for UK Telecommunications* (Communications Educational Services Publishing, London, 1991).

Part VI
The Future in Europe

18 Britain and European Telecommunications

The Bangemann Report Europe and the Information Society, submitted to the EU Council of Ministers in June 1994, recommended member states of the EU to accelerate liberalization by 'opening up to competition infrastructures and services still in the monopoly area'. Implementation of the subsequent directive is not obliged to begin until 1998. Many countries have enacted or are enacting the necessary legislation to pave the way for the licensing of new operators. The crucial decisions will be those about how these new licensing powers of governments are actually to be used in practice. There is an opportunity which may be unrepeatable to take stock of policy in readiness for the twenty-first century before these are finalized. This Part of the book is intended to stimulate and to contribute to this stock-taking.

The political forces making for favourable presentation of the British regime are powerful, and British experience has played a big part in influencing the thinking of Bangemann and the Commission. BT itself has continued to improve since 1984 and we should have nothing but respect for the BT operating achievements of the last few years. But as we have seen, the contribution which the changed regime and network competition in particular have made to the improvement in BT is much less clear or impressive than is generally assumed, and the business prospects of the competitors to BT remain basically uncertain. All the odds are that similar experiences will be repeated across Europe before too many years are out. It is important that opinion-formers in the continental countries should take the reality of the British experience and its implications on board while their new regimes are still in the formative stages.

In considering the future we should take account of British experience before as well as after privatization. To recapitulate, UK telecommunications priorities in the 1970s were concentrated on the network. They had to do with meeting the great acceleration in demand for telephone service as it spread through the general population, with the pressing need for modernization of the network of exchanges and transmission links, with the provision of proper modern facilities for international communications, and with the search for efficiency in the use of resources and the introduction of proper disciplines in the immense capital programme. As Part II showed, these challenges were met by the monopoly operator with remarkable success. The network was expanded in size by a factor of nearly three in fifteen years. The modernization programme planned and initiated by the PO stands as one of the most successful (and least recognized) British utility achievements of the last hundred years.

These advances in the network area were brought about by a nationally unified management. Once the government had decided on the introduction of network competition, it was awaited as impatiently inside the senior management of the business as outside, because we believed what we were told. The stimulus it would give held the answer to a lot of our remaining problems. The making of legislative provision for competition and the creation of Mercury both called forth highly positive responses inside BT. As Managing Director Inland Division I was myself an enthusiast for 'facilities-based' competition in the early 1980s. But our growing experience in Britain has led me to change my mind. In the rest of this book I want to develop my reasons and to suggest an alternative.

I want to make two important points here as background to this.

For a hundred years the *raison d'être* of telecommunications was the spread of service to the general population, starting with the telegraph and going on through the telephone to modern digital communications. This process has had profoundly constructive consequences. We shall never be able to measure the extent to which the immense political progress since the British Great Reform Act of 1832 and the European Year of Revolutions in 1848 has been due to the advance of the telegraph and the telephone. As the rulers of the communist states were well aware, the telephone has become a key ingredient of democracy. And the better public telecommunications have become, the better people have been able to organize research and production, to learn about products and services and place orders; and the more economies have expanded. It is not just a matter of a fair society to say that things must go on like this. Advances in telecommunications must never be allowed to become the preserve of privileged minorities, whether in big business or in government. The criterion by which policies for telecommunications are judged should similarly be the interest of the whole population and not just that of particular interest groups within it like the big business sector. The latest UK regulatory proposals are seriously deficient in this respect (see page 183).

The second point concerns the future of the industry itself. Historically telecommunications has been *par excellence* a growth industry and this is still very much its received image. But there are limits to its growth. The telephone service has been far and away the biggest single source of growth. The conclusion from Figure 6.1 is unmistakable. In Britain the rate of growth of telephone service measured in lines is slowing up; and Britain is typical of advanced countries so far as telecommunications are concerned.

The present-day national telephone services of the advanced countries and the networks which support them operate on a scale of tens or hundreds of millions of customers and tens of billions of calls. Many of the telecommunications developments of recent years are valuable enough in themselves but their markets are numbered in thousands or at most tens of thousands. Modern international business services, video-conferencing, data communications and many of the other sophisticated services and facilities developed recently are qualitatively impressive; but in the perspective of public telecommunications they are not much more than niche services, with only limited significance. The only serious exception has been mobile and hand-held radio service to people on the move. A key question for the future of telecommunications is whether there are new services out there capable of developing on the scale of the public telephone service. If there are not, the days of telecommunications as a growth industry on the scale of the 1970s and 1980s are numbered. Our approach to policy and especially to policy for the structure of the industry needs to do all it can to secure a positive answer to this question.

In the next chapter I look in depth at the arguments for and against infrastructure competition against this background. In the final chapter I make proposals for a fundamentally different approach to the structure of telecommunications in European countries.

19 The Engine of Telecommunications

Academic studies and business surveys suggest the most important factors discouraging investment are uncertainty about future demand and inadequate rates of return.

Michael Heseltine, *Financial Times*, 12 June 1996

The network is the engine of telecommunications. The technology and the capabilities of the network determine the range of facilities which customers enjoy and are formative for cost and quality of service. Without the network, customer apparatus and sophisticated services have no life of their own. The network contributes the core of the operators' revenue; and network capital and staff charges are the biggest single influence on their costs. The working of a telecommunications regime in network matters has to be the principal criterion for judging its success or failure.

As I pointed out earlier, the profitability and growth of telecommunications over the last twenty years have been due primarily to the telephone service; but the growth of telephony is fated to decline, and it is doing so. If the industry is to avoid stagnation and continue to satisfy investors it needs a new service or group of services comparable in scale with the telephone service. The big carriers have turned to international business services; but this market is limited and competition is fierce. In any case the issue is much wider than just the question of the business prospects of the operators. The scope for development of telecommunications network technology is anything but exhausted. It has great potential for the future of national economies and societies. The countries which find a viable way to exploit it further on a large scale will have a vital tool for social and political advancement and a decisive commercial advantage in a fiercely competitive world.

The public networks of most of the advanced countries of the world outside the United States were created by public authorities using very large amounts of money raised in one way or another from the public as distinct from the stock market. As they stand, these networks are important national assets. They have one crucial advantage not shared as far as I know by any other utility infrastructure. Properly exploited they can fund their own development, renewal and technological advance, in a way which can make them independent of the fluctuations of national economies or of the varying fortunes of the stock market. The former monopoly operators like BT and its fellow former PTTs have inherited a leading role in these processes which cannot and should not be denied.

The fact that many of the networks have been or will be privatized makes no difference to the fact that the starting point for policy should be to maintain them intact and to do nothing to impair their profitability and their power to fund their own renewal. By this criterion it is just as wrong to divert an undue proportion of network income into dividends for private shareholders as it is to divert it into central state finances and to use it as a way to reduce taxes. It is also wrong to encourage competition in infrastructure because it dilutes the profitability of the existing network operations and puts its future at risk.

There is no law of nature which says that competition is the right answer for everything. History alone should make policy-makers cautious. *The Wealth of Nations* is treated as gospel by its exponents. Adam Smith wrote his treatise in 1776. The British canals of the early nineteenth century were to become the first co-ordinated communications network in Britain since the Romans. But in the late eighteenth century even the canal network was in its infancy. The nineteenth century rediscovered the hard way through the early days of the railways the importance of ordered infrastructures. The later Victorians and the Edwardians did not hesitate to apply the lessons they had learnt from this experience to telegraphs and the telephone.

The history of telecommunications up to the First World War is of increasing concentration of services on monopoly operators. This was almost certainly an essential condition for the development of telecommunications as a universal service. It is highly improbable that competing private operators would have created the countrywide networks we take for granted today; or would have updated them to their present level of technology. This applies especially to those sectors of the network which serve the main population of residential users, which are notorious for being under-utilized. We shall never know whether competing operators working in a true market environment would have carried through the growth of the British network in the 1970s on the scale and at the pace accomplished by the demand-driven monopoly; but the odds are that they would not.

Identical issues are going to arise in one form or another for the next generation of telecommunications, whatever form it finally turns out to take. An approach based on competing networks will load the dice unacceptably against the spread of the next generation of facilities to the general population.

As we have seen, huge sums are involved in the construction and renewal of modern telecommunications networks. Over the past twenty-five years BT and the PO have between them invested the equivalent at 1994 prices of well over £60bn or over £1,000 per customer to create the present BT network. The cable TV companies estimated they would have to invest £6bn just to cover the franchise areas existing in 1994. Such a scale of investment is an order greater than anything normally found or financed by companies in competitive business. And no one has suggested duplicating the Channel Tunnel or the rail network in the interests of competition.

It may be tempting to see a parallel between manufacturers' production facilities and the networks of telecommunications operators. But this is misleading. Because the investment per customer in factories is relatively low it often makes economic sense for manufacturers to expand and update their production facilities at frequent intervals. But telecommunications operators are in a quite different situation. By manufacturing standards, the investment per customer in telecommunications networks is huge. The creation of competing facilities adds an important dimension of risk. The higher the combination of investment and risk, the less the inclination to invest. The build obligations on British cable operators are living proof of this.

The market is seen at its best as a mechanism for optimizing the use of resources and for stimulating advance in design and technology in familiar consumer products like cars, detergents or radio sets; or in services like rival travel companies. Where physical products are involved in such cases, product life cycles are short. Product designers gain a short-term edge by what are often quite small advances in design which are worked out in secret until they are ready to be put on the market. Such advances are then leapfrogged by competitors developing similar advances with similar tactics; and so the process goes on. Telecommunications networks are in a quite different category. Product life cycles run into decades. Even with the rapid advances in technology and manufacturing technique of recent years it has taken thirty years for electronic switching really to pervade the UK network and even now there are still electro-mechanical enclaves. In the case of the renewal of an asset as big as the modern telecommunications network of an advanced country like Britain there will always be a fundamental physical constraint. The time needed to engineer the necessary technology, to marshal the resources and to complete execution will always impose a minimum time-scale, even if financial constraints are ignored.

The tactical secrecy taken for granted in other markets cannot apply in the circumstances of telecommunications, if only because secrets always leak over time. In any case it is foreign to the tradition of the industry and would almost certainly be counter-productive if enforced in telecommunications. Telecommunications has made the huge strides which it has through a deeply rooted tradition of international pooling of knowledge. Experience has shown over and over again that telecommunications engineers produce the biggest advances if they are allowed to share their secrets, if only because the technology and its ramifications are so complex and the problems are so challenging that no one group of people is likely to find the right answer. New techniques evolve through the collective consciousness of the industry. There is simply no room for the kind of secretive short-term shock tactics used in selling consumer products. Again in the car, detergent or radio set markets the end-consumers have direct acquaintance with the product and through their purchasing behaviour directly influence its characteristics. It is self-evident that the end-consumer of telecommunications does not have such acquaintance with or influence on exchanges or transmission systems.

The history of telecommunications is a history of creation of ever-increasing modules of capacity, economies of scale and reducing unit costs. The effect is most obvious in transmission. The very first transmission links between distant cities used copper conductors which provided a single speech channel per pair. They were replaced by first-generation carrier systems whose whole purpose was to get more channels out of one pair over longer distances; and then by successive generations each directed to getting more and more channels out of a single cable medium. Current Synchronous Digital Hierarchy (SDH) transmission systems using optical fibre cables have standard capacities up to 2.4 gbit/s, or 37,500 speech channels on a single optical fibre. Capacities and economies of scale are set to go higher still. The same is true if not more so of switching. Enormous concentrations of traffic are possible on single switches using the modern Asynchronous Transfer Mode (ATM) technology.[1] Single switches are being designed with a potential total throughput of 60 Ghz, enough for nearly a million simultaneous voice connections or the whole traffic of cities as big as London and New York. Very similar considerations apply to the economics of the high-tech distribution plant which may be expected to replace the inner part of copper customer distribution. The whole logic of the technology is moving relentlessly in the direction of ever-increasing modules of capacity and potential economies of scale. The potential seriousness of the loss of economies of scale due to duplication or further replication of plant is increasing in a corresponding way. It is too big to be recouped by competitive pressures.

Telecommunications networks are engineering artefacts. The logic that forms their affairs is not the logic of academic economics or of political doctrine, it is the logic of the industry and its engineering.

By 1984 the telephone service had been in existence for something just over a hundred years. In these hundred years it had advanced from manual exchanges serving a few hundred customers, with a few heavy copper conductors linking large cities, to circuit digital and packet exchanges and to plesiochronous digital transmission serving tens of millions. It had grown from nothing to a position as one of the largest single areas of organized human activity. Technology provided the central axis of this advance. The enormous business and profit volumes of telecommunications today are the product not of financial manipulation or of competition but of engineering effort. The present-day technologies – circuit digital switching, packet switching, plesiochronous transmission and cellular radio – were the last and finest product of engineers working in the monopoly environment.

Despite all the advances in switching and inter-exchange transmission, however, the former PTT networks still use copper pair cables today to connect customers to exchanges as they have done for a hundred years. The companies which provide combined cable TV and telecommunications service in Britain use a combination of standard telecommunications transmission technology, the traditional US coaxial cable technology and copper pairs to deliver TV and telecommunications service to customers. In other words both ex-PTT and competitors' telephone distribution technologies are still essentially the same as they were 50 years ago.

The industry was already beginning to speculate about the possibilities for introducing optical fibre as a new cable medium for distribution to customers towards the end of the 1970s. In the early 1980s the proposition was developed that, associated with the right switching and inter-exchange transmission, a fibre into each home and premises would make possible a complete new generation of 'broadband' communications, capable of much higher transmission speeds (bit rates) than conventional 'narrowband' facilities and therefore providing the 'super-highway' for a completely new family of visual and computer services for the mass market with which the future of the industry would lie. But the practical and economic hurdles to this have proved to be considerable. The early visions of 'fibre to the home' have faded in face of the economics. The cost is simply too high, though efforts continue to reduce it.

The industry is still wrestling with the question whether a viable technical approach can be found for providing broadband service for the general population.

The Asynchronous Transfer Mode (ATM) packet technology[1] which emerged in the 1980s can provide the necessary switching and inter-exchange transmission medium. It would make possible comprehensive public switched service at any speed or bit rate, right up to those needed for moving video and even virtual reality. As I write, ATM is still an immature technology with significant difficulties still to be overcome if it is to be used on an economic basis, especially for voice service. As of now its application on other than a trial basis is confined to the private communications market. So much is at stake, however, and the effort being devoted to the problems is so great that we may reasonably expect that solutions will be found by the turn of the century.

In principle the ATM transmission environment is capable of being extended right out to the customer, as the basis for comprehensive broadband service for the mass market. But ATM cannot reach out to customers' doorsteps in this way until the distribution problem is solved.

The engineering detail of the distribution situation is varied and changing all the time as the operators and suppliers vie with one another to solve the problem. As I write, the US cable TV industry is putting the finishing touches to a 'hybrid fibre-coaxial' technology which uses radio frequency bearers over optical fibre mains feeding directly into coaxial cables on the final leg to customers. This technology marks a significant step forward towards an economically viable solution for broadband distribution. It requires much less expensive electronics at the customer end than full fibre-to-the-home. At the cost of providing the necessary additional electronics this technology will be capable of being used to upgrade the cable TV companies' networks in Britain to provide broadband service.

The telecommunications operators in the USA have tried various permutations of technology to deliver TV pictures and interactive service to customers over their existing copper pairs, using electronics which adapt themselves to overcome the limitations of copper as a transmission medium (Adaptive Digital Subscriber Loop technology or ADSL and its variants). BT is trialling the same technology. There is every prospect that true high bit rates, up to 25 mbit/s, will be capable of delivery over copper using this technology. To the extent that it uses the existing copper cables it has an obvious economic advantage over the approach of the cable operators. Adaptive equipment is provided only for lines which need it and can be recovered if not required. But at present at least the electronics, which have to be provided on a per line basis, are expensive.

While all this has been going on, the existing telecommunications operators in Europe have been finding their own ways to exploit fibre in distribution. Customers for ordinary telephone service in the former East Germany are already served by fibre links to their buildings or apartment blocks. In the particular circumstances of BT, whose copper distribution cables are of patchy quality, there are solid grounds for replacing the old copper cables with optical cables purely in order to reduce the operating cost of conventional telephone service. BT has already announced its desire to provide conventional service to all businesses of five lines and above in this way.

Measures of such kinds will progressively create a pattern of fibre distribution spines with considerable transmission capacity over and above that needed for ordinary telephone service, or in the case of Spain that needed for conventional TV distribution. Several countries including Britain are pursuing the idea of linking hospitals, doctors, schools, universities and similar institutions with broadband links of their own, which will permit the development of broadband services for their specialized needs. The fibre spines will provide a valuable foundation for such arrangements.

Whatever form they turn out to take, broadband facilities for the general public are going to cost a lot of money. At macro-economic level there are two schools of thought in the world about how to approach paying for them.

In different ways Japan and Spain have opted for a kind of Keynesian approach. Working through their former PTT operators they have decided to incur the huge cost of making a countrywide investment, or at least an investment covering all urban areas at the outset, in the belief that once the facility is created it will be taken up and exploited. The underlying conviction is that the potential benefit to the societies and economies of the countries justifies the very considerable investment risk.

The companies in the USA and Britain, by contrast, are adopting a strictly commercial approach. As matters stand, the only firmly predictable sources of revenue in the whole field are conventional telephone service and cable television, both of which can be and are provided now over their respective forms of conventional distribution. Over the last two or three years in the USA and Britain great effort has gone into trying to identify a new family of 'interactive' applications growing out of conventional TV which would attract enough new business to justify large-scale investment in two-way broadband distribution; but no such applications have been found.

In the meantime the Internet and its derivatives are growing like wildfire, using the conventional telephone network with its copper distribution cables as the medium by which the general public gains access. The Internet grew up through co-operative effort by computer users in universities and similar establishments. The demand for it is completely spontaneous. Use of the Internet is now spreading rapidly to business and the general public. It owes nothing to selling effort either by telecommunications operators, who indeed are struggling to keep up with its implications for their conventional business, or by cable TV operators.

Many people believe that the users of the Internet and especially children and teenagers will become more and more impatient with the relatively slow data speeds available over copper pairs and conventional switching and the contribution these make to delays in operation of the Internet. Equally importantly, the pattern of services provided on the Internet seems set to evolve into multimedia, involving high-speed data transactions and still and moving video. These automatically require some form of broadband distribution.

The most promising scenario is probably one in which the requirements of Internet users for higher transmission speeds and bit rates and the developments in network technology come together. If the problems of ATM switching in providing voice service in an economic way can be solved there is likely to be a powerful case for complete replacement of the existing public switched network facilities of advanced countries with ATM-based switching and transmission purely on grounds of the cost and service advantages for ordinary telephone service. The new network resource thus created will have the ability to switch really high bit rates at marginal extra cost. With the explosive growth predicted for the Internet and with the continuing evolution of distribution technology there is a good prospect that by the turn of the century or soon after both means and demand will finally exist for universal broadband service for the general public.

The sums of money involved in such a fundamental recasting of networks will be very large indeed. If any approach is adopted short of out-and-out printing of money by governments to subsidize it, this will face the industry with one of its toughest ever financing challenges. Under conditions of privatization the investment required will be able to come only from company boards allocating internally generated funds or from the stock market. The quotation at the head of this chapter is correct. To attract money from the market or to justify investment of internal funds on the scale involved one must be able convincingly to demonstrate and predict profitability.

Britain is the country with the most experience of the regime of privatization and competition in the present format. The British experience set out in Chapters 16 and 17 leads to two conclusions. First, in regimes like the present British one, the government will always find ways to force prices down, through price cap regulation or otherwise, and to hold them down for reasons which are political in essence, even though they may not be acknowledged as such. Second, available savings in operating cost and the benefits of growth in business volume will be used up in holding down tariffs for existing services and protecting market shares, while maintaining dividends. At the same time infrastructure competition is visibly adding a new layer of costs, through loss of economies of scale and increase in idle capacity. The combined effect must be substantially to depress the future overall profitability of the operating industry. (These predictions about declining profitability were confirmed in a remarkable way by developments which occurred as I was finalizing this chapter. Depression of profitability has indeed recently become a major issue between BT, its competitors and the regulator.)

Major expansion into new services might of course go some way to restore profitability expectations. But on experience so far interactive TV does not seem to offer much of a chance in this respect. The Internet might possibly do so in the long run. But in the short term the Internet is worrying the major operators precisely because the way it works represents a threat, not a boost, to their mainstream revenues.

Competition in infrastructure inescapably constrains willingness to invest at a very basic level. The experiences of Gresham Street in persuading the PO Board to authorize the network modernization programme in 1972 and 1973 recounted in Chapter 11 show just how cautious Boards are obliged to be where investment in activities as exceptionally capital-intensive as telecommunications networks is concerned. Competition and uncertainties about market share add an extra dimension to this caution. Again this is demonstrated in Britain. In the interest of promoting the spread of infrastructure competition, as we have seen build obligations had to be imposed in the licences of the UK cable operators to counter-balance the natural (and sensible) caution of the managements in this respect.

Taking it all together and in strictly business terms the industry in Britain and in all countries which emulate the British regime is at risk to a vicious circle of declining profitability and declining investment, if present policies continue.

Duplication of infrastructure obviously increases orders for the supplying industry in the short term, and injects extra funds and jobs into the economies concerned. But in our case not all the orders for extra plant are going to Britain and in any case these effects will not last unless the flow of investment by new operators is maintained.

The other obvious short-term advantage of present policies in Britain is that they have increased the flow of inward investment. The majority of the funds invested by the overseas cable TV operators are being spent in this country. But the question that matters is whether Britain will have a properly laid-out and economically viable telecommunications infrastructure which will keep it abreast of its competitors in the world; and whether replication of infrastructure will help or hinder with this. This is much more important for the future than any short-term boost to inward investment, desirable though this may be in itself. And even looked at from the narrow perspective of the national ability to attract inward investment, as the significance grows of telecommunications as a key competitive resource it is obvious that investors will be more and more influenced by the character of telecommunications facilities in the countries they are considering.

There were what were seen as important practical reasons for encouraging network competition in Britain in the early 1980s. The idea at that time was that competition would make it possible for the service given by competing operators like Mercury to be independent of that of the original operators like BT. This was an important advantage in situations of breakdown or industrial action. I for one shared William Barlow's exasperation recorded in Chapter 8 with the power of monopoly unions to exert pressure by industrial action directed to service.

The argument had some validity when one was considering things like private facilities for the finance interests in the City of London. As I have pointed out, there was a better case for competition in provision of private facilities than I for one took on board at the time. But it was never watertight even for private facilities, let alone for the public service. Practical competing networks are always interdependent. The Mercury network cannot provide full service unless it can interwork with the BT network; and so on.

In fact the industrial relations argument was already losing force in other ways even in the early 1980s. PO and BT experience had shown that the automation of telecommunications networks had already reached the point where short of actual sabotage they would run for many weeks with only the kind of attention which could be given by engineering managers. Network technology has advanced considerably further since then. Modern networks really will function for months with no more attention than can be given by a small number of engineering managers working without supporting staff.

The advantages of replication of networks in circumstances of breakdown may be thought more telling. Experience has shown that large modern software-controlled networks are vulnerable to service breakdowns of an almost catastrophic kind. If such a breakdown occurs say on the BT network there are obvious advantages in having other completely independent networks which remain unaffected. But once again the competing networks can give only partial service in such situations. And in any case under modern conditions the consequences to customers and the loss of operator revenue due to major breakdowns are so serious that the problem of network vulnerability to breakdown has to be and undoubtedly will be cracked anyway. In properly designed networks in future the diversity, alternative routing and duplication of control equipment needed to afford proper protection against breakdown will be built in as a matter of course. The traffic volumes in modern networks are so great that this need not add very much to costs.

The arguments for diversity go up with distance. Landline communications between say London and Tokyo are obviously more vulnerable than those between London and Croydon. There is a practically unanswerable case for duplication of facilities for transoceanic and transcontinental telecommunications on security of service grounds. Even so far as long-distance inland communications go in a country like Britain, the arguments for duplication were significant ten years ago and they should not just be dismissed now. But they are not enough in themselves to justify replication of inland plant in a country like Britain for that reason alone today.

I am writing at a time when the situation on the continent is in its very early stages. It is impossible to say how matters will develop as time goes by. Certain features of the situation are however recognizable from British experience. For example in the present phase of threat both Telecom Italia and Telefonica in Spain have taken the view that if they are to hold their competitive position in the future they must take new initiatives involving construction of cable TV plant at local level now, just as BT did in 1983. Telefonica is well ahead with the construction of a completely new broadband distribution network of fibre cables out to nodes serving five hundred customers, which will be used initially for TV in the outward direction only but is engineered so that it could provide the foundation for two-way broadband service in due course. Telecom Italia earlier announced plans for a fibre/coaxial network to be constructed to pass ten million homes in the next three years, although this programme has now been halted by a decision that Telecom Italia is not to be allowed to carry entertainment services.

Generally speaking those continental PTTs which either have or are constructing cable TV or broadband networks are keeping their existing copper networks for telephone service in being and distinct. The idea of combining conventional telephony and broadband communications on the same distribution media, which is being pursued with such vigour by the US cable TV industry, has not so far taken root among the former PTTs on the continent. (There are signs as I write that the RBOCs in the USA may also retain their copper plant for telephone distribution, and may provide cable TV over separate networks.)

In the USA threat has finally become reality with the passing of the amending legislation through the Congress. The USA now faces similar question marks about the viability and impact of the *actuality* of competition in this format to those posed by the British experience. The economic parameters are obviously different because of the higher profitability of cable TV in the USA. But the fundamental question in both countries is whether, even with conventional telecommunications, entertainment TV and broadband all added together, there is enough revenue in the market to support two competing parties at local level each carrying the burden of its own infrastructure. Continental countries which do promote infrastructure competition will face the same questions in the future. British experience is definitely not encouraging in this respect.

The passing of the legislation empowering the Bell companies to enter long-distance service and to provide cable TV, and the cable companies to provide telecommunications in the USA, is bound to have a marked effect on their priorities. It seems inevitable that it will affect their attitude to their subsidiaries in Britain. Given also the growing uncertainty about the business prospects of the competing operations themselves, the future of this flow of inward investment into Britain is becoming more and more debatable.

As the situation stands BT seems bound to remain the principal national carrier for the foreseeable future. As I pointed out in Chapter 16, the regulator now has the final responsibility for ensuring that a balance is preserved in the operators' investment plans as between home and overseas markets. It is absolutely essential in the national interest that the regulator should ensure that a sensible level of future investment by BT in its home network is maintained into the future. Present policies are visibly not doing this. This is a very serious matter.

The BT distribution network is ageing and much of it is certainly in need of extensive renewal, if not replacement, just from the point of view of the conventional telephone service. In the areas where they operate the cable companies are creating modern distribution networks which in a sense amount to just such a replacement. Eventually these new networks could supersede that of BT across large parts of the country. In itself this might be held to be in the national interest. But equally in itself such a replacement process does not constitute competition. A more accurate presentation of what is going on would be that the cable companies are simply filling an artificial and regrettable gap created by the working of the regime. BT has felt constrained for many years by the entertainment bans and for the last five years it has been constrained also by the pressures of the price cap on investment. In consequence it has not carried out its own replacement programme, which is badly needed in the interest of the customers whom it still serves and who form the great majority of users.

There is one argument for the present pattern of replication which in itself is clearly valid. All the local competitors to BT and the main long-distance competitors have decided to create their own facilities. They must have had good reason for this and their judgement must weigh in the balance. In the present situation, where the only alternative is to use BT facilities, it is both natural and sensible for the competitors to prefer to have facilities of their own. This by itself may be thought a sufficient justification for the present situation. The point to be made, however, is that they had no other choice. The question of them using network facilities owned by a third party who was not a competitor either to themselves or to BT was never considered. We shall return to the questions this raises in the next chapter.

The justification for the policy of competing infrastructures depends in the final analysis on the belief that competition will lead to greater advances in technology and to greater economic efficiency than monopoly.

Looking back at British experience since 1981, there is absolutely no evidence that our regime of network competition has stimulated a higher rate of introduction of new network technology than monopoly. In the USA it is true that the prospect of competition has called forth the radio frequency bearer technology designed for the cable TV industry and the adaptive technology now being adopted by the telecommunications operators. But neither of these developments is attributable to the actuality of competition; and certainly neither of them is due to the British competitive regime. In the last twenty years of monopoly network operation, on the other hand, the USA and Europe between them produced Stored Programme Control, reed exchange technology, digital exchange and transmission technology and cellular radio. In fact worldwide the period since 1981 has seen fewer rather than more advances in network technology compared with the previous fifteen years. All the evidence is that whatever the factors are which drive advance in telecommunications technology and reduction in telecommunications unit costs, they are independent of monopoly or competition. The most recent advances are simply a continuation of the past.

So far as economic considerations are concerned, as the Beesley Report said, even with the technology of the 1970s the economic evidence for network competition was poor. The significance of the loss of economies of scale due to network competition is much greater with the technology of the 1990s and it will be greater still with the technology of the next century. And, as Chapter 16 demonstrates, there is no evidence that the present approach is producing decisive improvements in the economic performance of the former monopoly.

Chapters 16 and 17 showed how the present British regime has operated actually to discourage BT from playing its proper inherited role in network matters. The combination of the constraints on BT carrying entertainment on its network and the pressures from regulation on its cash flow must have this effect. A regime which operates to discourage the principal carrier from discharging its inherited and necessary role in this way is deeply flawed.

Although the arguments in this chapter have been developed mainly in the British context, in essentials they hold for all the countries of the present European Union and for many other countries in the world. Taken together, the British experience and the arguments set out above lead inexorably to the conclusion that European countries' inland public telecommunications networks should be kept unified under a single management.

Public infrastructure competition is the last thing the European telecommunications industry needs from the point of view of its future growth and viability. A basically different approach is needed. In the next chapter I propose one.

Note

1. Asynchronous Transfer Mode technology (ATM) works as follows. In conventional packet switching systems the information to be transmitted is divided into packets of defined length and structure. The network is synchronized end-to-end for the transmission of each packet. In ATM systems the information is similarly divided into packets but each packet includes the address of the end-destination customer. The packets are fed into the network without the need for synchronization and find their own way to the distant end. It has been found that this is a very efficient means of transportation. Vast numbers of packets can be routed through a single node; and the signals being transmitted can be of widely varying bit rates, up to the highest which is likely ever to be needed for communication purposes. The ATM 'environment' can be arranged to operate right from and to the final termination in the customer's premises.

   The engineering problems of making ATM systems work fully reliably and fully economically in large-scale public service applications have, however, yet to be finally solved.

20 A Better Model

Although competition from and between service providers can provide increased choice for consumers, this is not an adequate substitute for competition between networks. Only competition between networks can deliver competition in the supply of network services which are a necessary input into basic retail or enhanced services for consumers. Without network competition, even vigorous competition between service providers will not prevent customers being disadvantaged by any inefficient and/or expensive provision of such network services.

OFTEL, *Promoting Competition in Services over Telecommunication Networks*, 1996

This book demonstrates just how desirable and indeed overdue many of the changes affecting telecommunications made by the early Thatcher governments actually were. There was a pressing need for reform of industrial relations and for separation of posts from telecommunications. Liberalization of customer apparatus and of value-added services have been a success. But bold though it was we can see now that the decision to foster competing physical public networks was a mistake.

To sum up the argument for this conclusion:

- The British state monopoly made great progress in the 1970s (Part II).

- By 1980 it was notably more efficient, innovative and commercially oriented than it is currently given credit for, particularly in network matters (Part II).

- BT has continued to improve and as one would expect it is clearly better now than it was at the time of privatization; but on proper analysis network competition is found to have made remarkably little contribution to this continuing improvement (see Chapter 16).

- After fifteen years the network competitors' prospects remain discouraging. They have not impacted on the core of BT's operations and revenue. BT continues to hold a dominant position (see Chapter 17).

- The threat of network competition unquestionably impacted BT; but the force of the threat has not been borne out by the actuality (see Chapter 17).

- The ineffectiveness of network competition is tellingly underlined by the stringency of the price controls which the regulator continues to impose on BT using his own powers (see Chapter 17 and Appendix 2).

- Contrary to expectations the pace of innovation in network technology has actually slowed up since network competition was introduced in Britain (see Chapter 12 and Chapter 19).

- This catalogue of weaknesses is despite the fact that four of the most powerful and expert companies in world telecommunications (NYNEX, US West, Pacific Telesis and Cable and Wireless) have been involved.

- The administration of the network regime is getting into more and more serious difficulty, with no way out in sight; in particular the conflict between BT and its regulator is steadily deepening (see Chapter 17).

- It has proved impossible to create a genuine free market in local telecommunications networks (see Chapter 17).

- The regime is prejudicing the future profitability of the operating industry (see Chapter 17 and Chapter 19).

- In an industry which depends on investment in technology the regime is also prejudicing the chances of raising and justifying the investment of capital (see Chapter 17 and Chapter 19).

- The regime is distorting the investment priorities of BT as the principal national carrier (see Chapter 17).

In short, the British experiment with competition between public telecommunications networks is developing in a basically unsatisfactory way. It has much less to show by way of benefits than is claimed for it; and its downside is becoming more and more apparent.

The quotation at the head of this chapter postulates that infrastructure competition offers a unique guarantee of efficieny. The recent proposals for the future assume that the way to overcome the failings of the regime is to extend competition further; and that the ineffectiveness of existing competition can be rectified just by giving blanket anti-competitive powers to the regulator. The reliance on competition alone to control prices for larger users involves a particular act of faith. As we have seen the experience of the last fifteen years calls all these beliefs deeply in question. There is no proof at all that infrastructure competition has bitten into the core of the cost or price base of the former monopoly; and it has proved uncomfortably difficult to make it work properly. The regulator's wider powers are a recipe for endless sterile conflict with BT.

There is moreover no reason to think that network competition will be any more effective in the future than it has been in the past. The new entrant companies now appearing are essentially start-up operations in specialized markets, with much further to go to make an impact than the Regional Bell Operating Companies, the Cable and Wireless group and others of the present generation. The wave of take-overs and mergers which is affecting the industry as I write may save overheads and lend more weight to marketing but it is unlikely to make any real difference to the situation so far as public network matters are concerned.

These conclusions should not surprise us. As I showed in the preceding chapter, network competition is out of step with the real characteristics and circumstances of the industry. After fifteen years of the present regime Britain stands at a parting of the ways. It can either continue with present policies, with steadily diminishing expectation that they will succeed; or develop new ones. The clear national interest is to do the latter.

Parts II and III showed how the telecommunications priorities of the 1960s and

1970s were dominated by the massive problems presented by the growth and renewal of the original electro-mechanical public switched networks. These problems were successfully solved. In the 1980s so far as networks were concerned it was a matter of completing the execution of existing plans. The emphasis of innovation shifted to the interface with the customer, both in terms of matching the demands of the consumer revolution in the mass market for the way service is offered and delivered and in terms of responding to the very specialized communications needs of international business and finance. By the 1990s these challenges had largely been met and the emphasis shifted back to public network matters. The priority for the last few years has been to find a way to exploit broadband technology in the public network on a commercial basis.

All round the advanced world the network problems of the 1970s were solved by unified authorities. In logic there would have to a be a very strong and concrete case to justify departing from the unified model in addressing the public network issues of the 1990s. Part V showed just how far such case as exists for having competing authorities for public networks falls short of this requirement. In fact, as the Beesley Report went some way to recognize, there has never been a sound economic or engineering case for competing inland infrastructures for the main public service in countries like Britain, Germany and France. The sensible – indeed the only defensible – basis for policy is that at national level public networks should be run by unified authorities.

Network or 'facilities-based' competition has its roots in transcontinental communications in the USA. The character of national inland telecommunications systems in Europe, the scale of distance over which they operate and the value systems which have underlain their development are completely different. US telecommunications companies are very welcome as competitors in Europe. But this does not mean we have to import US regulatory approaches.

The US regime was a debatable enough model in the early 1980s. The regulatory system was a matter of widespread unrest in the US industry and outside; and it was clogged then as it is now by litigatory practices. The regime had been confused and hampered for years by the conflict between AT&T and IBM, which finally led to the breakup of the former in 1983. The USA is an even less useful model now, because it is so far back up the learning curve. Where the British legislation liberalizing networks and the experiment under it have been running for fifteen years, the USA has only just passed properly comparable legislation and is only now addressing the problems of using it in practice. It was not and is not sensible to map the US approach on to Europe, which should hammer out its own future pattern.

The starting points for considering policy in detail are of course different in continental countries today from that which obtained in Britain in 1980. In addition to the effects of differing national cultures and practices, with certain very distinguished exceptions notably in Scandinavia, continental European PTTs have until very recently still been at the stage the GPO was at in 1969. They have remained as state monopolies run by Civil Servants, often used as sources for revenue for central government; and very much less commercial in approach and very much less geared to business standards of operation than the BPO was in 1980, let alone BT in 1996.

Continental policy-making in telecommunications has been confused by its own set of arguments reflecting this situation. Certain PTTs have been determined to preserve the linkage between monopoly operation of the network and monopoly provision of the telephone service, in the context of the Open Network Provision debate. Such approaches are backward-looking and rooted in the past. Even the liberalizing approaches of the EU and the British government reflect the parameters of the past and of past technology. In an industry which needs to be driven by the future the present operators, competitors, policy-makers and regulators are sunk in obsolete concepts. Their ways of thinking have been overtaken by events.

Britain led the world in blazing the original trail in the early 1980s. It has the chance to do so again by learning from its own mistakes and redesigning its regime in readiness for the twenty-first century, taking more time to think and taking account of all the experience in the meantime; and by being imaginative and forward-looking in doing so. In the remainder of this chapter I want to suggest a new model to form the basis for this redesign, based on a completely new structural concept and excluding facilities-based competition.

There are certain points I want to emphasize in approaching this. The first concern regulation. The cards are stacked heavily against the regulator in the present British set-up. As I showed in Chapter 17, more is asked of him or her than he or she can humanly deliver in terms of expertise; and he is obliged to conduct a precarious balancing act between conflict with and regulatory capture by the principal operator. An important objective in designing a new regime has to be a much more limited and closely focused role for the regulators, so that they can become fully expert and independent authorities on the matters they have to regulate in their own right.

The privatized BT has two distinct roles which overlap. It is a competitor but it is also still something near a big monopoly. Monopoly-like operations demand regulatory disciplines tailored to monopoly characteristics. The requirements for promotion of competition are quite different. The two can easily conflict, as with the stringent holding-down of BT prices generally and of rentals in particular by the price cap mechanism in the early 1990s, which was obviously calculated to improve BT's position *vis-à-vis* its competitors. Such attempts to graft the psychology of the market on to near-monopoly operations can never work satisfactorily. The regime and the structure of its institutions need to distinguish much more clearly between monopoly and competitive activities than they do at present. The emphasis should be on maximizing the area for proper competition, separating it out completely and systematically *de*regulating it.

Britain has more experience of interconnection of competing public networks than any country in the world. This experience has shown that it is inevitable that the sitting tenant will have to carry the competitors' traffic to and from the majority of customers for an indefinite period of time and that its charges will dominate the competitors' cash flow and profitability. It is inherently unlikely that such a situation could operate without steadily mounting disputes. These become harder and harder to resolve. For this reason alone it will be an important objective to avoid the need for interconnection between networks carrying public traffic in designing an improved regime.

The second group of considerations arises from basic differences between the public and private telecommunications markets which are not properly recognized at present. Public telecommunications constitute a true mass market, in which low prices and low unit costs are of overriding importance. The end-customers in this market are not concerned at all with technical detail. The market for private business facilities and especially for the sophisticated business services on offer nowadays is quite different. It is made up of a small number of large customers who must have advanced communications and services to survive and who are motivated accordingly. Prices and costs are important but they take second place to the efficiency and up-to-the-minuteness of the facilities on offer. Most of these large customers employ specialists who can master the technical detail of their network arrangements.

Private services have their own importance to the operators as profit generators. But public network telecommunications dominate the overall finances and investment of the industry. They are formative for the role of the industry in society and for the future of the industry itself.

As Part II demonstrated, the unified national operator of the 1970s was good at matters concerned with the main public service but not so good at private facilities. By the same token the one place in the network area where there has been real improvement in Britain attributable to network competition has been in private facilities. We should be guided by this. In designing the future structure we should distinguish clearly between the requirements of the public service and those of private network services, in a way that has never been done in the past.

Part II also underlined the deficiencies of monopoly in the retail area, especially in terms of customer relations. We need to build on this. In addition to the distinction between public and private facilities the other requirement for the future is to distinguish between network matters, or what we might call the wholesale side of the industry, and first-hand dealings with customers, which we might regard as the retail side. There is no question that the majority of the things retailed directly by and to human beings in telecommunications are likely to be better done in a climate of competition than of monopoly. The issue we have to address is the best way to achieve this in terms of the overall make-up of the industry.

Finally may I stress that my concern here is with inland telecommunications. In the international area the case for competition, including facilities competition, has in my view been unanswerable in both public and private services for a long time.

With these considerations in mind we can turn to the rethink itself.

My basic thesis is that the infrastructure for inland public services should remain unified in European countries and that in the case of Britain it should be reunified.

But there is more to it than that. The trouble with the present arrangements lies not just in the idea of network competition but in the archaic structure of the industry. In Britain the present structure, combining network and service provision in a single industry, was taken over from the state regime in the early 1980s with far too little time taken for thought. The functions of the PO were transferred wholesale to BT. It still sets out to provide the network and the complete range of services to everyone, countrywide. This pattern dates back to nationalization in 1912, when there were at most half a million 'subscribers', the only services were telephones and telegraphs and the telephone was a luxury. There are now forty times as many subscribing customers; telecommunications is part of life for fifty-four million people; and its services and facilities have ramified out of all recognition. The task of internal management had in fact outgrown the old structure while I was still involved and well before privatization, without our realizing it.[1] The whole thing is quite spectacularly out of date.

Mutatis mutandis, these arguments apply or will apply before too long in most continental countries. Regardless of other considerations the case for each EU country including Britain radically to re-examine its operating structure at national level is unanswerable.

One important argument for re-examining structure arises from the experience in Britain itself with competition over the last ten years. As I pointed out earlier it is not surprising in present circumstances that the local competitors to BT and the majority of the long-distance competitors have decided to create their own facilities. The only alternative so far has been to use BT facilities. No one wants to be at the mercy of a big competitor. The possibility of them using facilities owned by anyone other than themselves or BT was not considered when the present regime was formulated. Conversely, it might seem that it would make sense for BT itself to be allowed to use the new networks the competitors are constructing and to let its old one progressively go out of service. But such arrangements would be at risk of colliding with competition and anti-trust law; and in any case it is simply not credible that they could be negotiated in present circumstances. It follows that if the inland network is to be reunified it must be owned by some body other than BT or its competitors in their present capacities. This in itself requires change in industry structure.

Engineering developments in recent years have gone a long way to help us in designing a new structure. There is now a natural structural boundary at the periphery of telecommunications infrastructure, in the street. It has been the practice of the cable TV industry ever since it started to lay its distribution plant out in such a way that cables reach all multi-occupation buildings and 'pass the front doors' of all distinct dwelling houses in the districts it serves. The plant of the new networks being laid out now for cable TV is systematically laid out on this basis. In countries like Britain where telecommunications penetration has reached high levels this has become the normal practice also for new and replacement construction by existing operators in the urban and suburban areas in which the great majority of customers live. It would be surprising if the plant of the embryo broadband networks which BT and other ex-PTTs are beginning to construct did not develop on the same principles. The days and problems of partial and selective provision of distribution plant described in Part II are past.

With infrastructure already passing along every street in this way, the work which remains to be done to connect a customer is either to put in the last few metres of cable or overhead wiring to connect the house or office (the final 'drop') or to install the internal wiring within the apartment or office block. This work is quite distinct from that of construction of the main infrastructure; and its time frame is quite different. Where construction of the infrastructure is a one-shot operation, the work of connection and disconnection continues throughout the life of the plant, as customers come and go. It is a natural field for competition among retail operators; and it has strong affinities with the provision of customer apparatus, which is already successfully liberalized. In designing regimes for the future this work of providing the final connection to the customer can and should be treated quite separately from the construction and running of the infrastructure of the network.

Other valuable pointers to future structure have become apparent in the course of the British experience. The extensive outsourcing of work by BT has tested and established the principle of devolving blocks of the work of principal telecommunications operators to outside firms. And Mercury's service to the bulk of its customers is provided over BT or cable TV company distribution plant. In

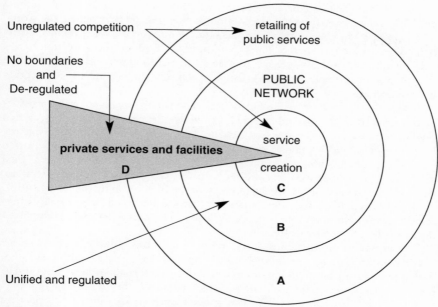

Figure 20.1   Proposed new industry operating structure

other words the customer facing functions are provided by one company and the wholesale (network) functions by another. A similar distinction between retail and wholesale (network) functions has been made in UK cellular radio from the outset.

Against this background my proposals are as follows:

- The creation and retailing of public telecommunications services, the provision and operation of the infrastructure of the main inland public service and the provision of private telecommunications facilities should henceforth be treated as three completely distinct sectors of the industry.

- In the retail public services sector unregulated companies in competition with one another should create and retail all services, including the provision of the final drop to connect individual customers to the network infrastructure.

- In continental countries the public network infrastructure should remain unified. In Britain it should be progressively reunified.

- There should in future be a single organization in each country responsible for this unified inland public infrastructure, which is subject to national regulation.

- This public network organization should be owned by a group of the principal telecommunications public service retailers on a co-operative or consortium basis, with no provision for outside shareholders to hold equity shares in it.

- The private services and facilities sector should be thrown open to full unregulated competition by local and international firms.

The point to be stressed is the fundamental difference in concept between these proposals and any past or present telecommunications regime anywhere in the world. The provision of public network infrastructure would be the sole province of the unified network co-operative. The provision of the final 'drop' connection to this infrastructure and of all services and associated hardware and software would become the province of a completely separate family of companies in deregulated competition with one another.[2]

The proposals are illustrated in Figure 20.1. The public-service-providing activities include two elements, marked A and C. C involves the creation of services, carried out at points which as the user sees them are located 'inside' the network, like the host computers which provide Internet services. A involves the functions carried out directly for individual consumers, like the provision and maintenance of final drops and of customer apparatus and the actual marketing and retailing of services. Between A and C comes B, the inland network, which is run by the co-operative.

A and C would be fully deregulated at national level and open to all comers subject to a bare minimum of rules about safety, technical compliance, exclusion of pornography and similar matters.

The provision of private networks and facilities forms a distinct vertical sector of the industry (D). This sector would be completely deregulated, with companies free to provide any permutation of services and network facilities they chose and to construct infrastructure or resell other people's circuits as they wished.

If individual national governments so wished the network co-operatives operating in sector B could be empowered to provide and retail private network services in sector D for business at home or abroad, in competition with others on the deregulated basis; whether they actually did so would be for their owners to decide. But they should have no other retail functions at all.

In the main public service market many companies, among them Internet providers, might choose to combine both A and C functions. Others might concentrate on permutations of A, like the present specialist customer apparatus providers, or on particular services like telephony or visual services. It is basic to the proposals that any permutation would be permitted involving A or C or both. This would be a genuine free market.

The extent of deregulation of international activities would of course remain a separate matter of policy for individual national governments as now.

A basic rule would be necessary to establish the balance between public service retail competitors which is so lacking at present and which experience has shown to be essential. In countries the size of Britain there would have to be a limit to the number and size of regions or cities in which any one service-providing company in sector A would be permitted to operate. Thus for example in the UK a company which operated in both Leeds and Newcastle might not be permitted to operate in London and so on. In smaller countries no such rule might be needed.

There would be provision for any smaller service providers and private network providers, including new entrants, who wished to do so to purchase shares in the national network co-operatives. Governments themselves should take a stake of say twenty per cent in these co-operatives to enable them to protect consumers' interests and as a guarantee of fair play. There would be no provision for shares to be held by anyone else and they would not be traded on the market.

These network co-operatives would have professional boards, including the executives of the co-operative itself but otherwise made up exclusively of their owners' representatives, including at least one government Director and at least one Director to represent the smaller service providers. Their Managing Directors and top executives would be appointed by the owners on regularly renewable contracts.

It would be crucial to the whole idea for these public network co-operatives to be run efficiently.

A starting point – though certainly not the finishing point – in designing this part of the new arrangements would be the treatment of the BPO in the 1970s. To recap, it was regulated on the basis of a return on capital target not to be fallen below or exceeded. It appraised its capital projects according to strict discounted cash flow procedures, with a discount rate prescribed by Treasury in the role of owner. It had sophisticated procedures for relating capital plant capacity to need. It tailored its staff closely to requirements, on the basis of factors of efficiency improving constantly from year to year. It is to be stressed that in these respects the BPO of 1980 was ahead of many continental PTTs of today. It provides a correspondingly demanding model on which to base new regimes throughout Europe. But even more rigorous arrangements are needed if full efficiency of operation is to be guaranteed.

The second of my points of emphasis comes into play here. The network co-operative licences granted by governments should recognize unambiguously that they will have a monopoly-like position. These licences should include a new formula in respect of operating efficiency. They should require the major part of the pay and remuneration of the Managing Director and the Operations, Technical and Finance Directors of the co-operative to be performance-related. The cash value of this performance-related component should be determined not by the executives' board colleagues but by the national regulators, by reference to the progress made each year with agreed targets for efficiency. The value of these targets would be set in the light of performance in well-managed outside business.

I showed in Chapter 17 that the price cap system is unsatisfactory. The profits and price levels of the public network co-operatives would be determined by a return on assets requirement not to be fallen below or exceeded, set to correspond to the upper quartile of returns being earned by blue chip companies generally and fixed by the regulator. Profits would be re-invested or distributed by agreement between the owners. The initial and later investment requirements of the co-operatives not met from profits would be found by the owners or from the market on a non-equity basis. The co-operatives would represent an excellent investment proposition for outside investors on this basis, with low risk and solid and respectable returns.

It would be a basic feature of the new regimes and of the network co-operative licences that anyone who wished to create and/or retail services to the public would be entitled to use the co-operative's network, paying standard charges ratified by the national regulator. The private network providers in segment D would be free to lease circuits from the co-operatives and to resell them.

A most important question is how governments which accept these proposals should bring them into operation. The starting point would have to be promulgation of these policies by government itself. Government would announce that it intended for the future to move to a structure of the kind proposed and in particular to use its licensing powers to share out the functions of the present big public operators – that is, BT and its competitors and their continental equivalents – between the new network co-operatives (B) on the one hand and the families of service providers (A and C) on the other.

As to how government would go about this in practice, in the UK the powers of the government under the 1984 Act should go some way to equip it to enforce the new arrangements by compulsion if it so chose. Parliament is sovereign and these powers could be supplemented by new primary legislation – a new Act – if this proved unavoidable. But in all countries it would be very much preferable to treat all such legal processes as in reserve only and to proceed by persuasion and negotiation.

Britain of course presents the most challenging situation, because a significant number of BT's competitors have already constructed their own network facilities. Their rights and those of BT have to be respected. In Britain the process of reunification can be completed only over time. It has taken fifteen years to get to where we are and it would take at least ten to get back to a properly integrated network.

The practical approach in Britain would be to move progressively towards the new regime over a period of perhaps ten years, with government making judicious use of levers already available to it to steer the process. For example experience with the reaction of the British cable operators to changes in the law on capital allowances in the 1980s showed how powerful fiscal changes can be in such a capital-intensive industry. It would be open to government to use changes in tax law as an incentive to encourage the companies to move to the new arrangements.

So far as factors within the industry itself are concerned, the starting point for government would be to develop the arguments which I have put forward in earlier chapters to convince them that their own business interest lies in the creation of a unified network run by a co-operative on the lines proposed above, rather than in the continued building-up of their own competing infrastructures.

In the British case the competing group with the biggest stake in infrastructure of their own is the cable operators. A major attraction of the new arrangements for them would be that they could be relieved of the build obligations in their present licences and of the corresponding requirement to continue to invest very large sums in a market of growing uncertainty. The other group of competitors affected would be those like Mercury and Energis who have created long-distance facilities. In their case the effect of technical developments in increasing the significance of economies of scale discussed in Chapter 19 would be important. It would in any case be open to them if they so chose to continue to operate as independent providers of facilities for private networks.

Persuading BT to subdivide itself and to surrender its network facilities to a co-operative would be a challenging undertaking. Persuading its shareholders to do this might be even more difficult. But within the present structure BT is visibly fated to more and more difficult relations with its regulator; and condemned to everlasting restriction of core parts of its prices and profits in one way or another. In the long run it cannot possibly succeed as a big-league company on the world market with a home base subject to such difficulties. A properly negotiated change of structure which would get them away from such restrictions and reduce the cost and risk of investment in new technology should have overwhelming attractions both for BT Board members and for their shareholders.

At the time of transition to the new arrangements BT's existing shareholders would have the option of assuming non-equity stakes in the co-operative or of choosing one or more of the successor service companies in which to hold equity; or both. The big profit potential for the future lies in the development of services and applications, especially for broadband. The prospects of the shareholders holding stakes in the new service retail companies would be very much better than their prospects in BT under the present regime.

This discussion of the situation in Britain demonstrates many of the questions that would arise in continental countries, but the transition would be less complicated. The majority of European countries still have unified networks at the present time. The important issue for them will be to separate the network and service functions of their existing PTT or ex-PTT operators; and then to give effect to the rest of the proposals and to form the network co-operatives, preferably by persuasion as in Britain, with whatever powers they have under existing law or to enact new legislation in reserve.

The argument I have developed here concentrates on wired infrastructure through to the customer. At the time of writing there is renewed interest in radio (wireless loop) systems as a vehicle for competition. As I pointed out in Chapter 17 I have myself been arguing publicly for the potential of radio in the loop for over ten years. I am not to be seen as arguing against competition from radio in principle if it can be made to stick; or indeed against the use of radio loop systems as first comers for provision of telecommunications service in greenfield situations. There is no way of telling at present the extent to which loop radio systems will develop as a vehicle for competition to through wired service. But the structure of systems for radio service to end-customers fits well with the structural ideas I am advancing here. The arguments for unified public infrastructure provided by a co-operative apply with just as much force to the base station and network infrastructure of radio systems as they do to that for wired service; and the actual provision of radio services using this infrastructure is a natural for deregulation (apart from frequency spectrum controls).

In the next chapter I consider briefly some objections which may be raised to these arrangements and review their advantages at the policy level.

Notes

1. For a more detailed discussion of the managerial issues arising from the size and character of the PO and BT organization see J. M. Harper, *A 21st Century Structure for UK Telecommunications* (Communications Educational Services Publishing, London, 1991).
2. Special arrangements would probably be needed for the final drop in sparse areas like the Highlands of Scotland and their equivalents in continental countries, where the work might be carried out by the network co-operative on a repayment basis

21 Objections and Advantages

In this chapter I should like to consider certain objections which may be raised to the proposals in Chapter 20; and then to consider the advantages which the proposals offer at the level of policy.

First, the objection of principle to the reduction of competition, which theory says will result in better resource allocation and more efficient pricing. It is a fundamental objective of the proposals to *increase* competitive pressures on the retail prices offered to end-customers. But it is true of course that the effect of the proposals would be to remove competitive pressure on inland public network operations, costs and charges, which will always be a major component of these end retail prices.

The first part of the answer to this has to be the remarkable lack of evidence of any actual effect of this kind in the last fifteen years. For whatever reason network competition does not seem to produce in practice the benefits which theory says it should. As I established in earlier chapters there is no evidence that it has of itself pulled down BT's costs or the overall level of its prices; nor has it stimulated more innovation in technology or products and services.

The reasons for these failings seem obvious. As I explained in Chapter 19 the basic concept of competing physical networks runs counter to many of the most distinctive characteristics of telecommunications as an industry. Also, experience says that the nature of the network telecommunications market in a country like Britain is such that competitors do not succeed in gaining enough market share to constitute the kind of real nail-biting threat that would be needed to make an impact. As I pointed out in Chapter 20 there are no grounds to think that the regime will be any more effective in the future in this respect than it has been in the past. Whatever theory says, this bit of economic doctrine does not seem to apply in practice in public telecommunications networks.

The second part of the answer is concerned with the theory of the economics of the capital plant. It well illustrates the difficulties of regulation founded on economic theory in coming to terms with the realities of telecommunications technology to which I referred in Chapter 17.

Network competition must result in loss of economies of scale. As the Beesley Report said, in the late 1970s economic evidence about loss of economies of scale was poor, whether for or against competition. I myself recognized that with the technology of that time there would be certain large long-distance inland relations on which competition could be introduced without loss of economies of scale (see Chapter 14). But the technology has moved on. The module capacities inherent in the digital switching and transmission technology of the present day are significantly higher than those of the electro-mechanical switching and plesiochronous digital transmission systems of the 1970s, so that the damage done by loss of economies of scale due to duplication must be that much greater. The inherent module capacities and therefore the potential for loss of economies of scale due to competition in the ATM switching and transmission environment of the future will be greater still.

So far as the distribution network is concerned, economy of scale arguments obviously do not apply to the individual customer pairs which account for a significant part of the cost inherent in conventional local distribution over copper. They do however apply in full to the high-technology systems which are reaching out further and further towards the customer in the modern distribution network.

To sum up this argument, in any given technology there is a threshold level of volume of business relative to inherent module sizes below which the potential for loss of efficiency due to loss of economies of scale will outweigh any potential gains due to competitive pressures. Even in 1981, with the technology of that time, Beesley could find no decisive evidence that inland network telecommunications was above this threshold level. Inherent module sizes have increased and continue to increase so much since then that objections to my proposals on these grounds have less and less chance of being made to stick.

The third part of the answer lies in the new machinery I proposed in Chapter 20 to bring efficiency pressures to bear on the management of the unified public network. If performance-related pay is as effective a motivator as we are told, the system I have proposed in which a powerful performance-related element in the pay of the top managers of the unified network is administered by the regulator acting on the public's behalf should provide a new and better spur to efficiency either than the pressures we were under in the PO in the 1970s or than competition in the form it has been found to take in Britain in the 1980s and 1990s.

A second objection to the proposals concerns their legal implications from the point of view of competition law and the re-creation of monopoly. In the USA they might be seen as liable to collide with anti-trust law. But the proposals are not for creation of anything resembling a monopoly of service to end-consumers – indeed the reverse, since the idea is completely to deregulate retail service provision. Also, they involve a new kind of telecommunications network company which was not conceived when existing anti-competitive rules were framed on either side of the Atlantic; and they relate to Europe, not America. It would be for US companies operating in Europe to decide whether US law would allow them to participate in European companies of the kind proposed. It would be a pity if they could not but it would in no way be fatal to the basic idea. In the UK, where Parliament is sovereign and government acts by virtue of its Parliamentary majority, the position is clear. The only question that matters is whether government is satisfied about a policy on its merits. If a government in power were satisfied by the arguments in the present case it would be able to legislate to modify existing law in respect of any difficulties which might arise.

A third objection which may be seen in technical circles in the industry concerns the separation from network operation of service creation on the intelligent network platform. This is a subject with a long and very loaded history. The issues involved lay at the centre of the disputes between computing and telecommunications interests in the USA which led to the division of the old Bell system into AT&T and RBOCs. These issues can no longer be pushed to one side. The proper development of advanced services is so important for the industry's future that they must be properly faced. This is true whatever view one takes of the future and of my proposals for change in structure.

There is good reason to believe that if a structural separation is enforced by governments at this boundary the industry will rapidly accommodate to it. In the late 1970s there was strong engineering resistance in Britain to the idea of structural separation out of customer apparatus, on the grounds that the telephone instrument was an integral part of the network. Such separation was enforced for wider reasons of policy and it has been accommodated at engineering level with remarkable success. The customer premise sector is now distinct from the rest of telecommunications operations in all respects. The separation of the service platform from the physical network is a close parallel. It presents complex engineering problems. I have myself argued in the past that in the normal run of things engineering considerations should weigh considerably more heavily in the formation of policy than they do. I still believe this as a general matter; but when issues as important as those involved in future industry structure arise it is the responsibility of the engineering community to accommodate policy rather than the other way round. I am confident that, given the right policy lead, the engineering community will successfully meet the technical challenge of separation between the service platform interface and the physical network.

Finally on the downside, the proposals in the preceding chapter leave the operator of the unified inland public network free to compete in the private facility market. In doing so he might be seen as having unfair advantages from economies of scale in the actual provision of private circuits, since he can draw them from the pool of capacity provided for the public service. But private circuit capacity, including capacity used in virtual private networks,[1] is nowadays a commodity, which is sold and resold between and by competitors as a matter of course. The competing providers of private networks in Britain are nowadays free to resell circuits leased from the public network operator and they must remain so in the new structure. But the private services market is driven more and more by the sophistication of the value-added services on offer and by marketing techniques like 'one-stop-shopping', in which the public network operator has no natural advantages. In any case its competitors are likely to be, or to be subsidiaries of, large international operators and companies which are powerful enough to be able to compete effectively with it without special protection.

There would be no reason why companies constructing facilities for customers requiring private communications should not sell capacity on their plant also to the unified public network co-operatives to use for public traffic, in a form of 'reverse resale'. It is quite possible that in suitable circumstances such operators who had capacity on routes heavily used by private traffic – for example between major business centres – would be able to offer spare capacity on their plant to the public network co-operatives for use in the public service at prices competitive with the cost to the co-operatives of using their own plant.

Coming to the advantages of the proposals, far and away the most important would be the unleashing at last of true free competition in the retail public service market. I cannot stress too much the disappointment which I feel personally at the failure of the present arrangements in this respect, especially as regards the role of competition in fostering new services and applications.

At the same time the whole clumsy apparatus of interconnection would be swept away. Both network and service operators would be freed up to concentrate their attention on their real job without constantly having to look over their shoulders at the complexities of the interconnection process.

Importantly also the role of the regulator in the proposed structure would match the requirements I suggested earlier. The regulator's functions would be limited to a specific area which he or she and staff could fully master. The role of telecommunications regulation would still be demanding and specialized and it would require a specialized regulatory organ. It would still need to be kept separate from the regulation of broadcasting and content generally, which is a quite different matter involving quite different kinds of issue. On the other hand the business of regulating the electricity grid and its gas equivalent could well be found to have a good bit in common with telecommunications network regulation. This is not the place to pursue the idea in detail, but subject obviously to the structure of the other two industries it could well be that all three networks should be supervised by a single regulator with the functions suggested.

The Director General of Telecommunications, like the other regulators, is a non-Ministerial officer of government, with no day-to-day answerability to anyone. Regulation in the strict sense has something of the character of a quasi-judicial function and there are obviously good reasons for making the body charged with regulation in this sense as independent as possible. In practice in the 1980s the advice of OFTEL as given to successive Secretaries of State came to be recognized (for example in the 1990 White Paper) as playing a large part also in the determination of policy for telecommunications. The practice grew up of taking account of the views and interests of users and of the public at large primarily through the mechanism of consultation with bodies like consumer groups and trade associations, conducted independently of Parliament. Such consultation has its own value but it is no substitute for the Parliamentary process. Policy should be formed only by Ministers at the heads of departments directly answerable to Parliament, as it always had been before 1984.

The ideas in Chapter 20 and in this chapter are worked out in a British context. Some of the starting points on the continent would obviously be different. But the principles which underlie the argument should be capable of application in most European countries, *mutatis mutandis*. They provide a much better basis of approach than the present policies of the EU, not least because they are founded in the logic of the industry itself.

Finally, to summarize the principal arguments in favour of the proposals, recasting of the old structure on the basis proposed would markedly help service competition and network development right across Europe. The most important single advantage is that all telecommunications service provision would be deregulated and set free to benefit from the full working of the market. The investment expenditure and the risks of individual companies would be greatly reduced. With the security of their asset bases and the mechanism I propose for securing predictable returns, the new unified network co-operatives should find it very much easier than the present competing operators to raise capital when they need it and to justify its investment internally as the years go by. The technical and commercial problems of interconnecting competing networks would disappear. The regulators would be left with a manageable role concentrated on the pricing of public network facilities to the retail companies and on key levers of public network performance. Finally, the permanent danger, so clearly being illustrated in Britain as I write, that the principal national carriers may be induced by regulatory pressures to divert abroad investment which should be going into the home market would be eliminated.

Note

1. Virtual private networks are private facility networks created by software control on existing physical networks without the necessity for any physical rearrangements.

22 Conclusion

telecoms is the lifeblood of the financial services sector. Furthermore, the value and concentration of business in the financial services sectors of the main industrialized countries are powerful driving forces behind competition, liberalisation and innovation across the telecoms industry.

Andrew Adonis, *Financial Times*, 15 June 1994

To end the book I should like to suggest a way of my own of looking at developments in telecommunications over the last twenty-five years.

I want to start on a note almost of triumph. The British Post Office was numbered among the main PTTs of Europe. Whatever our faults in the old PTT regimes we had a job to do and we did it. The priority for us was creation and renewal of national telecommunications infrastructure. The world network which we created by our collective action is the largest single human artefact. It has been immensely satisfying to me, looking back to my eight years in charge of forward planning in the 1970s and early 1980s, to see how the vision to which were working has been realized on the foundations we laid. The industry *has* expanded, its services *have* proliferated and its profits *have* grown in the way we believed they would in the dark days of 1975; and the infrastructure we built up has been the foundation on which all this has happened.

Over a hundred years we PTT engineers and administrators created a huge base of capability, which has now passed under the control of a brisker, competitive world of managers. We are only at the beginning of the new era, even in Britain. The question is what the new generation will make of their inheritance. The jury is still a long way from a verdict.

The British state corporation of the 1970s was a long way from perfect. But in terms of the challenges it faced and the progress it made in meeting them it was successful. The private company is well run today. It has benefited greatly from separation from posts and from the reform of industrial relations; and, twelve years on, it has naturally enough put right the most obvious deficiencies which it inherited, just as we did in terms of the situation of the 1970s. The changes of the early 1980s were made with boldness and many of them have been a success. Privatization and the threat of competition have certainly been followed by an improvement in the way service is offered. But as I showed in Chapter 16, on proper analysis the image of a general revolution in the performance of BT due to these causes is seen to have been contrived.

It is instructive to look closely at the basics of the industry. In Britain provision of telephone connections has always been demand-driven. Even by 1987, well after privatization and with penetration at quite a high level, (the real problems of the operator were still characterized by the difficulty of accurately forecasting demand and of mobilizing resources to meet it in a fluctuating economy, as distinct from those of selling service.)The same goes in essence for calls. The network is essentially a blank sheet on which users paint their own enormously diverse pattern of uses; and it is they, not the operators, who generate the enormous growth of call demand. Generation after generation of Ministers and Chairmen from outside tried to push the organization into marketing lines and calls but it never had any convincingly measurable effect.

The fundamentals of the Internet are exactly the same. It owes nothing to initiatives by the carriers. It has grown up spontaneously out of co-operation between an informed group of users in the defence and academic communities in the USA. Its dramatic growth owes nothing at all to the telecommunications operating industry. There is no central marketing organization behind the Internet at all.

Cellular mobile telephone systems and the peripherals of the telecommunications industry – PABXs, call-connect systems, advanced customer services like the BT Star services, luxury telephones and niche services like alarms by carrier and so on – are well suited to marketing as we understand it today. But the main core of the industry's activities is not. In this fundamental sense the industry is outside the general run of business; and policy for it needs to be determined with this in mind.

We are left with the question of why privatization and competition happened in the first place in Britain.

(The case for freeing UK telecommunications from Whitehall in 1969 arose from obvious deficiencies of performance and from the evident inappropriateness of trying to run it directly from within government.)This case was really beyond dispute and was accepted by both main parties, as Chapter 3 showed. It is perfectly true that our performance in the PO passed though a bad patch about 1980, when we were hit like everyone else by the overheating of the economy before we had reformed ourselves enough to cope fully with such abrupt pressures. But we were already out of this phase by 1981 when the decision to privatize began seriously to arise; and in fact BT plc was to pass through a similar phase of its own when service deteriorated in 1987.

I wrote Part II to show how far we had come by 1980 in terms of reform of management practice and service to the general market. The only real area of persisting operational weakness was in the provision of private network facilities, which we were not good at and where, as I pointed out in Chapter 20, competition was warranted and already legally provided for in its own right.

There was no general sense of public outcry for constitutional change in telecommunications in 1981 – or if there was it was not apparent to me, in one of the hottest seats in the business. As Deputy Managing Director in charge of operations I had to handle some extremely critical press and broadcasting interviews at the height of the service difficulties. The criticism was justified by the facts but never once did the question of privatization or competition arise. The dialogue was all about what we were doing to rectify our failings in our capacity as a public monopoly. As I said at the end of Chapter 9, internally we needed more drastic change than we had so far had if we were to get ourselves fully fit. But it cannot be said too often that George

Jefferson, who supplied this change, got it under way as head of the nationalized monopoly. What he was really doing was finally to enforce the logic of Tony Benn's original 1965 conception of a separate telecommunications corporation, which is why he was so welcomed in the business. Even the decision to privatize in principle came two years later. The act of privatization occurred two years after that.

One of the most persistent and least accurate complaints about the tele-communications operations of the PO state corporation is that they were in some way supported by taxpayers' money. This is factually untrue, and this ghost should once for all be laid. From 1976 onwards the current account operating expenses of telecommunications had to be and were met from income from customers; and, averaging out the last six years of the PO, 1976–7 to 1981–2, even our fixed asset investment requirements were more than met by internally generated funds. In other words we ran on money generated by our own operations and efforts.

It was indeed the obvious profitability of our operations which put us at the top of the list for privatization. As the authoritative passage I quoted from Lord Howe's book in Chapter 15 makes abundantly clear, the decision to privatize BT did not arise primarily from considerations internal to our industry. The special needs of the City of London for telecommunications facilities (brought out by the perceptive statement quoted at the head of this chapter) and their exasperation, shared by William Barlow, with the power of unions in state monopolies certainly played a part. But it was general political priorities and the City's eye to a chance to make money which really led to the decision to privatize BT.

(The privatization of BT was a political act.) It will stand or fall on its political merits as the years go by. Judging by British experience, a lot will depend on whether the public feels that the profits of the utilities and the salaries of top managers are being sufficiently moderated in the privatized regimes. If it is felt that they are not, pressures will grow for a return to public ownership, where such matters can be directly controlled by government.)

Privatization is not the key characteristic of the new era in telecommunications. What really matters is competition. There can be no going back on the principle of competition in telecommunications. The problem is to make it work.

Competition in customer apparatus and in services was a great and overdue advance and in the right environment it will deliver the goods. It is very much better to have an unrestricted number of enterprising companies thinking up ways to use and exploit telecommunications facilities than to be dependent on a single monolith. Private telecommunications services and facilities nowadays form a closely focused market with highly knowledgeable customers, which is a natural for competition. But public network infrastructure needs to be looked at in a completely different light.

The linking of competition in services to competition in public infrastructure is wrong. The present regime was grafted on to an obsolete industry structure, based on concepts dating from Edwardian times, still really rooted in monopoly thinking and dominated by the former monopoly operator. It is not surprising that it has not worked properly. A fundamentally new structure is needed, which starts from the principle that service to the public should be retailed by companies of comparable and manageable size in genuine competition with one another. I have suggested a way of achieving this.

Appendix 1

Patrick Jenkin's Statement
of 19 July 1982

The text below is reproduced in the White Paper The Future of Telecommunications in Britain, Cmnd 8610 (HMSO, London, 1982).

With permission, Mr. Speaker, I would like to make a statement about the future of telecommunications in Britain:

It is the Government's aim to promote consumer choice. Wherever possible, we want industrial and commercial decisions to be determined by the market and not by the State. We believe that consumer choice and the disciplines of the market lead to more stable prices, improved efficiency and a higher quality of service.

Since the British Telecommunications Act 1981 received Royal Assent less than a year ago, some progress has been made in breaking the State Monopoly in telecommunications. I have licensed the Mercury Consortium to provide a new telecommunications network in competition with BT. I intend shortly to issue a general licence permitting all bona fide value-added network service operators to use the BT and Mercury networks. The way is now opening for the private sector to sell telephone apparatus direct to the public. Liberalisation of telecommunications has started and we intend to see it through. For BT, the prospect of competition and the advent of new technology are now stimulating them to provide a wider range of competitive services. I pay tribute to the way Sir George Jefferson and his Board are transforming what was not so long ago a Government Department into a commercially oriented business. Mr. Speaker, we now want to take the next step.

As a nationalised industry BT does not have direct access to financial markets. Its borrowing is controlled by Government and counts against the PSBR. To bring inflation under control these borrowings have inevitably to be subject to strict limits. But external finance is only part of the picture. In the past monopoly power has allowed BT to raise prices to finance investment without doing all that could be done to increase efficiency. Around 90 per cent of BT's investment programme, about £2,200 million this year, has been self-financed. By 'self-financed', I mean of course 'customer financed'; BT's charges to customers not only cover current running costs, but are also paying for 90 per cent of new investment. As a result, charges have risen steeply while investment is still not enough. Unless something is done radically to change the capital structure and ownership of BT and to provide a direct spur to efficiency, higher investment would mean still higher charges for the customer. The Government, BT and the general public would find that unacceptable. We need to free BT from traditional forms of Government control.

We will therefore take the earliest opportunity to introduce legislation which, while keeping BT as a single enterprise, will enable it to be converted into a Companies Act company, 'British Telecommunications plc'. The legislation will allow the sale of shares in that company to the public. It is our intention after the next election, to offer up to 51 per cent of the shares on the market in one or more tranches.

Once half of the shares have been sold, the Government will give up control over the commercial decisions of BT plc. BT plc will be outside the public sector; its borrowing will cease to be subject to Exchequer control, and it will look to its shareholders and the markets for its external financing. It will be for the Board of the company to decide when and how much to borrow taking account of internal factors and market conditions in the same way as any other private sector company. This will mean not only a greater flexibility for BT and less pressure on consumers and taxpayers, but also that BT will be subject to proper market disciplines. BT will be in a position to provide better services which are more responsive to customer needs like those provided by the privately-owned telephone companies in the United States.

BT plc will nevertheless dominate the British market for telecommunications for some years yet. The Government considers therefore that there will be a need for regulatory arrangements for the industry to balance the interests of those supplying telecommunications services, their customers, their competitors, their employees, their investors and their suppliers. The legislation will reform the arrangements for licensing telecommunications so as to end BT's exclusive privilege and its role in licensing. Instead, there will be new Office of Telecommunications, modelled on the Office of Fair Trading, under a Director General appointed by me. He will have powers similar to those of the Director General of Fair Trading. He will operate with the same degree of independence from Government. It will be his job to ensure fair competition and fair prices.

The legislation will contain provision to safeguard existing pension obligations. There will also be special provisions to ensure that those employed in BT can acquire shares in the company.

Finally, the legislation will reform the Telegraph Acts which were passed in the last century. We need to recast the law to make it relevant to the technology of today and tomorrow. I will be issuing a consultative document on this aspect shortly.

Because these proposals are far-reaching and will affect a lot of people, I am today publishing this statement, with some additional background information, in the form of a White Paper.

Mr Speaker, these proposals follow naturally from the liberalising measures passed by the House last year. It would make no sense to stop half way. If those who work in telecommunications are to provide the range and quality of service which modern technology now permits, and if they are to do so in competition with each other, it cannot be right that BT should remain subject to the web of government interference and controls which are the inevitable lot of an industry which enjoys the privilege of Exchequer finance.

The quality of the service which any enterprise provides depends upon the skills, energy, and leadership of the people who work in it. We want to provide those people with the environment – market, financial, legal and structural – which will free them to give of their best.

In the view of the Government, that is what the proposed legislation will do. I look forward to its early introduction.

Appendix 2

Prices and Volumes

1. Figure A2.1 plots PO and BT income at constant PO and BT prices as a measure of the trend of volume of business over the twenty-five-year period (I am indebted to Mr J. J. Wheatley, former BT plc Chief Economist and now a consultant, for both graphs in this Appendix).

2. The rate of growth of business approximates remarkably closely to 7.5 per cent compound over the whole period up to 1989. Growth effectively stopped around 1990, but despite competition it has now resumed on the long-term trend.

3. Figure A2.2 plots real changes in PO and BT prices overall (i.e. including both regulated and unregulated prices) for the years 1966 to 1995.

4. The most striking single feature is the violent increase in real prices at the time of combined violent inflation and recession in 1975–6. As Figure A2.1 shows, the check to volume growth due to the three-day week in 1974 and the recession in 1975 was limited. But the business still ran seriously into deficit in 1974–5 because price increases had been artificially held back in preceding years for political reasons. A very marked increase was essential if the business was to be restored to profitability.

5. As Chapter 5 makes clear, the year 1975 was an important milestone in reform of telecommunications finances. A proper budgetary system and current account cost mechanisms were introduced for the first time; and pricing policy was set up properly on those foundations.

6. As will be seen, real prices reduced steadily in most other years after the reforms of 1975. The only exception was in the years 1981 and 1982, when inflation and wage settlements reached unusual levels nationally and when telecommunications prices had been held down as a matter of PO policy in the preceding period (see Chapter 8). The real increase in prices in 1981 and 1982 was very much smaller than in 1975–6, owing no doubt in part to the improvement in cost control. The increases actually caused overshoot of the financial target (see Table 5.1).

7. If anything the annual reductions in real prices tended actually to be less after 1984 than in the years immediately before 1981. Despite the exceptional events of 1980 the average real reduction in the whole period 1976 to 1984 was 3.9 per cent a year. In the period 1985 to 1995 it was 4.5 per cent. This is a remarkably small difference, bearing in mind that in marked contrast to the 1970s the national economy was stable from 1984 right up to the 1990 recession and how radically the national industrial relations climate and the incidence of pay disputes had improved.

8. Throughout the whole twenty-five-year period from 1970 the most important single reason for the reductions in prices has been the steady growth in volume of business visible in Figure A2.1 and the associated increase in revenue, plus the effect of technology on unit costs. The cost control record both of the PO and of BT is examined in more detail in Appendix 3.

9. The regulated sector of BT prices accounts for about two-thirds of income. It is regulated by the price cap mechanism. This mechanism had no obvious effect on the overall trend of prices up to 1990, nor did competition (see Chapter 16, note 2, p. 169). The rate of real price reduction actually began to decrease in 1990, rather than increasing as one would have expected if competition was biting. The price cap has however had a noticeable effect since about 1992. In the years commencing 1 August 1990 the permitted changes and the BT achievements for regulated prices were as follows, after allowing for carry forward of unused allowances or shortfalls from previous years:

	1990	*1991*	*1992*	*1993*	*1994*
Permitted value	+5.52	−0.23	−0.95	−6.94	−4.86
Actual change	+5.34	−0.73	−0.47	−6.95	−3.57

In other words between 1991 and 1994 BT was required by its regulator to make a cumulative real reduction of no less than 12 per cent in the prices for the regulated services, which produce two-thirds of its group revenue. It is to the credit of BT management that at the time of writing it has achieved actual reductions amounting cumulatively to about 11 per cent without any deterioration in service so far (a further reduction of over 1 per cent remained to be implemented at the time the table was compiled). There can be few precedents for an enforced price reduction on this scale for such a big utility. It clearly contributed to the marked reduction in overall prices in 1995. It was more than enough to drown out any effect of competition and privatization as such. No conclusion one way or the other can be drawn about their effects from these events.

10. To sum up:

- Before 1975 the business had no proper budgetary or cost control system.

- There was an very large price increase indeed in 1975–6.

- That year was also a milestone for reform in the financial management of the business.

- With the exception of the exceptional years 1980 and 1981, real prices have reduced in every year since then.

- The stringent price caps imposed after 1990, coupled with the very sharp check to volume growth as a result of the 1990 recession, clearly affected prices overall; and undoubtedly contributed in an important way to the forces which caused management to make economies (see Appendix 3).

- At no time in the period since 1984 have there been any detectable effects on the overall price envelope attributable to privatization or competition as such.

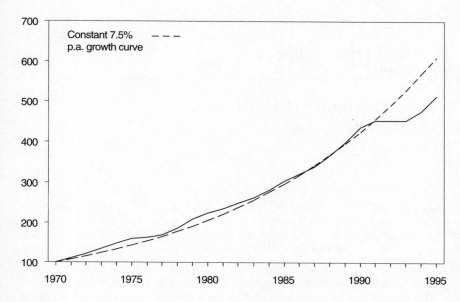

Figure A2.1   PO and BT volume 1970–95 (income at constant PO and BT prices)

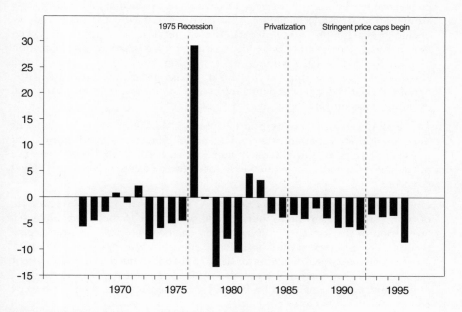

Figure A2.2   Real change in overall BT prices 1967–95

Appendix 3

Operating Performance

1. Figure A3.1 sets out annual PO and BT current account (operating) expenditure for the period 1971 to 1995 (depreciation at historic cost and exceptional payments for redundancy in recent years are excluded). Figure A3.2 plots the same expenditure at constant 1990 prices, using retail price inflation as the deflator.

2. One technical complication should be noted. Historically, the PO had capitalized expenditure on connecting customers up and installing their apparatus. In 1981 this expenditure was decapitalized and became a charge on current account operating expenditure. Detailed figures in respect of this expenditure were not published after 1983 and it is not therefore possible to plot expenditure on a fully consistent basis throughout the period. Figure A3.3 however puts the change in perspective for the years up to 1983. The pattern of a reduction followed by a rise around 1982–3 visible in Figure A3.2 is visible also with the main body of operating expenditure plotted separately from installation. Figure 6.1 showed how network growth in lines has decreased since privatization. This reduction of itself has reduced the volume of installation work to be done and the corresponding expenditure. It has also of course progressively decreased the significance of the decapitalized installation expenditure as a factor increasing total operating cost compared with the period before 1981.

3. The staffing record is discussed in Chapter 16. As Figure 16.1 showed, staff numbers remained substantially constant up to 1990. A marked rundown did however begin then. Since then staff numbers have reduced by 40 per cent; but in constant price terms the reduction in total current account spending is only 9 per cent.

4. One would not expect a *pro rata* reduction. Total current account expenditure of course includes many non-staff costs; and, as Chapter 16 showed, a substantial proportion of the staff shed will have been engineering staff paid from capital account. These factors may not however be enough wholly to explain the size of the difference between reduction in head count and reduction in total current account cost. Outsourcing is an obvious explanation for the rest. Work done previously by staff employed by BT and now shed is being done by outside contractors. It still has to be paid for.

5. As Figure A2.1 shows, under modern conditions the traffic and revenue of telecommunications operators like BT rises at a considerably higher rate than

costs, for reasons largely independent of the day–to–day actions of the operating managements. The primary reason is the inexorable growth of customer demand for communication, varying in the short term in line with the national economy, which the operators can affect only in a marginal way, if at all. Various other factors characteristic of the industry also play a part. For example the traffic-handling plant which forms the core of the revenue-earning and capital-charge-generating assets is provided to meet peak hour requirements; but a large part of it is loaded approaching capacity for most of the working day, on a favourable load factor pattern determined by users and influenced only in a limited way by tariffing and other measures taken by the operators themselves. There are various such multiplying factors for growth which do not apply to costs. At the same time product improvements by the telecommunications manufacturers have for many years been reducing the unit cost to the operators of new capacity in revenue-earning plant. These improvements have been driven by competition and technological advance in the manufacturing industry rather than the operating industry. Revenue-based unit cost indicators of operating efficiency, like the Real Unit Cost (RUC) indicator used by government for PO telecommunications before privatization, are therefore of limited value as a measure of the effectiveness of telecommunications operating management over time. They should not be relied upon in analysis.

6. One can however make a reasonable approximation of the behaviour of unit cost over time by dividing total operating cost by the number of connections working on the system (Figure A3.4). Using this indicator the change of trend at the time of the formation of BT is if anything more apparent than in Figures A3.1 and A3.2. The new trend was not halted until 1988 and not significantly reversed until 1991.

7. Appendix 2 shows, that coupled with the recession and the drop in inflation, the price cap values imposed by the regulator after 1990 have been enough by themselves to oblige management to make stringent reductions in cost after 1991. These price cap values are determined from time to time by the regulator as an administrative matter. The price cap system of price regulation is a separate matter from privatization and competition. It could have been imposed without either being implemented. No conclusions can be reached about gains in economic efficiency attributable to privatization or competition from this evidence.

8. BT service deteriorated seriously in 1987 (see the quotation at the head of Chapter 16). It was restored within a year or two. The effect is clearly visible in Figure 11.1, which plotted network performance. Other features of service were affected also.

9. To sum up:

- The success of the PO in containing costs after 1975, in face of the steady increase in volume of business noted in Appendix 2, contributed to the steady reduction in real prices after that year also noted in Appendix 2.

- Even making allowance for the effect of decapitalization of installation expenditure in 1981, Figures A3.1, 2, 3 and 4 taken together indicate a *relaxation* in current account expenditure control in the years following the formation of BT compared with the closing years of the PO.

- There was a marked decline in service in 1987.

- Service was restored within a year or two. But the improved trend of spending did not resume until the regulator intervened with unprecedentedly stringent price caps from 1991 onwards.

- The price cap system of regulation is a separate matter from privatization and competition.

- In short there is *no* evidence of gains in efficiency attributable to privatization or competition as such.

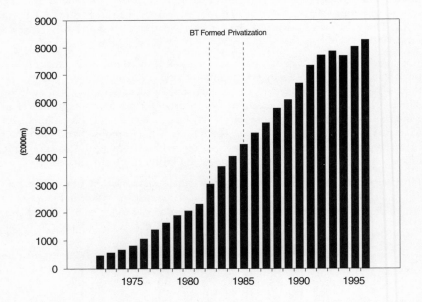

Figure A3.1   Operating expenditure at constant prices 1972–95 (year ended March, depreciation and exceptional payments due e.g. to redundancy excluded)

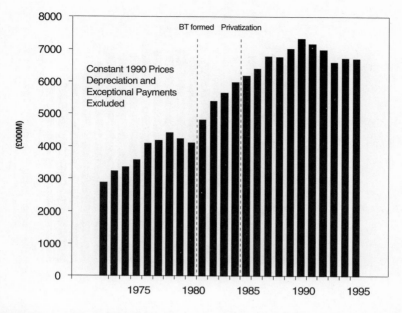

Figure A3.2   Operating expenditure at constant prices 1972–95 (£m, constant 1990 prices, depreciation and exceptional payments excluded)

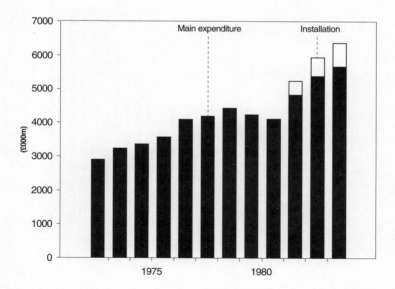

Figure A3.3   Customer installation expenditure at constant 1990 prices 1972–83

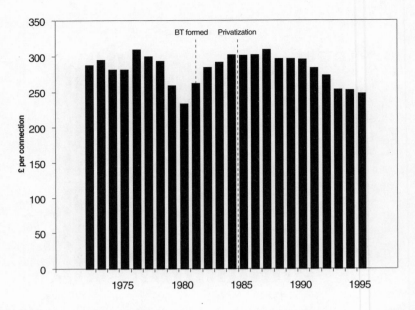

Figure A3.4 Operating expenditure per exchange connection 1972–95 (constant 1990 prices; depreciation and redundancy and other exceptional payments excluded)

Appendix 4

Chronology

	External events	Internal events	Industry and technology
1960			Highgate Wood trial
1961	PO Act 1961	GPO finances separated from Exchequer	
		Quarterly financial review system instituted	
1964	Benn PMG		
1969	PO Act 1969	PO Board appointed	Bulk supplies agreements end
		Hall Chairman	AGSD formed
		Fennessy Managing Director	
1971		UPW Strike	
		450,000 waiting list	
1973	Oil shock		PO programme cuts
1974	Three-day week		Further cuts
1975	Inflation and recession	PO economies	Cable scandal
	Carter Committee	Management accounting reforms	Further cuts
		Asset utilization disciplines	
1977		Ryland and Fennessy retire	System X development contracts
		Barlow Chairman	
		Shorter working week dispute	
1978		Benton Managing Director	

	External events	*Internal events*	*Industry and technology*
1979	Thatcher in power	THQ reorganized	
	Inflation and pay settlements rocket	Ferment in products and services	
		Monarch, Herald, Prestel Viscount, Statesman etc.	
		Service deteriorates	
1980	Keith Joseph announces competition	Jefferson appointed to PO 250,000 waiting list	
	Beesley Report commissioned		
1981	British Telecommunications Act 1981	BT formed as nationalized Board	System X large local pilot
	Beesley Report	Jefferson Chairman	
	Mercury formed	THQ reorganized	
1982	Intention to privatize BT announced	Inland Division subdivided into National Networks and Local Communications Services	
1983	White Paper on cable systems		
	1980s boom starts		
1984	Telecommunications Act 1984		
	BT privatized		
1987	Native cable companies falter	Service deteriorates	
1988	RBOCs and others enter cable		
1989		Project Sovereign reorganization	
1990	Competition and Choice White Paper		Peak of digitalization programme
1991	Stringent price caps		
1995	Mercury falters		

Index